A READER'S GUIDE
TO NABOKOV'S
"Lolita"

Studies in Russian
and Slavic Literatures,
Cultures and History

Series Editor: Lazar Fleishman

ACADEMIC
STUDIES
PRESS

A Reader's Guide to Nabokov's "Lolita"

Julian W. CONNOLLY

Boston
2009

Library of Congress Cataloging-in-Publication Data

Connolly, Julian W.
  A reader's guide to Nabokov's Lolita / Julian W. Connolly.
      p. cm. — (Studies in Russian and Slavic literatures, cultures and history)
  Includes bibliographical references and index.
  ISBN 978-1-934843-65-9 (hardback) — ISBN 978-1-934843-66-6 (pbk.)
1. Nabokov, Vladimir Vladimirovich, 1899-1977. Lolita. I. Title. II.
Series: Studies in Russian and Slavic literatures, cultures and history.
  PS3527.A15.L6325 2009
  440'.045—dc22
        2009032505

ISBN 978-1-934843-65-9 (hardback)
ISBN 978-1-934843-66-6 (paperback)

Book design by Ivan Grave

Published by Academic Studies Press in 2009
28 Montfern Avenue
Brighton, MA 02135, USA
press@academicstudiespress.com
www.academicstudiespress.com

CONTENTS

ABBREVIATIONS

AnL	*The Annotated Lolita*. Ed. with preface, introduction, and notes by Alfred Appel, Jr. 1970. Revised edition: New York: Vintage International, 1991.
Des	*Despair*. 1966. New York: Vintage International, 1989.
En	*The Enchanter*. Trans. Dmitri Nabokov. 1986. New York: Vintage International, 1991.
Gift	*The Gift*. Trans. Michael Scammell with the collaboration of the author. 1963. New York: Vintage International, 1991.
L	*Lolita*. 1955. New York: Vintage International, 1989.
LL	*Lectures on Literature*. Ed. Fredson Bowers. New York: Harcourt Brace Jovanovich / Bruccoli Clark, 1981.
Lo Screen	*Lolita: A Screenplay*. 1974. New York: Vintage International, 1997.
NWL	*Dear Bunny, Dear Volodya. The Nabokov-Wilson Letters, 1940–1971*. Revised and expanded edition. Ed., annotated, and with an introductory essay by Simon Karlinsky. Berkeley: Univ. of California Press, 2001.
PP	*Poems and Problems*. New York: McGraw-Hill, 1970.
SL	*Selected Letters, 1940–1977*. Ed. Dmitri Nabokov and Matthew J. Bruccoli. New York: Harcourt Brace Jovanovich / Bruccoli Clark Layman, 1989.
SO	*Strong Opinions*. 1973. New York: Vintage International, 1990.

CHRONOLOGY OF NABOKOV'S LIFE AND CAREER

Dates before the departure of the Nabokov family from Russia in April 1919 are given in Old Style (Julian Calendar); the New Style date (Gregorian Calendar) is given in parentheses. In the nineteenth century, the Julian Calendar lagged the Gregorian Calendar by twelve days; in the twentieth century, the difference increased to thirteen days. For example, April 10, 1899 (the date of Vladimir Nabokov's birth in Russia) was April 22 in the West, and it became April 23 in 1900. This chronology is based on information found in Brian Boyd's two-volume biography of Nabokov (*Vladimir Nabokov: The Russian Years* and *Vladimir Nabokov: The American Years*), the chronologies Boyd prepared for the Library of America editions of Nabokov's English-language novels and *The Garland Companion to Vladimir Nabokov*, Michael Juliar's *Vladimir Nabokov: A Descriptive Bibliography*, the volume entitled *Nabokov's Butterflies* (edited and annotated by Brian Boyd and Robert Michael Pyle), and Stacy Schiff's *Véra*.

1899	Vladimir Vladimirovich Nabokov (VN) born on April 10 (April 23) at 47 Bolshaia Morskaia Street, St. Petersburg. Parents are Vladimir Dmitrievich Nabokov (VDN [1870–1922]), a teacher of criminal law at the Imperial School of Jurisprudence, and Elena Ivanovna Nabokov (née Rukavishnikov [1876–1939]).
1900	Brother Sergei born February 28 (March 13).
1901	VN's Rukavishnikov grandparents die. Mother inherits country estate Vyra, and VN's uncle Vasily inherits country estate Rozhdestveno. Véra Evseevna Slonim (VN's future wife) born in St. Petersburg on December 23 (January 5, 1901).
1902	VN and Sergei learn English from British governess, Rachel Home. Sister Olga born December 23 (January 5, 1903).
1905	January 9 (January 22) — "Bloody Sunday" — tsarist troops fire on demonstrators in St. Petersburg. VDN deprived of court title after denunciation of the incident in the St. Petersburg Duma

(City Council). VDN becomes one of founders of Constitutional Democratic (CD) Party.

1906   Sister Elena born March 18 (March 31). VDN elected to First State Duma in March and advocates for major political reform. Duma is dissolved in July.

1907   VN seriously ill with pneumonia; studies books on butterflies while recovering.

1909   Family travels to Biarritz, where VN falls in love with nine-year old girl, Claude Deprès ("Collette" in VN's memoir *Speak, Memory*).

1911   VN enters Tenishev School in St. Petersburg. Brother Kirill born June 17 (June 30).

1914   VN composes first poem. Germany declares war on Russia. St. Petersburg is renamed Petrograd.

1915   VN begins romance with Valentina ("Liusia") Shulgina. In November he co-edits school literary journal, in which his first published poem, "Osen'" ("Autumn") appears.

1916   VN publishes collection of poetry entitled *Stikhi* (*Poems*) at his own expense. Uncle Vasily Rukavishnikov dies, leaving VN his Rozhdestveno estate, worth several million dollars.

1917   February 27 (March 12) — February Revolution. Tsar Nicholas II abdicates; VDN accepts post in new Provisional Government. October 25 (November 7) — Bolshevik Revolution. VDN sends family to Crimea. Arrested and imprisoned for several days by the Bolsheviks, VDN leaves Petrograd and rejoins his family in December. VN composes first chess problems.

1918   German army takes Crimea in April. After departure of German troops, VDN becomes Minister of Justice in Crimean Provisional Government.

1919   Facing approach of Bolshevik troops, Nabokov family leaves Sebastopol for Athens on Greek ship on April 2 (April 15). From Athens, Nabokov family travels to London. VN enters Trinity College, Cambridge in October; begins studying zoology and then modern languages (French and Russian). Writes poetry in Russian and in English; also writes first entomological paper (published 1920).

1920   Nabokov family moves to Berlin; VDN helps establish Russian-language newspaper *Rul'* (*The Rudder*).

1921	VN publishes poems and the short story "Nezhit'" ("The Wood-Sprite") in *Rul'* in January, using for the first time the pen-name "Vladimir Sirin." During summertime visit to Berlin, falls in love with Svetlana Romanovna Siewert.
1922	On March 28, VDN is shot and killed while trying to defend Pavel Miliukov from assassination by two monarchist gunmen. In June, VN receives B.A. degree and moves to Berlin, where he becomes engaged to Svetlana Siewert. Collection of poems entitled *Grozd'* (*The Cluster*) published in December.
1923	Poetry collection *Gornii put'* (*The Empyrean Path*) appears in January. Engagement with Svetlana Siewert terminated due to her parents' concern about Nabokov's financial standing. *Ania v strane chudes*, Nabokov's version of *Alice in Wonderland*, is published in March. Nabokov meets Véra Evseevna Slonim at a charity ball in May.
1924	Publishes several short stories in Russian periodicals. Drama *Polius* (*The Pole*) published in August. While supporting himself by giving private lessons in tennis, boxing, Russian, and English, Nabokov publishes several short stories in Russian periodicals.
1925	Marries Véra Evseevna Slonim in May. Writes first novel, *Mashen'ka* (*Mary*, published in March 1926).
1928	Novel *Korol', dama, valet* (*King, Queen, Knave*) published in September.
1929	Completes work on novel *Zashchita Luzhina* (*The Defense*). Novel appears serially in *Sovremennye zapiski* in 1929–30 and in book form in 1930. Collection of stories and poems entitled *Vozvrashchenie Chorba* (*The Return of Chorb*) appears in December.
1930	Short novel *Sogliadatai* (*The Eye*) published in *Sovremennye zapiski* in November.
1931	Novel *Podvig* (*Glory*) published serially in *Sovremennye zapiski*, and in book form in 1932.
1932	Nabokov travels to Paris to give public readings of his work. Novel *Kamera obskura* (*Laughter in the Dark*) appears serially in *Sovremennye zapiski* in 1932–33, and in book form in 1933.
1933	Adolf Hitler appointed Chancellor of Germany in January.
1934	Novel *Otchaianie* (*Despair*) appears serially in *Sovremennye zapiski*, and in book form in 1936. Son Dmitri born May 10.

1935	Novel *Priglashenie na kazn'* (*Invitation to a Beheading*) published serially in *Sovremennye zapiski* in 1935–36, and in book form in 1938. Nabokov translates *Otchaianie* into English.
1936	Véra loses job at engineering company because she is Jewish.
1937	Nabokov leaves Germany for a reading tour in January; he never returns. Becomes involved in romantic liaison with Irina Guadinini in Paris. Travels with family to Cannes; ends affair with Guadanini. *Despair*, Nabokov's translation of *Otchaianie*, appears in England. Last Russian novel, *Dar* (*The Gift*), begins serial publication in *Sovremennye zapiski*; novel is published 1937–38, with the exception of Chapter Four, which editors refuse to publish because they disapprove of the treatment of its subject, the life of the nineteenth-century writer N. G. Chernyshevsky.
1938	Two dramas, *Sobytie* (*The Event*) and *Izobretenie Val'sa* (*The Waltz Invention*), published. *Laughter in the Dark*, Nabokov's translation of *Kamera obskura*, comes out in the United States. *Sogliadatai*, a collection of short fiction, appears in October.
1939	Writes *The Real Life of Sebastian Knight*, his first English-language novel. Travels to England looking for employment. Mother dies in Prague on May 2. Germany invades Poland on September 1. France attacks Germany on September 7. Nabokov accepts offer to teach summer course in Russian literature at Stanford University. Writes *Volshebnik* (*The Enchanter*).
1940	Germany begins invasion of France on May 12. Nabokov departs France with Véra and Dmitri on ocean liner *Champlain*. Arrives New York May 27. Writes reviews for the *New Republic* and the *New York Sun*. Works on Lepidoptera at the American Museum of Natural History.
1941	Begins one-year appointment as Resident Lecturer in Comparative Literature at Wellesley College in the fall. Begins helping put Lepidoptera collection at Harvard's Museum of Comparative Zoology in order. *The Real Life of Sebastian Knight* is published by New Directions in December.
1942	Appointed Research Fellow at the Museum of Comparative Zoology. Short poem "The Refrigerator Awakes" becomes Nabokov's first published *New Yorker* poem.
1943	Begins teaching non-credit Russian language course at Wellesley College. During summer, collects butterflies and works on novel *Bend Sinister* in Utah.

1944   Short monograph entitled *Nikolai Gogol* published by New Directions. Nabokov appointed lecturer at Wellesley College.

1945   Collection of translations entitled *Three Russian Poets* published by New Directions. First short story published in the *New Yorker*— "Double Talk" (later retitled "Conversation Piece, 1945") — appears in June.

1946   Works on lectures for course on Russian literature at Wellesley. Finishes *Bend Sinister*.

1947   *Bend Sinister* published in June. Nabokov offered teaching appointment at Cornell. Collection *Nine Stories*, containing stories translated from Russian as well as English-language stories, appears in December.

1948   Excerpts from *Conclusive Evidence*, first version of autobiography, published in the *New Yorker*. Nabokov begins teaching Russian literature at Cornell.

1950   Begins working on novel entitled *The Kingdom by the Sea*, which later evolves into *Lolita*. Begins teaching major course on European fiction at Cornell.

1951   *Conclusive Evidence* published in February. Nabokov continues work on *Lolita*. Near Telluride, Colorado in July, Nabokov catches first female of *Lycaeides argyrognomon sublivens*, male specimens of which he had studied at the Museum of Comparative Zoology. Nabokov later uses this setting for a key passage in *Lolita*.

1952   Teaches Russian literature and a course on the novel as a Visiting Lecturer at Harvard during the spring. *Dar* published in (complete) book form. Returns to Cornell to teach in the fall. Collection of Russian poems, *Stikhotvoreniia 1929–1951* (*Poems 1929–1951*), published in Paris.

1953   Takes leave from Cornell to work on translation of Pushkin's *Eugene Onegin*. Publishes first chapter of *Pnin* in the *New Yorker*. Finishes writing *Lolita* in December.

1954   *Drugie berega*, a revised Russian version of Nabokov's autobiographical memoir, published. Nabokov unsuccessful in finding an American publisher for *Lolita*.

1955   *Lolita* accepted for publication by Maurice Girodias, owner of Olympia Press in France. Named one of the best books of 1955 by Graham Greene in the London *Sunday Times*.

1956   John Gordon denounces *Lolita* in the London *Sunday Express*, sparking controversy over the novel. Nabokov's collection of Russian short stories, *Vesna v Fial'te i drugie rasskazy* (*Spring in Fialta and Other Stories*), published in New York. French government bans *Lolita* along with several other Olympia Press titles.

1957   *Pnin* published; receives nomination for National Book Award. The *Anchor Review* publishes passages from *Lolita* together with Nabokov's essay, "On a Book Entitled *Lolita*," and a critical essay by F. W. Dupee.

1958   *Lolita* published by G. P. Putnam's Sons; achieves instant success. Collection of short stories, *Nabokov's Dozen*, appears. Nabokov takes a year's leave of absence from Cornell.

1959   Resigns from Cornell. Travels to Europe. Small collection of poetry entitled *Poems* appears. *Invitation to a Beheading*, Dmitri Nabokov's translation of *Priglashenie na kazn'*, published. *Lolita* published in England.

1960   Works on screenplay for *Lolita*.

1961   Works on *Pale Fire*, finishes novel in December. Takes rooms in Montreux Palace Hotel, Switzerland.

1962   *Pale Fire* published. Stanley Kubrick's film version of *Lolita* released.

1963   *The Gift*, translation of *Dar* largely completed by Michel Scammell with Nabokov's corrections, appears in May. *Notes on Prosody* published.

1964   Translation of *Eugene Onegin* with extensive notes and commentary published in June. *The Defense*, Michael Scammell's translation of *Zashchita Luzhina*, appears in September.

1965   Edmund Wilson's critical review of *Eugene Onegin* triggers heated debate in periodical press. *The Eye*, Dmitri Nabokov's translation of *Sogliadatai*, appears in the fall.

1966   *The Waltz Invention*, translation of *Izobretenie Val'sa*, published. *Despair*, Nabokov's revision of his early translation of *Otchaianie*, appears.

1967   Short story collection *Nabokov's Quartet* appears. Revised version of Nabokov's memoir, *Speak, Memory: An Autobiography Revisited*, published. Nabokov's Russian translation of *Lolita* published.

1968	*King, Queen, Knave*, Dmitri Nabokov's translation of *Korol', dama, valet*, extensively revised by Nabokov, appears in April. Anthology entitled *Nabokov's Congeries* (later entitled *The Portable Nabokov*) published in September.
1969	*Ada* published in late spring.
1970	*Mary*, the translation of *Mashen'ka* by Michael Glenny and Nabokov, published in September.
1971	Collection of poetry and chess problems entitled *Poems and Problems* published in March. *Glory*, Nabokov's translation of *Podvig*, published in December.
1972	*Transparent Things* published in October.
1973	*A Russian Beauty and Other Stories*, a collection of stories originally written in Russian, appears in April. *Strong Opinions*, a collection of interviews and notes, appears in November. Nabokov awarded the National Medal for Literature in the United States.
1974	*Lolita: A Screenplay* published. His last complete novel, *Look at the Harlequins!*, appears in August.
1975	A second collection of early stories, *Tyrants Destroyed and Other Stories*, appears in January.
1976	Third collection of early stories, *Details of a Sunset and Other Stories*, published in March. Nabokov selects poems for extensive collection of Russian poetry entitled *Stikhi* (*Poems*) that will not be published until 1979.
1977	Hospitalized in Lausanne with fever and influenza from March to May. Returns to hospital in Lausanne in June. Dies on July 2. After cremation, body is interred in Clarens cemetery.
1991	Véra Nabokov dies on April 6.

CHRONOLOGY OF *LOLITA*

This chronology is based on information gathered from the text of Nabokov's *Lolita* as well as from the chronological reconstructions prepared by Carl Proffer in his *Keys to Lolita* and Dieter Zimmer's online chronology at <http://www.d-e-zimmer.de/LolitaUSA/LoChrono.htm> (last accessed on November 13, 2008). For a discussion of the problems of chronology in the novel, see Zimmer's site. The page numbers in parenthesis refer to passages in the text where the information on chronology can be found.

1910	Humbert Humbert born in Paris, France (9)
1911	Clare Quilty born in Ocean City, Maryland (31)
1913	Humbert's mother dies from a lightning strike (10)
1923	Summer: Humbert and Annabel Leigh have romance (11) Autumn: Humbert attends *lycée* in Lyon (11) December (?): Annabel dies in Corfu (13)
1934	Charlotte Becker and Harold E. Haze honeymoon in Veracruz, Mexico; Dolores Haze conceived on this trip (57, 100)
1935	January 1: Dolores Haze born in Pisky, a town in the Midwest (65, 46) April: Humbert has brief relationship with Monique, a Parisian prostitute (23) Humbert marries Valeria Zborovski (25, 30)
1937	Dolly's brother born (68)
1939	Dolly's brother dies (68) Humbert receives inheritance from relative in America (27) Valeria discloses to Humbert that she is having an affair; divorce proceedings ensue (27, 32)

1940	Winter: Humbert spends winter in Portugal (32) Spring: Humbert arrives in United States and takes up job devising and editing perfume ads (32) Over next two years Humbert writes comparative history of French literature for English-speaking students (32)
1943–44 (?)	Humbert spends more than a year in a sanatarium due to psychological problems (33)
1944	Summer: Dolly under supervision of Miss Phalen (56)
1945	The Haze family moves from Pisky to Ramsdale, which is located in New England (46, 74, 35)
1945 (?)	Valeria dies in childbirth
1946 (?)	Humbert has "another bout of insanity" and is institutionalized (34)
1947	May: Humbert moves into Haze household in Ramsdale (40–41) June 5 (Thursday): First diary entry provided by Humbert (41) June 22 (Sunday): Humbert's encounter with Dolly on living room couch (57) June 26 (Thursday): Charlotte drives Dolly to Camp Q (65) Late June or early July: Humbert marries Charlotte (74–75) July 29 (Tuesday): Charlotte's and Humbert's last swim at Hourglass Lake (82) August 5 (Tuesday): Charlotte receives letter from the second Miss Phalen "exactly a week after our last swim" (93) August 6 (Wednesday): Humbert goes to doctor to get a prescription for sleeping pills (94); Charlotte reads his diary; Charlotte is hit by a car and dies. August 13 (Wednesday): Humbert leaves Ramsdale (105–6), spends night in Parkington (109) August 14 (Thursday): Humbert drives from Parkington to Camp Q to pick up Dolly. They drive on to Briceland and the Enchanted Hunters Hotel (112, 115) August 15 (Friday): Humbert and Dolly leave Briceland and go to Lepingville (139, 141)
August 1947– August 1948	Humbert and Dolly travel across the United States (154).
1948	August: Humbert and Dolly arrive in Beardsley and take up residence at 14 Thayer Street (176) December: Humbert meets with Miss Pratt to discuss Dolly's conduct (193)

1949   January 1: Humbert buys Dolly a new bicycle (199)
            May: Dolly participates in a "very special rehearsal" of the school
            play (202)
            May 27 (Friday): Dolly's piano teacher mentions in phone con-
            versation with Humbert that Dolly has missed two lessons (202);
            Humbert and Dolly fight, Dolly escapes, and then she decides to
            abandon the play and start a new road trip (207)
            May 29 (Sunday): Humber and Dolly leave Beardsley (208)
            Early June: Humbert and Dolly stay at the Chestnut Court in Kas-
            beam, where she surreptitiously meets with Quilty (212–15)
            Mid-June: Humbert and Dolly arrive in Wace, where they attend
            Clare Quilty and Vivian Darkbloom's play (220)
            Late June: Dolly plays tennis at Champion Hotel in Colorado
            (233), and frolics by the pool under that watchful gaze of Clare
            Quilty (237)
            June 27 (Monday): Humbert and Dolly arrive in Elphinstone at
            the Silver Spur Court (238). Dolly is ill and is taken to the local
            hospital (240)
            June 28 (Tuesday): Humbert attempts an early morning visit to
            the hospital (242)
            July 2 (Saturday): Humbert visits Dolly in the hospital for the
            last time and spies suspicious envelope (242)
            July 3 (Sunday): Humbert is sick, but he sends Dolly's two bags
            to the hospital (244)
            July 4 (Monday): Still sick, Humbert hears "some great national
            celebration in town" (245); Dolly leaves hospital (246)
            July 5 (Tuesday): Humbert telephones hospital and learns that
            Dolly had left the day before (246); Humbert leaves Elphinstone
            July 5–November 18: Humbert searches for Dolly and her new
            companion (248)
            November 18: Humbert arrives in Beardsley for a few days
            (248, 252)

1950   January 1: Humbert sends a collection of Dolly's belongings to
            a home for orphaned girls in Canada (255)
            Winter-Spring: Humbert stays in a Quebec sanatorium (255)
            May: Humbert picks up Rita (258) and spends two years with
            her (259)

1951   September: Humbert takes up position at Cantrip College until
            June 1952 (260)

1952   June: Humbert gets Rita out of jail and returns to New York City
            with her by way of Briceland (261)
            September 18 (Thursday): Dolly writes Humbert from Coalmont
            (267)

1952   September 22 (Monday): Humbert receives Dolly's letter and
              leaves New York for Coalmont (267)
              September 23 (Tuesday): Humbert arrives at Schiller home on
              Hunter Road, Coalmont (268–69); at around 4:00 PM, he departs
              for Ramsdale (281)
              September 24 (Wednesday): Humbert arrives in Ramsdale at
              around noon (287); he learns Clare Quilty's address from Quilty's
              uncle Ivor (291); and he drives from Ramsdale to Parkington
              (292)
              September 25 (Thursday): After spending the night at Insomnia
              Lodge, Humbert goes to kill Quilty at Quilty's house on Grimm
              Road (293); after the murder, Humbert is arrested by police (307)
              November 16 (Sunday): Humbert dies of coronary thrombosis (3)
              December 25 (Thursday): Dolly Schiller dies in childbirth in Gray
              Star (4)

1955   August 5: John Ray, Jr. finishes his foreword to Humbert's
              memoir (6)

A Reader's Guide to Nabokov's "Lolita"

PREFACE

Vladimir Nabokov's *Lolita* is one of the most fascinating novels of the twentieth century. Since its publication in the mid 1950s, it has stirred up a tremendous range of responses, from furious outrage to sheer delight. In Humbert Humbert, the novel's protagonist and narrator, Nabokov created a figure of considerable imagination who possesses a remarkable facility with language. At the same time, however, the figure commits heinous acts and coerces a twelve-year-old girl into becoming his reluctant sexual partner. This clash of verbal eloquence and despicable conduct creates a distinctive kind of cognitive dissonance for the reader. My book seeks to guide the reader through the intricacies of Nabokov's novel and to facilitate an understanding of the writer's elaborate artistic design. I have supplemented a detailed analysis of the work with chapters on its genesis and publication, its precursors in Nabokov's work and world literature, a discussion of the character of Dolly Haze (Humbert's "Lolita"), and a commentary on the critical reception and cultural afterlife of the novel. The volume concludes with an annotated bibliography of selected works for further reading. I should note here that Nabokov famously declared that "one cannot *read* a book: one can only reread it" (*L* 3). This reader's guide is meant to enhance the experience of both the first-time reader and the devoted rereader; it should in no way be seen as a substitute for the novel itself. Only direct immersion in Nabokov's text will enable the reader to appreciate the novel's true richness and depth. This brief guide aims to provide readers with the material they may need to grasp the full complexity and sweep of Nabokov's unique creation.

I would like to thank the Sesquicentennial Fellowship program at the University of Virginia for providing research funding for this project. I dedicate this book to my wife, Monica.

1

Chapter One

THE CREATION OF *LOLITA*

Vladimir Nabokov declared that the "first little throb" of *Lolita* went through him in 1939 or early 1940 when he was living in Paris ("On a Book Entitled *Lolita*"; *L* 311). As we shall see below, however, the specific theme of an older man being attracted to a much younger woman (or girl) long predates this period in Nabokov's life. Nonetheless, in the fall of 1939 Nabokov sat down to write his first extended treatment of the *Lolita* plot: an adult man marries a widow in order to gain access to the widow's young daughter. This tale, entitled *The Enchanter* (*Volshebnik* in Russian), was written from a very different perspective than *Lolita*. The story of the protagonist's obsession in *The Enchanter* is told from an external, third-person point of view, whereas *Lolita* is narrated by the obsessed man himself, and this shift in point of view opened up for Nabokov the opportunity to attempt his daring artistic experiment: he allows his abhorrent criminal protagonist the chance to plead his own case and to cloak his beastly crimes in language and images that are as intriguing as they are disturbing.

Nabokov perhaps had this later perspective in mind when he expanded upon his remark about his "initial throb." He states that this "initial shiver of inspiration" was prompted by a newspaper story about an ape in the Jardin des Plantes who was coaxed by a researcher into producing a charcoal drawing. The drawing showed the bars of the "poor creature's cage" (*L* 311). If this story has any relevance to *Lolita* (and curiously, no one has been able to identify the original source of the story, although Brian Boyd speculates that Nabokov may have seen a photograph of a chimpanzee in a London zoo with a paintbrush in his hand[1]), then it is surely the image of an imprisoned beast drawing the bars of his own cage. Humbert's narrative not only depicts the chastened criminal locked in prison awaiting trial, but the very words out of which he constructs his narrative form, in a metaphorical sense, the bars of his cage. As he writes in an imagined address to Dolly: "I have only words to play with" (*L* 32).

Nabokov was unable to publish *The Enchanter* at the time of its composition, and although he rediscovered the manuscript years later, it did not see the light of day until after his death: it was not published until 1986. Perhaps the failure of this text to appear in print in 1939 or 1940 was fortuitous, for when Nabokov began thinking about the theme again at the end of the 1940s, he did not have to worry about repeating himself in print. His first mention of a new work in progress in a letter to Edmund Wilson in 1947 reveals little. He merely states: "I am writing two new things now 1. a short novel about a man who liked little girls — and it's going to be called *The Kingdom by the Sea* — and 2. a new type of autobiography" (*NWL* 215; the second project would turn into *Speak, Memory*). A subsequent description of the novel in a letter to Pascal Covici in 1951 provides a bit more specificity: "I am engaged in the composition of a novel, which deals with the problems of a very moral middle-aged gentleman who falls very immorally in love with his stepdaughter, a girl of thirteen" (*SL* 128). Between these two points, as Nabokov himself put it, he was faced with the difficult task of "inventing America" (*L* 312).

To ground his story of a middle-aged European man pursuing a young American girl in the details of "real" life, Nabokov conducted research into every aspect of this story. Brian Boyd's biography of Nabokov sets forth the kinds of material Nabokov perused and the extent to which he sought specificity for the social and psychological milieu he would create in his novel. He rode local buses to record the way schoolgirls talked with one another. He read manuals on the physical and emotional maturation of adolescent girls. He studied gun catalogues, read teenage magazines, learned the titles of popular songs, and perused Havelock Ellis.[2] During his journeys across the country in the late 1940s and early 1950s he gathered material for his description of Humbert's and Dolly's own cross-country trips. Speaking engagements for women's groups gave him ideas on how to fill in the portrait of Dolly's mother Charlotte. A night at the Royal York Hotel in Toronto prompted him to record the nerve-jarring noises of the place in images that would find their way into his novel, including "the violent waterfalls of one's neighbor's toilet."[3] He read with interest newspaper accounts about the fate of a girl named Florence Sally Horner who had been abducted as an eleven-year-old by a fifty-year-old mechanic named Frank La Salle and kept as a "cross-country love slave" for twenty-one months. As Alexander Dolinin has persuasively demonstrated, Nabokov used key details from this incident in *Lolita*, and he even has Humbert refer to the incident by name (*L* 289).[4]

Despite his intense work on the project, he occasionally despaired of its ultimate success and, on more than one occasion, he was ready to destroy the notes he had made for the novel. In his essay on *Lolita* he writes that once or twice he was on the point of burning the unfinished draft but was stopped "by the thought that the ghost of the destroyed book would haunt my files for the rest of my life" (*L* 312). Nabokov's wife Véra played a key role in this rescue: upon at least one occasion, she saved his papers from the flame.[5] The work proceeded slowly, and if he had written a draft of the first twelve chapters of Part One and several passages from Part Two by mid-1950, it was not until December 6, 1953 that he would write in his diary: "Finished *Lolita* which was begun exactly 5 years ago."[6]

Having completed the daunting task of writing the novel, Nabokov now faced the similarly daunting challenge of finding a publisher for the work. Concerned about the security of his teaching position at Cornell, he initially explored the idea of publishing the novel under a pseudonym, but the publishers he contacted discouraged this idea. Nor were they themselves willing to undertake the risk of publishing what would surely be seen as a controversial work. Nabokov approached five American publishers — Viking Press; Simon and Schuster; New Directions; Farrar, Straus and Young; and Doubleday — but all turned him down; several were fearful of the complications that would ensue if the book were to be banned at its release. Nabokov also contacted an agent in France, Doussia Ergaz, to see if she might be able to find a publisher there, and she had better luck. In April 1955 she met Maurice Girodias, the owner of Olympia Press. Unlike his American counterparts, Girodias was happy to take on Nabokov's project, but the reason for this was apparently not obvious to Ergaz, and certainly not to Nabokov. Eager for success as a publisher, Girodias took under his wing a broad assortment of literature, from works by Samuel Beckett and Henry Miller to outright pornography. In fact, a large number of his titles were targeted at the English-speaking traveler looking for erotica. Several years later, Nabokov wrote that he subsequently pondered the question of whether he would have agreed "so cheerfully" to Girodias publishing *Lolita* if he had been aware of "what formed the supple backbone of his production." "Alas," he writes, "I probably would, though less cheerfully" (*SO* 271). Cheerfully or not, Nabokov signed a contract with Girodias in June 1955, and the book appeared in two slender paperback volumes in September of that year.

Given its humble origins and the unlikely company in which it was published (other titles produced by Olympia at the time included *Until She Screams* and *How To Do It*), *Lolita* might easily have languished in obscurity if Graham Greene had not named it one of the best books of 1955 in the Christmas edition of London *Sunday Times*. This declaration led others to look for a copy of the book, and one of those who did, John Gordon, wrote a searing rebuke to Greene in the London *Sunday Express* at the end of January 1956. Asking "Has Mr. Graham Greene...been pulling the leg of the sedate *Sunday Times*?" Gordon denounced *Lolita* as "the filthiest book" he had ever read and "[s]heer unrestrained pornography." He further declared that anyone who published the novel in England would surely go to prison, and he scolded the *Sunday Times* for "stepping into the business" of publicizing pornography.[7] Greene reacted to Gordon's criticism with a cutting rebuke of his own in February 1956, and a bracing controversy began percolating. Readers in the United States became acquainted with the dispute when Harvey Breit reported the Greene-Gordon fracas in the *New York Times Book Review* at the end of February, although he identified *Lolita* only as a "long French novel about nymphets" with no author's name attached to it.[8] Breit followed up the story a month later, with more detail about the novel sent to him by reader, and this time he named its author.[9]

Nabokov was concerned about the charge that his work was pornographic, and he defended his work in nearly identical terms in two letters written in March 1956 (one to Morris Bishop and one to Pascal Covici): "I know that *Lolita* is my best work so far. I calmly lean on my conviction that it is a serious work of art, and the no court could prove it to be 'lewd and libertine.'" He continued: "*Lolita* is a tragedy. 'Pornography' is not an image plucked out of context; pornography is an attitude and an intention. The tragic and the obscene exclude each other" (*SL* 184, 185).

The controversy brewing in Britain piqued the interest of the American reader, and in the fall of 1956, the first American review of the novel, written by John Hollander, appeared out in the *Partisan Review*. Hollander was very complimentary in his review, highlighting its comic and parodic elements, and declaring it to be "just about the funniest book I remember having read."[10] With interest in *Lolita* on the rise, Nabokov's supporters in the States saw an opportunity to begin a campaign to publish the novel on these shores. Hoping to smooth the way for the eventual publication of the novel, Jason Epstein of Doubleday developed the idea of using the *Anchor Review*, a Doubleday publication, to print a large extract from the novel accompanied by an essay from Nabokov ("On a Book Entitled *Lolita*") and an introduction by F. W. Dupee. The review came out in 1957. Although the excerpts totaled nearly one hundred pages, the editors tactfully decided to omit some of the passages that would be most likely to elicit controversy, including some details of Humbert's early sexual encounter with Annabel Leigh, Humbert's definition of the "nymphet," the masturbation scene in the Haze living room, and the night Humbert spent with Dolly in the Enchanted Hunters Hotel. At the same time, the publication of Nabokov's novel *Pnin* to high acclaim in March 1957 further bolstered Nabokov's reputation as a serious writer of talent and distinction.

Meanwhile, back across the Atlantic, things were boiling apace. At the urging of the British government, which was disturbed by the prospect of its citizens bringing home pornographic material from France, the French government had decided in December 1956 to ban two dozen Olympia Press titles, with *Lolita* among them. Maurice Girodias sued the government, the French press took interest in the matter, and by 1957, "l'affaire *Lolita*" was making news. The suit dragged on throughout the year, until Girodias won the case in January 1958 and the ban was temporarily lifted, only to be reimposed under a new law later in the year. It was formally lifted in September 1959.[11]

Hopes for publishing *Lolita* in America continued to rise during this period, but Nabokov now found himself embroiled in a dispute with Girodias over the rights to publish the novel in the United States. Increasingly frustrated with the demands and evasions of his French publisher, Nabokov was happy to let Walter Minton of G. P. Putnam's Sons negotiate with Girodias on his behalf. Eventually they came to an agreement, and in March 1958 Nabokov at last signed a contract with Putnam's to publish *Lolita* later in the year. Nabokov showed great concern about how his novel might be presented to the public, and in a letter to Minton written on March 1, he put forth his vision about the cover design for the book: "Who would be capable of creating a romantic, delicately drawn, non-Freudian and non-juvenile picture for *Lolita* (a dissolving remoteness, a soft American landscape, a nostalgic highway — that sort of thing)? There is one subject which I am emphatically opposed to: any kind of representation of a little girl" (*SL* 250; see also *SL* 256). He returned to this topic a month later: "I want pure colors, melting clouds, accurately drawn details, a sunburst above a receding road with the light reflected in furrows and rust, after rain. And no girls" (*SL* 256). He even preferred to have a simple black-and-white cover design rather than one that would offer up a girl's image to whet the reader's imagination. When the novel finally appeared, no female images adorned the simple dust jacket.

The publication of *Lolita* on August 18, 1958 was accompanied by a host of reviews. Most were positive, but one, by Orville Prescott, called the book both "dull, dull, dull" and "highbrow pornography."[12] Walter Minton sent

Nabokov a telegram that day reporting: "YESTERDAYS REVIEWS MAGNI-FICENT AND NEW YORK TIMES BLAST THIS MORNING PROVIDED NECESSARY FUEL TO FLAME...BOOK STORES REPORT EXCELLENT DEMAND" (*SL* 257). "Excellent demand" indeed: within three days, the novel was into its third printing with 62500 copies in print, and within the first month, the novel had sold over 100000 copies. By the end of September *Lolita* was at the top of the best seller list where it remained for seven weeks until it was displaced by Boris Pasternak's recently released *Doctor Zhivago*.[13] A movie deal for $150000 was soon signed, and deals to translate the novel into numerous languages followed apace. It would take another year for the novel to be released in Great Britain, but, for the first time since his family's fortunes had been devastated by the Russian Revolution, Nabokov could look forward to absolute financial security as well as genuine world renown.

Notes

1. Brian Boyd, *Vladimir Nabokov: The Russian Years* (Princeton: Princeton University Press, 1990), 512.
2. See Brian Boyd, *Vladimir Nabokov: The American Years* (Princeton: Princeton University Press, 1991), 211; and Stacy Schiff, *Véra (Mrs. Vladimir Nabokov)* (New York: Random House, 1999), 180.
3. Boyd, *Vladimir Nabokov: The American Years*, 184.
4. Alexander Dolinin, "What Happened to Sally Horner? A Real-Life Source of Nabokov's *Lolita*," *Zembla*, 18 November 2008 <http://www.libraries.psu.edu/nabokov/zembla.htm>.
5. See Schiff, *Véra*, 166–67; and Boyd, *Vladimir Nabokov: The American Years*, 184.
6. Boyd, *Vladimir Nabokov: The American Years*, 169 and 226.
7. Quoted in Brian Boyd, *Vladimir Nabokov: The American Years* 295; and Michael Juliar, *Vladimir Nabokov: A Descriptive Bibliography* (New York: Garland, 1986), 692.
8. Harvey Breit, "In and Out of Books," *New York Times Book Review*, 26 February 1956, 8.
9. Harvey Breit, "In and Out of Books," *New York Times Book Review*, 11 March 1956, 8.
10. John Hollander, "The Perilous Magic of Nymphets," *Partisan Review* 23.4 (1956): 560.
11. See Boyd, *Vladimir Nabokov: The American Years*, 364; and Michael Juliar, *Vladimir Nabokov: A Descriptive Bibliography*, 695.
12. Orville Prescott, "Books of the Times," *New York Times*, 18 August 1958, 17.
13. Boyd, *Vladimir Nabokov: The American Years*, 365 and 370.

Chapter Two

THE PRECURSORS OF *LOLITA*

Although Nabokov declared that the "first little throb" of *Lolita* went through him in 1939 or early 1940, the theme the sexual attraction felt by an adult male for a young girl, and the torment that derived from that attraction, had piqued his interest much earlier. A poem composed in Berlin in 1928, entitled "Lilith" ("Lilit" in the original Russian) deals with the subject in a particularly expressive way. The poem begins with the male narrator announcing "I died" and declaring his impression that he is in Paradise. He sees a naked little girl standing in a doorway exposing a "russet armpit," and this sight triggers a memory of a scene from his youth when he saw the youngest daughter of a miller emerging from the water "all golden / with a wet fleece between her legs" (*PP* 51). The girl leads him into a house and opens her legs before him. The narrator begins having sex with her, but as he approaches a climax, the girl pulls away, and he finds himself outside the house again, now surrounded by a mob of bleating youngsters. As the crowd increases, the man suddenly "spill[s] his seed" before them all, and he now realizes: "I was in Hell." When Nabokov published the poem with an English translation in his collection *Poems and Problems* in 1970, he characteristically warned his readers not to leap to interpretive conclusions about the work: "Intelligent readers will abstain from examining this impersonal fantasy for any links with my later fiction" (*PP* 55). At the risk of seeming unintelligent, however, we can easily point out some broad affinities between this poem and Nabokov's later treatments of the theme, from *The Enchanter* to *Lolita*.

To begin with, as in *Lolita* we find in the poem a first-person narrator describing his sexual attraction to a young girl, an attraction that results in disaster. In describing his initial attraction to the girl, the narrator makes reference to an earlier experience from his own childhood — his observation of the miller's naked daughter. Corresponding to this episode in *Lolita* is Humbert's description of his brief relationship with Annabel Leigh, which left him with a longing that would only be fulfilled in his encounter with Dolly. The overall arc of the plot, in which the protagonist's fantasy of being in paradise is replaced by torment when he discovers that his paradise is only a mask for an underlying hell, is duplicated in *Lolita*, both in small moments and in the novel as a whole. In Chapter Five of Part One, Humbert tells how he would become sexually aroused by observing through a neighbor's window "what looked like a nymphet in the act of undressing" (*L* 20). As he approaches orgasm, however, the "tender pattern of nudity" he had been looking at is "fiendishly" transformed into the image of a man in his underclothes and Humbert's "one-sided diminutive romance" ends in a "rich flavor of hell" (*L* 20). Similarly, after Humbert has first had sexual intercourse with Dolly, he remarks: "Whether or not the realization of a lifelong dream had surpassed all expectation, it had, in a sense, overshot its mark — and plunged into a nightmare" (*L* 140). He subsequently describes the typical motel room they stayed in as "a prison cell of paradise" (*L* 145) and he characterizes his "elected paradise" as having skies that were "the color of hell-flames" *(L* 166). What is more, the figure of Lilith (who, according to Talmudic legends, was the first wife of Adam) is herself specifically invoked in *Lolita*. In Chapter Five of Part One Humbert acknowledges: "Humbert was perfectly capable of intercourse with Eve, but it was Lilith he longed for" (*L* 20). In the same chapter Humbert comments on how his heart would beat when he spied "a demon child" among an innocent set of children (*L* 20).

Of course there is one vastly significant difference between "Lilith" and *Lolita*. In the poem, the girl is depicted as an integral part of a demonic realm. Her youthful age belies her guileful and deceptive nature. Yet although Humbert himself would call Dolly "hopelessly depraved" (*L* 133) with "nymphean evil" breathing through her pores (*L* 125), and he would portray himself being in thrall to her power to enchant him, the fact is that there is nothing remotely demonic about her. She appears to the reader as an essentially ordinary girl who becomes the victim of Humbert's own entrapment. It is he who forces himself upon her repeatedly, and holds her captive for nearly two years. Although the novel retains the poem's use of a first-person narrative in which the narrator presents himself as the victim of forces beyond his control, the emotional core of the novel lies in the depiction of a young girl's vulnerability and of the pain that is inflicted upon her by a callous and self-centered adult. In "Lilith" the child's function is to serve as the agent of the narrator's own torment; she is not given a distinctive personality or individualized identity. In *Lolita*, in contrast, despite Humbert's early assertion that his fantasy Lolita has "no will, no consciousness — indeed, no life of her own" (*L* 62), the emotional richness of the novel stems from the fact that Dolly does have an internal life, with a desires and fears that are distinctly her own, even though they are generally ignored by Humbert.

The treatment of an adult-child interaction in "Lilith" is set in what is appears to be an otherworldly realm. Another early glimpse of this theme occurs in the short story "A Nursery Tale" ("Skazka," written in 1926), which also displays an otherworldly connection. The tale centers on a demonic contract between a timid man named Erwin and a female incarnation of the devil who grants him the right to enjoy as many women as he desires one night on the condition that he must choose an odd, and not even, number of women during the preceding period from noon to midnight. His first selection is a girl he sees playing with a puppy in a park; his eye avidly recalls every detail of her figure: "the ripple of her verterbrae [...] the tender hollow between her shoulder blades, and [...] fiery strands in her chestnut hair" (*Stories* 165). Later in the evening he sees a "tall elderly man in evening clothes with a little girl walking beside — a child of fourteen or so in a low-cut black party dress." As he looks at the girl's face, he finds something odd about it, and he thinks "if she were not just a little girl — the old man's granddaughter, no doubt — one might suspect that her lips were touched up with rouge" (*Stories* 170). This girl becomes his twelfth selection, and Erwin realizes he must choose one more to achieve an odd number. Finally he sees a woman walking ahead of him, and he rushes to overtake her. He wonders: "What enticed him?" It's not her shape, he thinks, but "something else, bewitching and overwhelming [...] mere fantasy, maybe, the flutter, the rapture of fantasy" (*Stories* 171). As he finally catches up to her, he suddenly recognizes her as "the girl who had been playing that morning with a woolly black pup" (*Stories* 171), and he realizes that he has broken the terms of his contract: his thirteenth choice is the same as his first; the resulting number is even, not odd.

Two things should be noted in Nabokov's handling of the adult-child attraction theme here. First is the sense of utter enchantment that the adult feels in the presence of the child. His sight of her catapults him into the realm of desperate fantasy and desire. Second is the ultimate outcome of this desire. As in "Lilith," the man's attempt to realize his fantasy results in failure and loss. It is as if in Nabokov's world such transgressive desire inevitably invites punishment, and this pattern holds true for the subsequent, more pronounced treatments of the theme.

Several scholars have detected a precursor of the situation depicted in *Lolita* in Nabokov's novel *Laughter in the Dark* (*Kamera obskura*, published 1932–1933). The central protagonist of the novel, Albert Albinus (Krechmar [Kretschmar] in the Russian original) is a married man who becomes infatuated with a sixteen-year-old movie theater attendant. Ultimately he abandons his wife and child for the younger woman (named Margot in the English-language version and Magda in the Russian original), and as if in fulfillment of the saying "Love is blind," he loses his sight in a car accident. He is subsequently tormented by Margot and her former lover, Axel Rex (Robert Gorn [Horn] in the Russian), whose role as Albinus's nemesis has been compared to that of Clare Quilty in *Lolita*. It should be noted, however, that at sixteen, Margot is significantly older than Dolly at twelve, and as Nabokov himself declared: "Margot was a common young whore, not an unfortunate little Lolita" (*SO* 83).

A foreshadowing of the core plot of *Lolita* also shows up in Nabokov's last Russian novel, *The Gift* (*Dar*), which appeared in Russian in installments in 1937 and 1938 (with the exception of Chapter Four), and as a book (with all chapters intact) in 1952. One of the characters, the stepfather of Zina Mertz, the protagonist's love, tells the protagonist about an idea for a novel he would write if he had the opportunity:

> Imagine this kind of thing: an old dog — but still in his prime, fiery, thirsting for happiness — gets to know a widow, and she has a daughter, still quite a little girl — you know what I mean — when nothing is formed yet but already she has a way of walking that drives you out of your mind [...] What to do? Well, not long thinking, he ups and marries the widow. Okay. They settle down the three of them. Here you can go on indefinitely — the temptation, the eternal torment, the itch, the mad hopes. And the upshot — a miscalculation. Time flies, he gets older, she blossoms out — and not a sausage. Just walks by and scorches you with a look of contempt. Eh? D'you feel here a kind of Dostoevskian tragedy? (*Gift* 186)

Although this character may be giving voice to some private fantasies he may have had about his own stepdaughter, the story line he presents is not developed in *The Gift*. Nabokov, however, would return to the idea of a man marrying a widow to gain access to her young daughter in one of the last prose pieces he wrote in Russian, the short novel *The Enchanter* (*Volshebnik*), which is the very work he discusses in his essay on *Lolita* in connection with his recollection of the "first little throb" of the later novel (*L* 311–12). When Nabokov wrote his essay on *Lolita*, he believed that he had destroyed the work after moving to America in 1940, but he subsequently discovered it among his papers in 1959, and it was eventually translated into English by his son Dmitri to be published in 1986.

The Enchanter is the clearest precursor in Nabokov's work to *Lolita*, and the affinities between the two are numerous. The title character is a dealer in gems who burns with a secret desire for young girls and thinks of it as a "unique flame" (*En* 21). Like Humbert, he claims that only certain girls excite this desire: "I'm not attracted to every schoolgirl that comes along, far from it" (*En* 23). This anticipates Humbert's extended discussion of the difference between his enchanting "nymphets" and ordinary girls: "are all girl-children nymphets? Of course not [...] Within the same age limits the number of true nymphets is strikingly inferior to that of [...] ordinary [...] essentially human little girls" (*L* 16–17). *The Enchanter's* protagonist regards himself as protective of a child's innocence: "I cannot even consider the thought of causing pain or provoking unforgettable revulsion. Nonsense — I'm no ravisher" (*En* 22). We can compare this to Humbert's protestations: "Humbert Humbert tried hard to be good. Really and truly, he did. He had the utmost respect for ordinary children, with their purity and vulnerability, and under no circumstances would he have interfered with the innocence of a child" (*L* 19–20); "We are not sex fiends! We do not rape as good soldiers do" (*L* 88).

The Enchanter's protagonist is weighed down by the feeling that his desires will never find fulfillment, until he sees a twelve-year-old girl roller-skating in the park (*En* 26). He learns from the woman who accompanies her that the child's mother is severely ill, and he begins to visit the mother, gradually winning her confidence to the point where she accepts his proposal of marriage. To his dismay, however, the woman insists that her child remain with the woman who has been taking care of her, because the child's presence disturbs her. (This lack of tolerance for the child's presence anticipates Charlotte's uneasiness with Dolly's presence, but here, the reason for the mother's stance is that she needs peace and quiet, whereas in *Lolita* it may be that Dolly's presence threatens Charlotte's desire to be alone with Humbert.) The protagonist becomes

13

increasingly frustrated with his wife's intransigence, and even considers poisoning her, but her illness finally overcomes her, and she dies suddenly after an operation.

On his way to retrieve the child from the care of her mother's friend, the protagonist thinks about taking the girl on an extended trip with no fixed destination, much like the trip that Humbert takes with Dolly after Charlotte's death. When the protagonist first sees the child at the friend's house, he undergoes an experience of estrangement very similar to that which Humbert undergoes in the analogous scene when he picks Dolly up at camp: "at this very first instant he had the impression that she was not quite as pretty as before, that she had grown more snub-nosed and leggier." We can compare this to *Lolita*: "She was thinner and taller, and for a second it seemed to me that her face was less pretty than the mental imprint I had cherished for more than a month" (*Lo* 111). And, like Humbert, for an instant he feels something akin to compassion for the orphaned child: "Gloomily, rapidly, with nothing but a feeling of acute tenderness for her mourning, he took her by the shoulder and kissed her warm hair" (*En* 76). After a long journey, the two end up in a hotel where they are unable to find a room with twin beds because a flower show is in town and has brought many visitors to the place; they are given a room with one double bed instead. (A flower show comes together with a religious convention to create the same congestion in *Lolita*, and instead of twin beds, Humbert and Dolly are also offered a double bed.)

The subsequent events in *The Enchanter* unfold in quite a different fashion than they do in *Lolita*, however. After a brief episode involving an odd interaction with a local policeman, the protagonist returns to the hotel room to find the girl sleeping soundly and clothed only in a loose robe. Sexually stimulated by the sight and by physical proximity, the man is on the verge of an orgasm when the girl suddenly awakens and catches sight of his "rearing nudity." She begins to scream frantically as his orgasm erupts, and unable to calm her, he rushes outside the room and into the hallway where he is confronted by a growing set of inquisitive onlookers. In this sequence of events we find an echo of the ending of "Lilith." His sense of "the simplicity of paradise" (*En* 92) is quickly snuffed out, to be followed by exclusion from his chamber of pleasure and a humiliating exposure to a crowd of hostile beings. Shattered by the entire experience, the man runs out of the hotel where, in a desperate attempt to end the nightmare, he runs in front of a truck and is killed.

Although the broad theme of illicit pedophiliac desire and some specific supporting elements (such as the theme of enchantment and references to fairy tales) are common to both *The Enchanter* and *Lolita*, there are some major differences to be noted as well. One of the most important of these is the fact that the earlier tale is not narrated as a personal memoir by the protagonist. Although the third-person narrative does contain extensive passages of interior monologue, and the reader witnesses an ongoing conflict between ruthless desire and a recurring awareness of guilt that is also present in *Lolita*, the tone of the earlier work is entirely different. It is nearly devoid of the mordant humor and penetrating irony that permeates Humbert's narrative. More importantly, very little of the young girl's personality is revealed to the reader, and she remains nameless, as does her mother and the protagonist himself. If the female figure in "Lilith" functions purely as an agent of demonic deceit, the girl here functions purely as a figure of defenseless innocence. Despite a fleeting reference to the girl's recent "outbursts and tantrums" by her mother's friend (*En* 78), her character is not given any scope for development, and the story ends without any provision for the kind of resourcefulness and cleverness that Dolly cultivates during the period of her cohabitation with Humbert. Although some of the broad outlines of *Lolita* can be discerned in the earlier tale, it was not until Nabokov returned to the theme in an American context that he began to give robust life to his European enchanter and his surprisingly resistant American teenager.

While the specific theme of an adult male's obsession with an adolescent or pre-adolescent child has a few distinct antecedents in Nabokov's oeuvre, there is a larger theme in the novel that runs throughout his preceding career — the theme of subjective vision. Nabokov had an abiding belief in the unique value of individualized perception, the personal attention to the world that gives vibrancy and life to all that surrounds one. In his essay on *Lolita* Nabokov proclaimed that "reality" is "one of the few words which mean nothing without quotes" (*L* 312). In an interview conducted in 1968 he explained his position more fully: "To be sure, there is an average reality, perceived by all of us, but that it not true reality: it is only the reality of general ideas [...] Average reality begins to rot and stink as soon as the act of individual creation ceases to animate a subjectively perceived texture" (*SO* 118). His entire life's work represents a sustained exploration of this concept.

Broadly speaking, one can observe a distinctive evolution in his treatment of the theme in his early growth as a writer. The brief story "Terror"

("Uzhas"), published in 1927, features a man who becomes terrified one day on a trip away from home because he suddenly ceases to understand the meaning of the world he sees around him: "My line of communication with the world snapped. I was on my own and the world was on *its* own, and *that* world was devoid of sense" (*Stories* 177). What has happened is that the everyday world around him has been stripped of its conventional meaning, and he has found no new meaning with which to apprehend it. Such a state, as the narrator describes it, is akin to madness and even death.

Once Nabokov had portrayed this state of absolute meaningless, he began to explore what happens when a person strips the world of its everyday meaning, but instead of staring at a meaningless jumble of impressions, he or she endows the surrounding world with entirely new meaning, meaning created by this very observer. A fine example of this occurs in the short novel *The Eye* (*Sogliadatai*), published in 1930. There the first-person narrator records how, in an act of despair after a humiliating beating, he picks up a gun and shoots himself. He then goes on to describe his life after death: he was introduced in to a family of Russian émigrés, became infatuated with one of the daughters, and was ultimately rebuffed by her for another suitor. The reader soon realizes, however, that the narrator had not really died after all; his account of his post-death experience is merely an attempt to create a defense against the insults of life. He fantasizes that *he* has created this new world and its inhabitants, and much of the humor and pathos of the tale results from the continual clash of his unlikely fantasies against that which seems to be authentic reality.

Not long after *The Eye*, Nabokov wrote *Despair* (*Otchaianie*), published in 1934. Here he returns to the theme of a person stripping the world of its everyday meaning and charging it with new, more personal meaning but now, in place of the essentially harmless fantasies of the narrator of *The Eye*, he endows his protagonist with a more aggressive and sinister orientation. The first-person narrator of the novel, one Hermann Karlovich, encounters a man who he believes is his identical double. He plans to dress the man in his (Hermann's) own clothes and then kill him, and thereby to begin a new life with the proceeds of his insurance policy which will be collected by his gullible and pliant wife. After the murder, though, it becomes apparent that the supposed double bears little, if any, resemblance to Hermann. The resemblance is merely Hermann's projection and reflects the fundamental solipsism at work in the way he view people and things around him. But Nabokov has added a new twist to this tale of solipsistic projection. Hermann views his act of murder not as a simple crime, but as a work of *art*. He considers himself to be an original artist of great distinction, and as he writes his account of the crime he recalls how he longed, "to the point of pain, for that masterpiece of mine [...] to be appreciated by men" (*Des* 178). Hermann's hopes for such recognition, however, are thoroughly dashed by the end of the novel, and Nabokov's text underscores in multiples ways Hermann's failure as an artist.

In point of fact, Hermann's delusion points to one of the most important themes of Nabokov's own art, with particular relevance to *Lolita*: the pernicious misapprehension of the powers and sphere of influence that properly belong to the artist. Nabokov himself held decisive views on the power and control he exercised over his creative world. As he told an interviewer in 1966: "I am the perfect dictator in that private world insofar as I alone am responsible for its stability and truth" (*SO* 69). In a similar vein he declared: "My characters are galley slaves" (*SO* 95). The crucial point to note here, however, is that the control which an artist exerts over his or her created world does not extend to the world of beings who surround the artist. In other words, the latitude granted to an author creating a work of fiction on paper is not granted to those who seek to manipulate or control others according to their own visions or desires, no matter how "artistic" those visions may be. Many characters in Nabokov's works make the essential error of regarding the world and its inhabitants around them as the material or medium for their own solipsistic art. This is how Hermann viewed and treated his supposed double Felix, and this is how Humbert Humbert will view and treat Dolly Haze. As he writes in the notorious masturbation scene in Part One of the novel: "What I had madly possessed was not she, but my own creation, another, fanciful Lolita [...] and having no will, no consciousness — indeed, no life of her own" (*L* 62). Lolita, he declares, "had been safely solipsized" (*L* 60). Nabokov would later highlight the connection between Humbert and Hermann when he wrote the foreword to his English-language translation of *Despair*: "Hermann and Humbert are alike only in the sense that two dragons painted by the same artist at different periods of his life resemble each other. Both are neurotic scoundrels, yet there is a green lane in Paradise where Humbert is permitted to wander at dusk once a year; but Hell shall never parole Hermann" (*Des* xiii). (We shall discuss the possible reasons for this glimmer of leniency in Humbert's case later.)

While *Lolita* displays many of the central themes of Nabokov's own art, it also reflects the artistic achievements of a myriad of other writers as well. Nabokov's art is deeply syncretic at its core. He enjoys combining elements from and allusions to a broad range of external source material, from literature and art to popular culture and local crime stories. Alfred Appel, Jr., who compiled the immensely useful *Annotated Lolita*, characterized the novel as "surely the most allusive and linguistically playful novel in English since *Ulysses* (1922) and *Finnegans Wake* (1939)" (*AnL* xi). The list of works to which some allusion in *Lolita* has been detected by critics and scholars is extensive indeed, including Catullus, Dante, Shakespeare, Goethe, Keats, Byron, Browning, Baudelaire, Rimbaud, Verlaine, Flaubert, Joyce, Proust, and de Sade, to name just a few.[1] Yet in addition to the many casual allusions that flash by in the novel, there are several that contribute significantly to the generation of meaning there. In fact, one of the most interesting aspects of the novel is Nabokov's intricate use of literary or cultural subtexts. Whereas Humbert Humbert may refer to a literary figure or theme for one purpose (such as to bolster his claim that his desires are normal and should be regarded with tolerance), his creator may invoke the very same reference for very different reasons, especially to undermine those very claims. We should look briefly at some of the more important texts that figure prominently in Nabokov's *Lolita*.

One of the most striking features of *Lolita* is its very form. Subtitled by its putative editor, John Ray, Jr., as "the Confession of a White Widowed Male," the narrative produced by Humbert Humbert displays a remarkable blend of exposition, self-analysis, self-castigation, and self-justification. While the confessional genre has a long history in world literature, the type of confession presented here may be most most closely reflective of the famous confessional monologues created by Fyodor Dostoevsky, especially in *Notes from the Underground* (1864) and "The Gentle Creature" (1876). In each of these works, the narrator addresses an unseen (and perhaps only imaginary) audience: an audience who the narrator thinks will be sitting in judgment of him. As a consequence, the narrator shapes his monologue in anticipation of the audience's response, and he moves restlessly between postures of supplication and defiance, self-accusation and self-defense. In *Notes from the Underground*, for example, the narrator exclaims on the one hand, "I can assure you, gentlemen, I suffered terribly," and on the other, "I don't care a damn what you might think about it."[2] Humbert will similarly go from imploring his readers to imagine him with sympathy

("I shall not exist if you do not imagine me; try to discern the doe in me, trembling in the forest of my own iniquity" [*L* 129]) to calling them names ("Frigid gentlewomen of the jury!" [*L* 132]).

Humbert's repeated references to a jury in *Lolita* indicate the novel's special connection to "The Gentle Creature." Although the narrator of "The Gentle Creature" is not facing trial like Humbert, in his internal monologue he is trying to explain to himself and to his imagined audience the reasons for his young wife's suicide and the role he might have played in driving her to this act. At one point he explodes: "What do I care for your laws now? What are your customs to me? Your morals, your life, your State, your faith? Let your judges judge me. Let me be brought before your courts, before your public courts, and I will declare that I do not recognize anything."[3] This anticipates Humbert's challenge to his audience: "You may jeer at me, and threaten to clear the court, but until I am gagged and half-throttled, I will shout my poor truth" (*L* 278).

The links between "The Gentle Creature" and *Lolita* extend beyond form, however. Both works deal with the attraction felt by an older man for a younger woman, although the age difference in *Lolita* is even more glaring than in the Dostoevsky work. Dostoevsky's narrator thinks: "that I was forty-one and she was only sixteen. That fascinated me — that feeling of inequality. Yes, it's delightful, very delightful" (681). Humbert writes of the difference in ages between a nymphet and her admirer: "there must be a gap of several years, never less than ten I should say, generally thirty or forty, and as many as ninety in a few known cases [...] It is a question of focal adjustment, [...] a certain contrast that the mind perceives with a gasp of perverse delight" (*L* 17). Both narratives go on to unfold tales of manipulation and control, with the male narrators trying to transform their young companions into docile and compliant partners, but in both cases, the attempt ultimately fails, although the specific way the young woman "escapes" differs from Dostoevsky to Nabokov.[4]

Although both "The Gentle Creature" and *Lolita* depict one-side relationships between an older man and a younger woman, the characterization "younger woman" can only be applied in an accurate sense to the Dostoevsky work, for Dolly is twelve years old when Humbert first meets her, not sixteen. But there are other works by Dostoevsky that touch upon the theme of pedophilia, from the suggestion in *Crime and Punishment* (1866) that Arkady Svidrigailov drove a girl to suicide by abusing her, to the explicit treatment of sexual abuse in the suppressed chapter of *The Devils* (1871–1872) entitled "At Tikhon's," which was published for the first time only in 1922. In that work, Nikolai Stavrogin contemplates publishing a "confession" in which he depicts his violation of a young girl who was roughly Dolly's age at the time of the abuse. Nabokov was well aware of the Dostoevskian subtext, and he has Humbert acknowledge that he felt "a Dostoevskian grin dawning" as he comes to realize that by marrying Charlotte Haze he would gain easy access to her child (*L* 70). It is worth noting that Stavrogin's sense of haunting remorse over the injury he had done to the little girl (who committed suicide after he treats her coldly) finds representation in the form of a tiny spider he envisions in a dream. Humbert will portray himself as a spider as he mentally probes the Haze household looking for traces of Dolly's presence (*L* 49–50).

Dostoevsky was not the only Russian writer whose legacy finds reflection in *Lolita*. Priscilla Meyer argues that Nabokov reworked the central events of a work he much admired, Alexander Pushkin's novel in verse *Eugene Onegin* (published in installments from 1825 to 1832, and as a separate volume in 1833), into the plot of *Lolita*.[5] Nabokov was working on a translation of *Onegin* and a vast commentary to the work at the very time he was composing *Lolita*. Another Pushkin work that may have affected Nabokov's creative plans for *Lolita* was the unfinished play *Rusalka* ("Water Nymph"). The *rusalka* is an unusual figure in Russian folklore. According to some East Slavic folk legends, *rusalki* (the plural form of *rusalka*) were female spirits who lived in ponds and streams and who were believed to be the souls of unbaptized or stillborn babies, or of women who had died prematurely, perhaps because they had committed suicide, primarily because of unrequited love. Pushkin had begun work on a dramatic piece about a miller's daughter (let us recall here the episode featuring a miller's daughter in "Lilith") who committed suicide after her lover, a prince, had left her to marry someone else. The young woman had been pregnant at the time, and in Pushkin's final scenes, the woman, now a *rusalka* smoldering with desire for vengeance, sends her daughter to the shore to meet the prince and to tell him of her parentage. Pushkin worked on the play between 1829 and 1832, but he had left it unfinished when he died in 1836. Some one hundred years later, Nabokov decided to try to finish the piece. In his conclusion, which he wrote at the end of the 1930s, the young daughter meets the prince, who is initially puzzled by her appearance. When she explains who she is, and summons him to join them in the water, the prince masters his anxiety and follows her into the water. Several readers have noted the presence of the *rusalka* (or mermaid) theme in *Lolita*, and it has even been suggested that after Charlotte's death, she becomes an avenging spirit similar to the figure depicted in Pushkin's *Rusalka*.[6]

When weaving the theme of water spirits into his novel, Nabokov not only had Russian folk beliefs and Pushkin's treatment of the *rusalka* at hand, he drew upon West European sources as well. One such source was Hans Christian Andersen's *The Little Mermaid* (1837), which Nabokov may have read as a child (see *SM* 87) and which Humbert presents to Dolly during their first cross-country trip together (*L* 174). This tale offers a good example of the kind of subtle complexity that Nabokov could instill into his use of literary subtexts: Humbert's intentions in invoking the tale may be quite different from Nabokov's. Emily Collins has argued that Humbert introduces the tale to bolster his idea that it is the young nymph (the mermaid in Andersen, Dolly for Humbert) who is the instigator of their relationship; it is she who has a desire for a relationship with the male figure. Additionally, he hopes to show Dolly that pain should be accepted as a necessary part of their relationship (Andersen's mermaid could exchange her mermaid form for human legs, but to walk on these legs would be painful). Nabokov, in contrast, invokes the Andersen subtext to advance a different message: Humbert's treatment of Dolly has deprived her "of her voice, of the opportunity to express, and to build through expressing, her own identity."[7]

Readers have also noted the presence in *Lolita* of motifs from other fairy tales, most notably "The Sleeping Beauty." Susan Elizabeth Sweeney has provided a detailed exploration of "Sleeping Beauty" motifs, (both from the original tale and from its balletic adaptation) in *Lolita* and its predecessor *The Enchanter*.[8] Commenting more broadly on fairy tale elements in the novel, Steven Jones has identified several similarities between Nabokov's handling of plot and character and aspects of the fairy tale. For example, Dolly is depicted by Humbert as a "little princess" and "sleeping beauty," while the character of Charlotte is modeled on the jealous mother or stepmother who is so often a villain in fairy tales (as in "Cinderella" and "Snow White," for example). Jones notes, though, that Nabokov subverts the usual formula to show that "actual events and persons do not always fit these folkloristic fabrications," especially the prospect that the fairy tale couple "lived happily ever after."[9]

Nabokov, of course, looked beyond the fairy tale for inspiration. Scholars have commented on Nabokov's use of material from Catullus in the first century BC to literature and film in the early twentieth century.[10] The literature of romantic longing plays a major part here, and several scholars have noted parodic elements in Nabokov's handling of the subject. Does this parody serve to undermine the reader's willingness to take Humbert's professions of love seriously, or, as Thomas Frosch has argued, does Nabokov use parody as a way to clear away the worn-out clichés and offer in their place a modern, self-aware Romantic vision?[11] Perhaps this is Humbert's intention, but is it Nabokov's? We shall investigate this further when we discuss the critical reaction to *Lolita* in Chapter Five.

While on the subject of precursors, we might note that it has been suggested that Nabokov's choice of the name "Lolita" could have been influenced by a little-known work that treats a young man's romance with a Spanish girl—the short story "Lolita" (1916) by Heinrich von Lichberg (born Heinrich von Eschwege).[12] Lichberg's story, however, is poorly written, and the similarities between it and *Lolita* are quite tenuous, other than the name of the principal female character and scattered allusions to the demonic (in *Lolita,* Humbert refers to Dolly as a "daemon" [*L* 139] with considerable powers of enchantment, whereas in "Lolita," the title figure herself seems to under some kind of a curse). The few similarities are far outweighed by the differences.[13] It is instructive to see how much more rich and complex Nabokov's novel is than this particular work. It should also be remarked that "Lolita" had appeared as a name, even in the title, in numerous works before Nabokov's.[14]

While Nabokov could draw upon a vast store of material from Continental literature, it is not surprising that in a novel featuring a European man's encounter with the New World that Nabokov would make significant use of material from *American* literature as well. Clearly, the most important American writer as far as *Lolita* is concerned was Edgar Allan Poe. Alfred Appel, Jr. asserts that there are more allusions to Poe than to any other single writer in in *Lolita* (*AnL* 330). This web of allusions offers a good example of the way in which Humbert's conscious reference to a literary figure or theme might have a very different purpose than Nabokov's intention for that same reference. Whereas Humbert seeks to bolster the legitimacy of his behavior by invoking a distinguished genealogy, Nabokov expects his readers to scrutinize this association with more skepticism.

Lucy Maddox has sketched out the broad affinities that Humbert might feel he shared with Poe: "Poe, like Humbert, loved a young girl who died prematurely; as a writer, Poe was fascinated by the nature of obsession; and as a theoretician, he insisted that the artist himself must be obsessed with beauty and that the sole aim of art must be aesthetic pleasure, which comes through the evocation of a beauty so perfect it can only be glimpsed and never fully apprehended."[15] Let us briefly examine each of Maddox's points. In terms of biography, Humbert's link to Poe begins with their mothers: both mothers hailed from England (Poe's mother, Elizabeth Arnold Poe, was born in London; Humbert describes his mother as "an English girl, daughter of Jerome Dunn, the alpinist" [*L* 9-10]). Humbert's mother died when he was three; Poe's mother died when he was just a month shy of his third birthday. (Unbeknownst to Humbert, he would die at roughly the same age as Poe: Poe was forty at the time of his death, Humbert was forty-two [he was born in 1910, and died in November 1952].)

More salient for Humbert's "defense," however, is the fact that Poe married his cousin when she was very young. As he puts it, "Virginia was not quite fourteen when Harry Edgar possessed her" (*L* 43). In actuality, the situation is not quite so clear. Poe and his cousin Virginia took part in a public wedding ceremony on May 16, 1836. Virginia was thirteen years old at the time, and Poe was twenty-seven. There has been speculation, however, that the marriage was not immediately consummated. Poe seemed to treat his bride with tenderness, and she held him in high regard. Thus their relationship was quite different from Humbert's and Dolly's, whose unhappy sexual relations began when he was thirty-seven and she was twelve. Eager to signal his bond with Poe, Humbert adds the name "Edgar" to his own for an interview with the local newspaper on the day of his wedding to Charlotte. He would later use the name again when registering at the Enchanted Hunters hotel on his first night alone with Dolly — "Dr. Edgar H. Humbert" (*L* 118).

Beyond the biographical links, Humbert believes that he is on a quest to encounter and record transcendent beauty, much like that described by Poe in his essays and in his poetry. In "The Poetic Principle" Poe describes an "unquenchable" thirst in humans: "It is no mere appreciation of the Beauty before us — but a wild effort to reach the Beauty above. Inspired by an ecstatic presence of the glories beyond the grave, we struggle, by multiform combinations among the things and thoughts of Time, to attain a portion of that Loveliness whose very elements, perhaps, appertain to eternity alone".[16] Humbert describes something kindred when he characterizes the longing he would feel for semi-nude girls he thought he saw through nearby windows: "There was in the fiery phantasm a perfection which made my wild delight also perfect, just because the vision was out of reach" (L 264). He records a similar sensation over-coming him when he watched Dolly playing tennis. Stating that her play produced an "indescribable itch of rapture," he tries to define this sensation further: "the teasing delirious feeling of teetering on the very brink of unearthly order and splendor" (L 230).

Humbert's emulation of Poe, however, does not enhance his image in the eyes of the reader to the degree that he would like. Poe's creative interest in the theme of adoration of a dead love bordered on the obsessive, and this obsession finds a discomforting echo in Humbert's writing. Poe declared that the death of a beautiful woman was "unquestionably, the most poetical topic in the world" and that it was equally "beyond doubt that the lips best suited for such topic" were those "of a bereaved lover."[17] Poe himself tried to exemplify this in his own writing, and one of his most famous efforts, "Annabel Lee," becomes the very foundation on which Humbert would construct his own narrative about his obsession for young girls. (And, like Humbert's memoir, "Annabel Lee" was only published after the death of its author.) In Poe's poem, the narrator outlines his profound love for a girl who died at a young age many years ago "in a kingdom by the sea." The narrator asserts that they loved each other "with a love that was more than love" and that it was the very intensity of their love that aroused the envy of the "winged seraphs of heaven" who sent a chilling wind down to earth to take Annabel's life. Nonetheless, as he puts it, nothing can "ever dissever my soul from the soul / Of the beautiful Annabel Lee." Every night, he writes, he lies down by the side of his darling, his "life" and his "bride" in "the sepulchre there by the sea — / In her tomb by the sounding sea."

The poem provides Humbert with a crucial poetic vision that he uses to characterize his own youthful infatuation with a girl he met at the seashore one summer when he was thirteen years old. It was this infatuation, he asserts, that ultimately led to his obsession with Dolly Haze. As he puts it: "In point of fact, there might have been no Lolita at all had I not loved, one summer, a certain initial girl-child. In a princedom by the sea" (L 9), and he names the girl "Annabel Leigh." He continues to draw upon Poe's poem when he introduces his description of their relationship by stating that it was this relationship that "the seraphs, the misinformed, simple, noble-winged seraphs, envied" (*L* 9). Like Poe's Annabel, Humbert's Annabel also died prematurely, just four months after their summer romance. Humbert's account of the affair suggests that it shared some of the transcendent, supernal quality intimated in Poe's poem: "The spiritual and physical had been blended in us with a perfection that must remain incomprehensible to the matter-of-fact [...] youngsters of today. Long after her death I felt her thoughts floating through mine. Long before we met we had had the same dreams" (*L* 14). Despite their passion for each other, they were never quite able to consummate their relationship, and Humbert writes that he was was "haunted" by "that little girl" ever since that summer, "until at last, twenty-four years later, I broke her spell by incarnating her in another" (*L* 15), that is, his encounter with Dolly Haze.

Humbert's comment is highly significant. Not only does it imply that Dolly, as the object of Humbert's obsession, is somehow derivative and is appreciated not for her own unique qualities but for her resemblance to another. But, by giving her predecessor the name "Annabel Leigh," which is itself derived from that of a fictional character, Humbert indicates that his very creation of "Lolita" is to a certain degree a literary or verbal creation, a product of the creative imagination, and not an animate sentient being with a consciousness, a will, or indeed a life of her own (see *L* 62).

What is more, the image of "incarnating" Annabel "in another" moves beyond Poe's poem to evoke a second Poe work, the uncanny short story "Ligeia." "Ligeia" presents a first-person narrative about a man who was deeply in love with a woman of remarkable intelligence, wisdom, and passion who died and left him crushed by her absence. He takes a second wife, but feels no love from her. Not long after their marriage, she falls ill, and eventually, after a long series of illnesses, she dies too. As the narrator sits by her corpse, however, he begins to note signs that life may be returning her and he watches in horror as brief intervals of warmth and animation are followed by periods of corpse-like stillness. At the end of the story, the woman rises from her bed, and as the shrouds fall from her face, the narrator recognizes first the hair and then the "wild eyes — of my lost love — of the lady — of the Lady Ligeia."[18] We can compare this with Humbert's description of his first sight of Dolly — "It was the same child" — followed by a list of features that he finds her sharing with Annabel. He concludes by stating that "the vacuum of my soul managed to suck in every detail of her bright beauty, and these I checked against the features of my dead bride [...] Everything they shared made one of them" (*L* 39–40). Humbert's declaration that he had "incarnated" Annabel in Dolly, and that Dolly had the same features as his "dead bride," emits something of the creepy air of necrophilia that flows from Poe's fantasies.[19] This does not add much to the reader's appreciation of Humbert himself.

Then too, Humbert's invocation of his relationship with Annabel does not really contribute to his cause of trying to justify his obsession with Dolly. Humbert and Annabel were approximately the same age when they began their relationship. As he himself remarks, they had similar interests, similar dreams. Twenty-four years later, though, he is an adult, and Dolly is a child. Her interests, life experiences, and dreams are inevitably far removed from his own. His attraction, then, can only be a distorted mix of the physical (for her prepubescent body) and the imaginary (for his fantasy of some idealized "Lolita"). His invocation of the Poe subtexts to illuminate his own situation does not go very far in bolstering his defense.[20]

In addition to Poe, American writers ranging from Nathaniel Hawthorne to F. Scott Fitzgerald have been mentioned in connection with *Lolita*.[21] The important role played by travel in the novel has led scholars to consider it in light of other narratives of travel in America, such as the *Adventures of Huckleberry Finn* by Mark Twain (Samuel Clemens), and *On the Road* by Jack Kerouac, which came out in 1957. In fact, Michael Wood suggests that the America "invented" by Nabokov in *Lolita* "is constantly in dialogue with American literature."[22] Paramount in this engagement with American literature is perhaps Nabokov's own perception of his new homeland as a place that beckons the immigrant with wide open possibilities. Humbert arrives on American shores with some expectation of this, but he carries with him some preconceptions and prejudices as well. He is quick to point out and mock American customs and manners that he regards as inferior to the standards he has brought with him from his own culture and background. Yet gradually, just as he comes to learn that there is more to Dolly Haze than he originally cared to see, he discovers that America has a richness and beauty all its own. This, surely, reflects Nabokov's own appreciation of his adopted land. In the European Humbert's discovery of the intricate beauty of America we may find an emblem of something that Nabokov may have been striving to accomplish in *Lolita* itself. In this richly textured novel, the Russian American Nabokov blends literary elements from the Old World, especially Russia, with those of the New World to create a vibrant cultural synthesis that glows with an originality and vitality of its very own.

Notes

1. Carl Proffer lists over sixty writers to whom allusion is made in *Lolita*. See his *Keys to Lolita* (Bloomington: Indiana University Press, 1968), 21–23.
2. Fyodor Dostoevsky, *Great Short Works of Fyodor Dostoevsky* (New York: Perennial Library, 1968), 271 and 276.
3. Dostoevsky, *Great Short Works*, 713.
4. For more detail, see Julian Connolly, "Nabokov's Dialogue with Dostoevsky: *Lolita* and 'The Gentle Creature,'" *Nabokov Studies* 4 (1997): 15–36.
5. Priscilla Meyer, "Nabokov's *Lolita* and Pushkin's *Onegin*: McAdam, McEve and McFate," in *The Achievements of Vladimir Nabokov*, ed. George Gibian and Stephen Jan Parker (Ithaca: Center for International Studies, Cornell University, 1984), 179–211.
6. See Efim Kurganov, *Lolita i Ada* (St. Petersburg: Zvezda, 2001), 59–60; and Olga Voronina, "The Tale of Enchanted Hunters: *Lolita* in Victorian Context," *Nabokov Studies* 10 (2006): 161–62.
7. Emily Collins, "Nabokov's *Lolita* and Andersen's *The Little Mermaid*," *Nabokov Studies* 9 (2005): 93.
8. See, for example, Sweeney's "*The Enchanter* and the Beauties of Sleeping," in *Nabokov at Cornell*, ed. Gavriel Shapiro (Ithaca: Cornell University Press, 2003): 30–45; and "'Ballet Attitudes': Nabokov's *Lolita* and Petipa's *The Sleeping Beauty*," in *Nabokov at the Limits: Redrawing Critical Boundaries*, ed. Lisa Zunshine (New York: Garland, 1999): 111–26, reprinted in *Vladimir Nabokov's* Lolita: *A Casebook,* ed. Ellen Pifer (New York: Oxford, 2003): 83–109.
9. Steven Swann Jones, "Folk Characterization in *Lolita*," in *Lolita* (Major Literary Characters), ed. Harold Bloom (New York: Chelsea House, 1993): 68, 73.
10. See, for example, Gary R. Dyer, "Humbert Humbert's Use of Catullus 58 in *Lolita*," *Twentieth Century Literature* 34.1 (1988): 1–15; and Galya Diment, "From Bauer's Li to Nabokov's Lo: *Lolita* and Early Russian Film," in *Approaches to Teaching* Lolita, ed. Zoran Kuzamnovich and Galya Diment (New York: The Modern Language Association, 2008): 101–7.
11. See Thomas R. Frosch, "Parody and Authenticity in *Lolita*," in *Nabokov's Fifth Arc: Nabokov and Others on His Life's Work*, ed. J. E. Rivers and Charles Nicol (Austin: University of Texas Press, 1982): 171–87, reprinted in *Vladimir Nabokov's* Lolita: *A Casebook*, 39–56.
12. For a translation of the story with a commentary on its possible relationship to Nabokov's novel, see Michael Maar, *The Two Lolitas* (London: Verso, 2005).
13. See Dieter Zimmer's response to the Maar hypothesis in a letter to the *Times Literary Supplement*, 23 April 2004. Available online at http://www.timesonline.co.uk/tol/incomingFeeds/article747361.ece
14. For a brief discussion of some French works with "Lolita" in the title, see Maurice Couturier, "Narcissism and Demand in *Lolita*," *Nabokov Studies* 9 (2005), 21n3. Couturier also quotes a passage from Valéry Larbaud's *Des*

prénoms féminins (1927) that points out how different forms of the name "Dolores" can be used to signify different ages and statuses (e.g. "Lolita est une petite fille; Lola est en âge de se marier; Dolores a trente ans"); this reminds one of the second paragraph of *Lolita* with its definitions: "She was Lola in slacks. She was Dolly at school. She was Dolores on the dotted line. But in my arms she was always Lolita" (*L* 9). We can compare this last sentence with Larbaud: "Et le soir des noces, j'aurai Lolita dans mes bras."

15. Lucy Maddox, *Nabokov's Novels in English* (Athens: University of Georgia Press, 1983), 73.
16. Edgar Allan Poe, *The Selected Poetry and Prose of Edgar Allan Poe* (New York: Modern Library, 1951).
17. Poe, *Selected Poetry and Prose*, 369.
18. Ibid., 114.
19. Adding to this air is a comment Humbert makes when he thinks of Dolly being drugged by a sedative at the Enchanted Hunters Hotel: "by nine [...] she would be dead in his arms" (*L* 116).
20. Shoshana Milgram Knapp points out a similar disjuncture between Humbert's invocation of a literary subtext or precursor and Nabokov's intentions for the very same allusion when she discusses the treatment of references to *Les Misérables* in *Lolita*. Summarizing the situation, she writes: "Humbert Humbert may wish to see himself as Jean Valjean, or to see Jean Valjean as a version of himself. He may wish to say that he, too, was devoted to a helpless orphan [...] But the comparison makes him look worse." Knapp, "The Lesson of Jean Valjean: *Lolita* and *Les Misérables*," *Nabokov Studies* 9 (2005): 74.
21. For Hawthorne, see Elizabeth Freeman, "Honeymoon with a Stranger: Pedophiliac Picaresques from Poe to Nabokov," *American Literature* 70.4 (1998): 863–97; for Fitzgerald, see G. M. Hyde, *Vladimir Nabokov: America's Russian Novelist* (London: Marion Boyars, 1977), 120–21.
22. Michael Wood, "*Lolita* in an American Fiction Course," in *Approaches to Teaching Nabkov's* Lolita, 117.

Chapter Three

APPROACHING *LOLITA*

In his essay "On a Book Entitled *Lolita*" Nabokov conjures up an image of "Teachers of Literature" asking such misguided questions as "What is the author's purpose?" or, "still worse" according to Nabokov, "What is the guy trying to say?" (*L* 311). Actually, for the reader of *Lolita* (or the manuscript entitled "Lolita, or the Confessions of a White Widowed Male"), this is not a bad place to begin. It is important, however, to be a bit more precise in formulating these questions: *which* "guy" are we talking about when we ask the question? Are we talking about Humbert Humbert, the narrator of the novel (and ostensible author of the manuscript), or Vladimir Nabokov, the actual author of the novel?

The main part of the novel (that is, the entire text except for the foreword by one John Ray, Jr.) consists of a first-person memoir by Humbert Humbert about his destructive obsession for young Dolly Haze (whom he refers to as "Lolita"). But, of course, Humbert's words are given to him by his creator Vladimir Nabokov. Therefore, although Humbert may think that he's communicating (or trying to communicate) one thing, what Nabokov himself is trying to communicate may be entirely different. Indeed, quite often it can be diametrically opposed. It is from this gap or disjuncture between narrator and author that some of the confusion and much of the debate about the novel has arisen. From the reader's point of view, however, the communicative situation is even more complex than this simple division between narrator and author might suggest. First of all, one can find a further bifurcation within the figure of the main character. In a sense, there are two Humberts on display. One is the Humbert who underwent the experiences outlined in the novel, and the other is the Humbert who narrates these experiences and occasionally reflects upon their significance. Moreover, this latter Humbert's narrative is not a straightforward recitation of facts and impressions. Rather, it is a carefully constructed discourse that has been put together with a specific audience (or audiences) in mind.

According to both Humbert and John Ray, Jr., Humbert wrote his memoir while in "legal captivity" (*L* 3), first in a "psychopathic ward for observation" and later in a prison cell (*L* 308). Humbert states that he had originally thought that he would use his notes at his trial (*L* 308), and his narrative is sprinkled with various addresses to "[l]adies and gentlemen of the jury" (see, for example, *L* 9, 87, 123, 132). He goes on to say, however, that in mid-composition he realized that he could not "parade living Lolita" (*L* 308). Instead, he decides to immortalize his love by having the manuscript published after her death. Presumably, the audience who would read this memoir would be very different from jurors at a trial. Thus, in addition to the numerous references to "gentlemen" and "gentlewomen" of the jury, Humbert makes other references to a more generalized "reader" who, Humbert hopes, will view him more as an artist than a criminal.[1]

As we read the text, we become aware that Humbert is constantly trying to anticipate, forestall, and shape his readers' judgments and evaluations. In fact, as Nomi Tamir-Ghez has skillfully demonstrated, Humbert fashions many of his overt references to his supposed juror-readers in a covert effort to garner the sympathy of the more generalized future readers. For example, when Humbert exclaims at one point "Frigid gentlewomen of the jury!" (*L* 79), he is mocking or abusing the juror-reader in a subtle attempt to court the support of the general reader who would not wish to be thought of as "frigid."[2] It is this degree of conscious manipulation and near-constant self-awareness that makes Humbert's tract so slippery and deceptive. When one adds to this Humbert's frequent shifts in tone and register, his alternating postures of defiance and self-incrimination, his playfulness and his postures of naiveté, it becomes very hard for the reader to maintain an even perspective on what he or she is reading. Humbert himself proclaims: "You can always count on a murderer for a fancy prose style" (*L* 9) and "I have only words to play with!" (*L* 32). Yet even the first of these declarations reveals the complexities involved in reading Humbert's text: he adopts a playful, knowing tone that seeks to establish a rapport with his audience, but in the very middle of this utterance stands the word "murderer," a designation that few readers will find easy to identify with. On the other hand, the playful tone of the entire sentence works to defuse or minimize the potential import of the word itself. In sum, although Humbert indicates full awareness of the kind of damage he has inflicted upon Dolly Haze, he strives mightily to appeal to the reader's "understanding" and to have the reader view him through a lens of what his lawyer has labeled "impartial sympathy" (*L* 57). In other words, Humbert has tried not only to seduce Dolly Haze, but to seduce his reader too.

And sometimes, the seduction has worked. Many of the original reviewers and commentators on the novel displayed palpable sympathy for Humbert, and they often expressed views of Dolly that are in close accord with Humbert's own representations (or misrepresentations) of their relationship. Leslie Fiedler, for example, described the plot of *Lolita* as "the seduction of a middle-aged man by a twelve-year-old girl," rather than the other way around.[3] Lionel Trilling reflects upon the way the reader who might be expected to feel outrage when reading about the violation of a twelve-year-old girl has a different reaction: "I was plainly not able to muster up the note of moral outrage. And it is likely that any reader of *Lolita* will discover that he comes to see the situation as less and less abstract and moral and horrible, and more and more as human and 'understandable' [...] Humbert is perfectly willing to say that he is a monster; no doubt he is, but we find ourselves less and less eager to say so."[4] (We should note here that Trilling, following convention, uses the masculine pronoun to refer to the reader.) Martin Green goes further in describing the effect of Humbert's discourse on the reader: "The sexually perverse enterprises of the main character are made funny, beautiful, pathetic, romantic, tragic; in five or six ways we are made to sympathize with him in them." He then states: "Humbert Humbert is our protagonist, and we are unable to disassociate ourselves from him self-righteously, because he represents a part of ourselves we are normally proud of [...] He is ourselves, without our inhibitions, acting out our tendencies."[5]

Despite the affirmation of sympathy and even identity expressed by some readers, as time has passed a more common response (and surely a more welcome one from Nabokov's point of view) is one of shock and surprise. Humbert's readers may find themselves laughing along with him, appreciative of his self-deprecation or his witty observations of contemporary mores, but then, they catch themselves and are surprised at the degree to which they have been taken in by him. And then, they may even recoil with some horror, both at Humbert and at their own susceptibility to his rhetoric. Ellen Pifer has concisely analyzed this reaction: "The outrage expressed by many of *Lolita*'s readers over the past fifty years may be due, in part, to the discomfort they feel at finding themselves taken in by the narrator's rhetoric, at realizing they have unwittingly accepted — and even identified with — Humbert's perverse desire."[6]

What I would like to do in this chapter is to examine this complex text — a text that is both Humbert Humbert's and Vladimir Nabokov's — with an eye toward unlocking the ambiguities and contradictions it contains. In writing *Lolita*, Nabokov set himself a difficult task: to find a way to engage the reader's interest in a self-described monster like Humbert Humbert without having the reader either recoil in total disgust at the character's behavior or to be so charmed by Humbert that the reader either overlooks this behavior or regards it with an attitude of gentle forbearance. Commenting on this delicate balancing act, Steven Butler asserts that Nabokov succeeds in a task that Humbert tried to accomplish: to fix the borderline between "[t]he beastly and the beautiful" (*L* 135).[7] We can begin our analysis by examining Humbert's actual conduct as well as his attempts to justify or rationalize his behavior. We will provide a condensed summary here, and then offer more detailed commentary in the chapter on textual analysis.

In the opening pages of his memoir, Humbert describes himself as a "nympholept" (*L* 17), that is, someone who is sexually attracted to a certain type of pre-teenage girl. We immediately note that in choosing this term, Humbert reveals a characteristic penchant for dressing up his base desires: the word "nympholept" seems more elevated and poetic than the harsher and more common "pedophile." He then goes on to offer several arguments or mitigating factors behind his predilection and conduct. One explanation for his pedophilia is that he was prevented from consummating a sexual relationship with Annabel Leigh, a girl close to his own age when he was thirteen. He asserts his conviction that "in a certain magic and fateful way Lolita began with Annabel" (*L* 14). He further claims that the shock of Annabel's death prevented "any further romance" throughout his youth (*L* 14). There "might have been no Lolita at all," he states, if it were not for his love for this "initial girl-child" (*L* 9). Nomi Tamir-Ghez labels this explanation the "psychological" argument,[8] and we shall discuss it further below.

Humbert also tries to convince the reader that his particular obsession is something refined, with an aesthetic impulse at its core. He declares that one has to be "an artist and a madman" to discern the special "nymphet" from a crowd of ordinary girls (*L* 17). He further suggests that he belongs in the lofty company of such writers as Dante and Petrarch in his attraction to a young female: "Dante fell madly in love with his Beatrice when she was nine [...] in 1274"; "when Petrarch fell madly in love with his Laureen, she was a fair-haired nymphet of twelve" (*L* 19), but his reference to these loves plays fast and loose with the data. First, he conveniently omits the fact that Dante was nine when he saw eight-year-old Beatrice in 1274. Moreover, Petrarch's "Laura" was probably not twelve when Petrarch saw her; it is likely that she was an adult and already married when they met. Even more important, though, is the fact that these loves were indeed "poetic"; there is no evidence that they were sexually consummated.

It should be noted here that Humbert's reference to the "artistic" element in his character reflects a particularly troublesome aspect of his defense. Nabokov was mindful of the way that certain turn-of-the-century artists and writers tended to blur the distinction between art and life or argued that an aesthetic vision served as ample justification for whatever endeavor they may have chosen to pursue under that banner. Although Nabokov himself believed that artists should be free to choose and shape whatever subjects they wished to treat in their art, they did not have the same freedom to impose their artistic visions on others, or, in other words, to manipulate or even injure other people as part in fashioning their artistic project. To appropriate a phrase from Ellen Pifer, the artist does not have the right "to subject a fellow human being to the despotic rule of aesthetic creation."[9]

On top of the artistic defense, Humbert also offers a more sweeping rationale for his behavior: he argues that his desire is a natural one ("I have but followed nature" [*L* 135]) and that it is only arbitrary societal convention that prohibits the union of a man and a girl. To support this claim he cites sexual and marital customs of ancient Rome and Egypt, and he laments the legal state of affairs in the United States that prohibits marriage between adult men and child brides: "I found myself maturing amid a civilization which allows a man of twenty-five to court a girl of sixteen but not a girl of twelve" (*L* 18). As Tamir-Ghez accurately points out, however, Humbert himself is not twenty-five but even older (thirty-seven) and he does not "court" Dolly, but forces her into a relationship "which she detests."[10] Humbert's ultimate defense is that he was basically a good man: "Humbert Humbert tried to be good. Really and truly he did. He had the utmost respect for ordinary children, with their purity and vulnerability, and under no circumstances would he have interfered with the innocence of a child" (*L* 19–20). Even in regard to Dolly, he claims that he tried to give her "a really good time" (*L* 163).

In the face of all of these arguments, however, Humbert's actual behavior paints a very different picture. Indeed, even in the last "defense" — "under no circumstances would he have interfered with the innocence of a child" — we find a characteristic loophole: Humbert's sentence concludes with the phrase, "if there was the least risk of a row" (*L* 20). In essence Humbert is declaring that he would not molest a child if there were any chance of getting caught. By implication, then, he would have been willing to molest a child if he thought he could get away with it undetected. This, of course, is precisely how he initially envisions getting pleasure from Dolly. Indeed, his entire conduct with Dolly contradicts every element of the rhetorical defense he has mounted.

Refuting the first defense — the psychological argument — is his own admission that his relationship with Dolly "was to eclipse completely her prototype" (*L* 40). In other words, having met Dolly, he filled in the void left by Annabel's premature death, and therefore, he presumably would not be interested in other young girls. This, however, is not the case, for he continues to refer to his obsession with young girls throughout his time together with Dolly and even after she leaves him. We have already addressed the specious nature of his self-identification with Dante and Petrarch, and we have noted the hollowness of his claims that he is devoted to preserving the innocence of a child. Most damaging to his claims of moral probity, however, is his actual conduct with Dolly herself. Despite his assertion that he did everything in his power to give her "a really good time," the evidence of his own narrative reveals a record of relentless insensitivity and callousness to her emotional and physical well-being. It would be instructive to list briefly the myriad ways in which his selfish pursuit of pleasure runs roughshod over the sensitivities of the young adolescent.

From the very first weeks of his acquaintance with Dolly, Humbert takes advantage of the girl's emotional needs, her naiveté, and her inexperience. Fatherless, and going through difficulties with her mother, Dolly finds the European Humbert to be an exotic attraction. Humbert himself notes that she is drawn to idealized images of movie stars, celebrities, and the like, and he perceives that he may, in a very local way, exhibit some of this same appeal. He encourages her interest in him, and functions as a kind of co-conspirator against her mother's attempts a controlling her (for example, when she steals his bacon from his breakfast tray, she tells him not to inform her mother of this, and of course, he does not.) He engages in a kind of low-level flirtation with her, and she seems to develop something of a crush on him. (Ironically, however, this crush may be grounded on her earlier attraction to the playwright Clare Quilty. Humbert states the he is said to resemble "some crooner or actor chap on whom Lo has a crush" [*L* 43], and Dolly has cut out an advertisement featuring Quilty and put it over her bed. Humbert notes that there may be a "slight" resemblance between Quilty and himself [*L* 69].) In the notorious living room scene in Chapter Thirteen, Humbert takes advantage of Dolly's interest in him, and succeeds in bringing himself to orgasm while she squirms with her legs in his lap. Although he claims that "she had noticed nothing" (*L* 61), the evidence suggests otherwise, and it is quite likely that he chooses to disregard signs of her awareness to satisfy his own base needs.

As disturbing as Humbert's behavior around Dolly is *before* her mother's death, it becomes completely unconscionable after Charlotte's death. Although she is now an orphan, Humbert cold-heartedly withholds this crucial information from her until he has had the opportunity to gain full sexual satisfaction from her body. He plans to drug her and take sexual pleasure from her while she is in an unconscious and defenseless condition, without her knowledge or permission. As it turns out, his plans do not work, but he manages to achieve his sexual goals nonetheless because, as he puts it: "it was she who seduced me" (*L* 132). The veracity of this claim is in much dispute, and we will take a close look at it in the next chapter. In any case, as Humbert himself notes in referring to Dolly's apparent sexual involvement with a teen-aged boy at summer camp, the girl was "not quite prepared for certain discrepancies between a kid's life and mine" (*L* 134), and he conveys something of the true nature of his sexual aggressiveness when he acknowledges the next day: "This was a lone child, an absolute waif, with whom a heavy-limbed, foul-smelling adult had had strenuous intercourse three times that very morning" (*L* 140). At this moment, Humbert exhibits some awareness of what he has done to this child, and he feels "an oppressive, hideous constraint" as if he were "sitting with the ghost of somebody [he] had just killed" (*L* 140). Yet despite his seeming recognition of the damage he has inflicted upon Dolly, he goes on to speculate about how quickly he could have another sexual encounter with her. Finally, as the ultimate indicator of his supreme selfishness, he concludes his review of his morning experience not with further acknowledgment of Dolly's suffering but rather with a plaintive lament about his own state: "poor Humbert Humbert was dreadfully unhappy" (*L* 140).

This astonishing willingness to discount the child's emotional condition while focusing on his own sets the tone for his subsequent months of cohabitation with Dolly Haze.

Of course, it is only after he taken advantage of Dolly's sexual curiosity and had "strenuous" intercourse with her three times in the morning that he finally tells her of her mother's death, and he does so only because Dolly demands to know why she cannot contact her. Dolly is of course devastated, and that night she initially goes to bed in a separate room, but, in one of the simplest and most moving lines in the novel, Humbert declares: "in the middle of the night she came sobbing into mine, and we made it up very gently. You see, she had absolutely nowhere else to go" (*L* 142). Dolly's utter helplessness and absolute dependence on Humbert are made piercingly clear in these lines, and Nabokov reinforces this sense that Dolly has no other options available to her by ending Part One with these very lines. Dolly's state of childhood innocence has come to a decisive end. What the future holds for her is entirely unknown.

In the first few chapters of Part Two, however, the outlines of this future come into stark relief. Cropping up amidst Humbert's descriptions of the places they visited in their cross-country automobile trip appear examples of the way he treats the orphaned Dolly. Although Humbert claims that he did everything in his power to give Dolly a "really good time," the reader cannot help noticing the extraordinary number of ways in which Humbert tried to manipulate Dolly and to ensure her compliance with his selfish sexual demands. He himself acknowledges that he employed several "methods" to keep his "pubescent concubine in submission" (*L* 148). One of these was what he called "the reformatory threat" (*L* 149), in which he painted a stark picture of her confinement in some grim public institution if anything were to happen to him. On a child who has just lost her mother, this threat may have had an especially chilling effect. Humbert confesses that this threat did indeed work. As he puts it, "By rubbing all this in, I succeeded in terrorizing Lo" (*L* 151).

In addition to terrorizing her, Humbert attempted to keep Dolly isolated as much as possible from other people. When she caught sight of some acquaintances during their travels, she pleaded with Humbert to let her talk with them, apparently to no avail (*L* 157). He was similarly controlling when she sought to enjoy the company of kids her own age, especially boys. Along with these negative tools of threats and deprivation Humbert also resorted to monetary bribes to procure sexual favors from his companion. When they first settled in Beardsley, Humbert would pay her three cents a day "under condition she fulfill her basic obligations" (*L* 183). Over time, Dolly succeeded in increasing her "allowance," and Humbert is distressed to discover that Dolly had learned the value of her services and would demand extra pay for "a fancy embrace" (*L* 184). Incredibly, he characterizes Dolly's resourcefulness as a "definite drop" in *her* morals (*L* 183)! Yet even as he faults her for seeking some reward for her compliance with his sexual demands, he himself is quick to take back whatever he had agreed to pay her for that compliance. He recalls one such incident during their first cross-country trip when he had just satisfied himself sexually: "I had just retracted some silly promise she had forced me to make in a moment of blind impatient passion, and there she was sprawling and sobbing, and pinching my caressing hand, and I was laughing" (*L* 169). Later, in Beardsley, he conjures up an image of him doling out coins as he is "on the very rack of joy," but then, unless she could get away, he would "pry open" her "little fist" to retrieve the very coins he had just given her (*L* 184). He even resorted to searching her room to steal whatever funds she had managed to save up in order to prevent her from running away.

In addition to his threats, bribes, and broken promises, Humbert was not above using brute force to obtain what he desired. In the paragraph that begins with Humbert telling the reader that he tried to give Dolly "a really good time," Humbert goes on to describe how he would pull Dolly away from a playmate: "thrusting my fatherly fingers deep into Lo's hair from behind, and then gently but firmly clasping them around the nape of her neck, I would lead my reluctant pet to our small home for a quick connection before dinner" (*L* 164). Humbert's use of physical force escalates as Dolly begins to show signs of resistance and independence. He describes a "strident and hateful scene" at the end of their Beardsley stay in which he gripped her wrist tightly and "in fact hurt her badly [...] and once or twice she jerked her arm so violently that I feared her wrist might snap" (*L* 205).

And what did Dolly think of all this? As is his wont, Humbert does not attempt to tell the reader very much about her inner world. Indeed, as he himself acknowledges, he wasn't all that interested in it. Nevertheless, he does provide two crucial pieces of information about how she responded to his regime of control. First, he addresses the issue of whether Dolly took any pleasure from their sexual interactions: "Never did she vibrate under my touch, and a strident 'what d'you think you are doing?' was all I got for my pains" (*L* 166). Even more disturbing, however, is the admission he makes as he sums up their experience together on their first cross-country trip. He states that the "lovely, trustful, dreamy" country they had traversed "was no more to us than a collection of dog-eared maps, ruined tour books, old tires, and her sobs in the night — every night, every night — the moment I feigned sleep" (*L* 176). Clearly, Dolly was in deep despair, and she had so little trust in Humbert that she would wait until she thought he was asleep to release her private sorrow. And nothing could be a simpler and more devastating indictment of Humbert's regime than his chilling repetition "every night, every night."

Thus far we have seen the numerous ways in which Humbert tried to coerce Dolly into doing his bidding, and in the last quotation, we see something of how she responds to this situation. But we should note that Humbert's comment about her weeping is a purely external observation; we are not given direct access into the specifics of her thoughts and feelings. This is symptomatic of another aspect of Humbert's abusive relationship with Dolly. Throughout his years of cohabitation with her, he shows almost no interest in the person who inhabits the body that he seeks pleasure from on a daily basis. Indeed, he is impatient with and dismissive of Dolly's own desires and feelings. When he comments on her interests, it is almost always with contempt or derision: "Lolita, when she chose, could be a most exasperating brat. I was not really quite prepared for her fits of disorganized boredom, intense and vehement griping, her sprawling, droopy, dopey-eyed style [...] Mentally, I found her to be a disgustingly conventional little girl" (*L* 148); "I could never make her read any other book than the so-called comic books or stories in magazines for American females" (*L* 173).

Humbert himself seems only dimly aware of the paradox of his relationship to Dolly: while he needs her to be physically present for him to satisfy his desires, he views the individual who inhabits that body as a nuisance or distraction that he would like to ignore. Thus he is hypersensitive to her physical attributes — taking careful note of her measurements, her skin color, her bodily aromas — while trying to ignore her emotional and mental worlds. It is only after Dolly has left him that Humbert truly acknowledges that she had an inner world of thoughts and desires to which he had no access, and more importantly, which he had no interest in during their time together. Repeating a comment Dolly had made about the horror of dying alone, Humbert recalls his impression at the time: "it struck me [...] that I simply did not know a thing about my darling's mind and that quite possibly, behind the awful juvenile clichés, there was in her a garden and a twilight, and a palace gate — dim and adorable regions which happened to be lucidly and absolutely forbidden to me" (*L* 284). Humbert's perception that Dolly might have had a rich emotional world is, of course, accurate, but it is characteristic that he seems to be putting the blame for his lack of access to this world back on Dolly when it was his own sustained disregard for that world that led to it being closed to him.[11]

In Nabokov's moral universe, Humbert is guilty of extreme narcissism and solipsism: he evaluates everything and everyone only as they fit his own needs, dreams, and desires. Humbert's condescension is not only directed at Dolly and her tastes; it spills out onto everyone he mentions in his narrative: Charlotte Haze, the Farlows, Gaston Godin, the staff at the Enchanted Hunters Hotel, and even one-armed Bill in Coalmont. What is more, as we indicated earlier, Humbert is guilty of a major crime in Nabokov's world: he regards those around him — and especially Dolly — as constituent elements of his own designs, designs that he believes to be artistic. The clearest expression of this emerges from the living room scene mentioned earlier, when Humbert succeeds in reaching orgasm as Dolly squirms on his lap. We shall discuss the scene in detail in our analysis of the text, but for now, Humbert's evaluation of what he had achieved will suffice: "What I had madly possessed was not she, but my own creation, another, fanciful Lolita — perhaps, more real than Lolita; overlapping, encasing her; floating between me and her, and having no will, no consciousness — indeed, no life of her own" (*L* 62). Humbert has banished the real child, Dolly Haze, and replaced her with a fanciful creation of his own whom he calls "Lolita." From this point on, he continually tries to repeat his feat, ignoring or dismissing Dolly Haze in pursuit of pleasure with his imagined Lolita.

The results, of course, are tragic. As he would acknowledge years later, he had damaged Dolly forever by robbing her of her childhood, and his formulation of this acknowledgment is significant. As he puts it: "Dolores Haze had been deprived her childhood by a maniac" (*L* 283). We note here that for the moment at least, Humbert refers to Dolly by her real name, not by his preferred, personal moniker "Lolita." He seems to recognize that he has done real harm to a real child, and not just a fanciful creation. Michael

Wood sensitively explores the implications of Dolly's loss of childhood: Humbert's crime is "to have deprived Lolita not of an idyll but of whatever childhood she might have had, and the terrible thing about the ruin of children is not the ruin of innocence but the wreck of possibility, even malign possibility."[12]

Clearly, by almost any measure one can imagine, Humbert is guilty of sustained child abuse, and neither his actions nor his attitudes have anything commendable about them. Why then, have many readers found themselves charmed by him and even "conniving" with him (to use Lionel Trilling's term)? Nabokov provided Humbert with an impressive assortment of rhetorical tools intended not only to deflect the reader's disapproval, but to establish some rapport as well. One of the most important of these is Humbert's frequent use of humor. *Lolita* has been called "perhaps the funniest novel in the language,"[13] and Humbert deploys its humor to establish a sense of connection with the reader. His wry humor shows up in all sorts of contexts. For example, he evokes the air of discontent he sensed in his first marriage with the phrase "moth holes had appeared in the plush of matrimonial comfort" (*L* 27); his image conjures up the faded trappings of a bourgeois household in which he feels himself trapped. His droll observations about the decor and ambience of the various lodgings he stays at with Dolly — with their paper-thin walls, their fluctuating water temperature, and their insipid food — strike the reader as both funny and accurate. What is more, the targets of Humbert's mockery often include aspects of American culture that many of his highbrow readers might find flawed as well (for example, educational institutions that downplay "medieval dates" in favor of "weekend ones" [*L* 178]). David Rampton comments: "it is precisely the Humbert 'talk,' the marvelously intelligent discourse that devastatingly indicts not just himself but a whole society, that makes him so attractive and keeps us sympathetic and involved."[14]

In addition, Humbert often turns his humor back on himself. His commentary is frequently self-deprecating and even self-castigating. For example, he refers to himself as "bestial" (*L* 55) and as a "monster" (*L* 284), and he calls himself such names as "Humbert the Terrible" (*L* 29). The fact that he regularly chastises himself in this way may be designed to lessen the reader's need to do so. Supplementing Humbert's depiction of himself as blameworthy, moreover, is a corresponding tendency to present himself as a vulnerable and unhappy soul who should be pitied. Thus he writes: "how dreadfully stupid poor Humbert always was in matters of sex" (*L* 25);

and "Despite my manly looks, I am horribly timid" (*L* 53). Describing his frustrated attempts to get near to Dolly during the night they spent in the Enchanted Hunters Hotel he addresses the reader directly: "Imagine me [...] try to discern the doe in me, trembling in the forest of my own iniquity; let's even smile a little. After all, there is no harm in smiling" (*L* 129). Finally, Humbert also depicts his search for bliss with a nymphet as a kind of noble but hopeless quest. He presents himself as a misunderstood Romantic seeker, not a common pedophile.

Just as Humbert's satiric treatment of the kitschy aspects of American culture is intended to establish a rapport with his reader, so too is his liberal use of literary allusions, some quite obvious, and some less so. By making passing reference to the worlds of mythology and fairy tale, and to writers from Catullus to Poe, Humbert subtly flatters those readers who recognizes these allusions and who therefore can applaud themselves for their intelligence and broad literary knowledge. As has already been noted, Humbert also tries to curry favor with his general reader by denigrating down the supposed juror-reader. Tamir-Ghez argues that as Humbert's attitude toward the juror-reader becomes "more critical and cynical," his tone toward the external reader becomes "warmer and warmer."[15] Finally, the very style of Humbert's narrative — its dazzling use of language, with striking sound play, word play, and original imagery — exerts a palpable appeal to many readers. Some of these readers may be willing to overlook the seriousness of Humbert's actions because of the brilliance and energy of his style. As a result of all this, susceptible readers may find themselves laughing with Humbert, agreeing with his judgments, and ultimately, going along with his perspective on events, including his relationship with Dolly. We can cite Martin Green as an example: "That Humbert manages to love Lolita makes a powerful claim on our respect. He knows her completely, and he loves her completely, sensually and sentimentally and for herself, all at the same time [...] Humbert loves Lolita in the way Dante loved Beatrice, the way Petrarch loved Laura."[16]

Although we may disagree with Green after we have examined the specific way Humbert treats Dolly during his period of cohabitation with her, we must also point out that Nabokov does not abandon Humbert the way Dolly does in Elphinstone, and after Dolly's disappearance he has Humbert undertake a process of self-examination and self-reflection that had been absent earlier in the tale. Although notes of guilt and remorse had surfaced intermittently throughout the narrative up to the point of

Dolly's disappearance, it is after her departure that Humbert seems to realize exactly what he had done to her and what he had lost with her departure. Nabokov incorporates three episodes into the late stages of Humbert's narrative that suggest that his protagonist has undergone a kind of revelation regarding his treatment of Dolly, and it is the suggestion that Humbert has come to acknowledge his guilt that gives the character and the novel its final twist of complexity. Many readers are willing to entertain the notion that Humbert does at last feel genuine remorse for this conduct, although some readers remain skeptical on this point. We shall look at these three episodes briefly here, and discuss them in more detail in our analysis of the narrative.

The first of these episodes is Humbert's final meeting with Dolly Haze, now Dolly Schiller, in Coalmont. He has not seen her for three years, and when he now encounters her, she is married and "hugely pregnant" (*L* 269). The emotional highpoint of Humbert's description of their meeting occurs when Humbert pronounces his love for this woman, pregnant and married to another, and no longer the nymphet he had once pursued with such force. He writes: "there she was (my Lolita!), hopelessly worn at seventeen, with that baby [...] and I looked and looked at her, and knew as clearly as I know I am to die, that I loved her more than anything else I had ever seen or imagined on earth, or hoped for anywhere else" (*L* 277). For many readers, this is perhaps the most poignant and moving passage in the novel. Humbert is expressing his love for the real woman he sees in front of him, and not a fanciful being created ("imagined") in his mind. His declaration is meant to convey an acceptance of who she is, who she has become, and not who he wishes she might be. Humbert goes on: "I insist the world know how much I loved my Lolita, *this* Lolita, pale and polluted, and big with another's child, but still gray-eyed, still sooty-lashed, still auburn and almond, still Carmencita, still mine" (*L* 278). Again, one notes Humbert's insistence that he loves "*this*" Lolita, and not just a prepubescent body.

But not all readers are persuaded. They point to the fact that Humbert is still calling her by the pet names (such as "Carmencita") associated with his earlier fantasies about her, and he is still insisting on the possessive nature of his feeling: "my Lolita," "still mine." Michael Wood, for one, professes such skepticism: "I can't believe in Humbert's new love partly because there is nothing in his self-portrait to suggest he can rise to it, and partly because he is protesting too much, hooked on his version of *Carmen*, too anxious for us to *see* the change in him."[17] Other readers acknowledge some hesitation too, but end up accepting the evolution of Humbert's character. Alfred Appel, Jr. takes note of some parodic elements in the larger reunion scene, such as "the parodic echo of Billy Graham's exhortation ('Make those twenty-five steps. Now')," and asserts that these "almost annihilate Humbert's declaration of love," but he concludes that one believes in Humbert's love "not because of any confession, but in spite of it."[18] Appel may be reflecting here a problem that James Phelan identified in an article on the device of the unreliable narrator in *Lolita*. Nabokov may have been so successful in creating what Phelan calls "estranging" unreliability in Humbert's narrative that the reader ceases to believe in *anything* that the narrator says, even in moments of poignant confession such as this.[19]

I think that most readers, however, will choose to accept the notion that Humbert has undergone a certain degree of genuine change by this point in the story. Indeed, the emotional texture of the novel becomes immeasurably richer if it reveals genuine development within Humbert rather than being merely a sterile exercise in narrative unreliablity. Further evidence of Humbert's belated understanding of the damage he has done to Dolly comes in the chapters that follow his description of his reunion with her. In Chapter Thirty-One, Humbert offers broad reflections on his crime, such as "Alas, I was unable to transcend the simple human fact that whatever spiritual solace I might find [...] nothing could make my Lolita forget the foul lust I had inflicted upon her" (*L* 282–83). In the next chapter, Humbert provides several specific examples of moments when he caught a glimpse of Dolly's emotional world but chose to ignore what he saw ("it was always my habit and method to ignore Lolita's states of mind while comforting my own base self" [*L* 287]). He concludes that he finally understood that to his "conventional Lolita [...] even the most miserable of family lives was better than the parody of incest, which, in the long run, was the best I could offer the waif" (*L* 287).

If, before this point, Nabokov's readers had not fully appreciated the extent to which Humbert had injured Dolly, they do now. The jocular, jesting tone of the first part of Humbert's narrative is gone, replaced by sober accounts of Dolly's suffering and Humbert's lack of sensitivity to her pain. In fact, the change in tone is so distinctive that some have wondered whether it was only during the writing of the memoir itself that Humbert came to understand the true nature of his crimes. Thus, Lucy Maddox writes that Humbert "did not understand himself or Lolita until he began to write."[20] As these readers see it, if Humbert had really come to realize how much he had damaged Dolly at the time he tells the reader he "reviewed" his case, why wouldn't this have been reflected from the very beginning of his memoir? Why is there so much verbal clowning around at the outset? Humbert himself provides an answer when he discusses why he tried to reproduce the style of the journal he kept while staying with the Hazes, no matter how "false and brutal" the intonations seemed to him while working on the memoir. He chose to do so "for the sake of retrospective verisimilitude" (*L* 71). Yet even though the prevailing tone of the first part of the memoir is more light-hearted than the late stages of the text, one can find many signs that the narrating Humbert is aware of his guilt long before he approaches the end of his manuscript. One such moment occurs in the middle of the narrative when Humbert is describing how his sudden retraction of a promise made to Dolly causes her to begin weeping while he himself laughs. He writes: "the atrocious, unbelievable, unbearable, and, I suspect, eternal horror that I know *now* was still but a dot of blackness in the blue of my bliss" (*L* 169).

It is my view that Nabokov's intention was for Humbert to reproduce for the reader the kind of emotional evolution he himself underwent over the course of his experience with Dolly: from light-hearted, self-absorbed pursuit to a belated recognition of his crime. Some susceptible readers may have initially been swept along with Humbert in his pursuit of Dolly, but they, like he, now realize what has truly transpired. And, as Humbert's memoir draws to a close, Nabokov creates an opening for these readers to come to terms with Humbert's (and possibly their own) lack of sensitivity about what has taken place, and to discern a potential path toward repentance and attempted restitution.

In Humbert's tale, however, this attempt at restitution must await the murderous vengeance he takes out on Clare Quilty, the man for whom Dolly left Humbert. It is only after this murder scene that Humbert presents the third and final scene in which signs of an internal shift are evident. This is the memorable episode that occurs during Humbert's quest to find the missing Dolly. Standing on a hillside above a small mining town, he becomes aware of the simple "melody" of children at play in the valley below. As he absorbs these sounds, he has a moment of intense insight: "I stood listening to that musical vibration from my lofty slope, to those flashes of separate cries with a kind of demure murmur for background, and then I knew that the hopelessly poignant thing was not Lolita's absence from my side, but the absence of her voice from that concord" (*L* 308). Here Humbert seems to be moving beyond a selfish preoccupation with his own desires and registering a genuine understanding of the fact that his abuse of Dolly has forever taken her away from the natural state of childhood with its untold opportunities and possibilities.

For many readers of *Lolita*, this moment signifies an authentic epiphany within Humbert. Immediately afterwards, Humbert brings his memoir to a conclusion, first telling the reader that he has changed his intention to use these notes at his trial and then indicating that he wishes to enshrine his beloved Dolly in art: "I am thinking of aurochs and angels, the secret of durable pigments, prophetic sonnets, the refuge of art. And this is the only immortality you and I may share, my Lolita" (*L* 309). He has abandoned the belief that he could somehow transform the living child Dolly Haze into a fantasy creation Lolita whom he could live with and treat as he wished. Letting go of his specious desire to impose his "artistic" vision *onto* life, Humbert turns from a fraudulent artistic medium to an authentic one — the realm of verbal art — and he seeks to transmute the transient sorrows and joys of earthly life into something timeless and transcendent. He cannot restore Dolly's childhood or repair the damage he has done her, but he can attempt some faint recompense.

This is the traditional interpretation of the ending. On the other hand, not every reader has been persuaded that Humbert's epiphany is so clear-cut. Writing of the scene where Humbert hears the melody of children at play, David Rampton asserts: "Humbert's regret for Lolita's loss of her childhood is a threnody for time passing, including the loss of his own childhood, not a confrontation with his guilt."[21] And Brian Boyd has pointed out that Humbert's positioning of this supposed epiphany scene is significantly out of chronological order. It took place long before he visited the married Dolly Schiller, but Humbert places it in his memoir not only *after* that reunion scene, but right after the scene of his bloody murder of Quilty too. Perhaps he wishes to mitigate the grim impression made by his ruthless murder of Quilty, and to contrast his own undying love for Dolly with Quilty's apparent indifference to her fate. But the notion of a repentant Humbert does not entirely square with his behavior before and after the reunion with Dolly. He sets out to meet her in part because he is feverish with the desire to take revenge on the man who took her away from him. This man, he erroneously believes, is now Dolly's husband. Boyd points out the brutal insensitivity that this implies: Humbert is ready to kill this man, "regardless of what that would do to Lolita and the child he realizes she is bearing and would be compelled to rear on her own." He then continues: "How this planned murder of Lolita's unborn child's father would testify to Humbert's moral refinement [...] I cannot conceive."[22] Indeed, even after Humbert sees the pregnant Dolly in person he still intends to kill her husband until he realizes that Dick Schiller is not the man who spirited Dolly away. Once he learns Quilty's true identity, he rushes off to murder the man in cold blood, and he shows no signs of remorse at all. He acts as though the deed is inconsequential and he writes of his imagined judge: "Had I come before myself, I would have given Humbert at least thirty-five years for rape, and dismissed the rest of the charges" (L 308). So, whatever sense of guilt and repentance he feels, it extends only to his abuse of Dolly, not to the murder of another person. But perhaps his epiphany — his remorse over having deprived Dolly of her childhood — has eliminated his pedophiliac predilections? He admits that it has not: "My accursed nature could not change, no matter how my love for her did" (L 257). He goes on to relate how he would still be on the lookout for "the flash of a nymphet's limbs" after Dolly's disappearance, but, he claims: "never did I dwell now on the possibilities of bliss with a little maiden, specific or synthetic, in some out-of-the-way place [...] That was all over, for the time being at least" (L 257). What is remarkable about this declaration is its last phrase: "for the time being at least." Despite his supposed devotion to Dolly, and his recognition that he had cruelly torn her away from the company of other children, he cannot absolutely renounce a vision of bliss with some other nymphet. His renunciation is at best only a partial or temporary one, "for the time being at least." Even when he has finally seen Dolly again, and declares fervently that he loves "*this* Lolita, pale and polluted, and big with another's child" (L 278), he cannot overcome his ingrained habits. When he returns to Ramsdale from Coalmont and stops by the old Haze household, he notices "a golden-skinned, brown-haired nymphet of nine or ten" looking at him. He reports, "I said something pleasant to her, meaning no harm, an old-world compliment, what nice eyes you have, but she retreated in haste" (L 288). This sounds suspiciously like the old Humbert, and in his "old-world compliment" one detects an echo of the story of Red Riding Hood and the Big Bad Wolf, albeit with the speaking roles reversed.

An irreducible ambiguity persists into the very last lines of the text as well. When Humbert mentally sends his regards to Dolly in Alaska, he writes, among other things: "Be true to your Dick" (L 309). Is it possible that Humbert is not aware that this comes across as a vulgar, juvenile pun? Certainly Nabokov knows what *he* is doing. It is likely that Nabokov inserts the pun to indicate that Humbert remains true to *his* nature to the end: he cannot resist making one more foolish play on words, even though it may demean his beloved Dolly's husband. Even the last two words of the text evince something of Humbert's basic duality. In penning his final sentence Humbert writes: "And this is the only immortality you and I may share, my Lolita" (*L* 309). He uses his pet name "Lolita" here, not Dolly, and he refers to her as "my" Lolita. Is this simply a sign of "tender affection rather than solipsistic desire" as Ellen Pifer has asserted in reference to an earlier usage of the term?[23] Or does it signal Humbert's reversion to that idealized, solipsized figure he had pursued earlier? Or is it meant to evoke both possibilities at the same time?

I think we need to realize that Humbert's belated understanding of what he has done to Dolly is not meant to be viewed as a kind of magic, fairy-tale (or even Dostoevskian) model of instant spiritual conversion where the rank villain suddenly sees the light and becomes a chaste, angelic being. No, Nabokov has written a truer, more "realistic" ending. Humbert remains afflicted with his "pederosis" (*L* 257) to the end, and he does not find any reason to blame himself for taking another person's life. But, he *has* come to recognize the terrible damage he had done to Dolly, and I think we can accept that acknowledgment as genuine. I think it is also likely that the combined effect of his loss of Dolly and then seeing her again as a more mature woman helped to push him beyond his exclusively narcissistic frame of mind. Seeing Dolly married and pregnant, Humbert realizes that he loves this particular individual, not simply his fantasy of prepubescent girlhood. Nonetheless, he remains Humbert Humbert, and the mixed signals he sends in the final pages of his memoir suggest something fundamental and unchanging about his character. For his part, Nabokov chooses to keep his readers off balance until the very end. Yes, we can come away with the hope that brutal and tragic experiences can be transmuted into the enchanted realm of art, but we have also learned to be wary of the smooth talker, one who can twist words to deceive, distract, and mislead the gullible reader.

At this point we might do well to ask: what did Nabokov himself have to say about his protagonist? Did he view him as an incorrigible villain, or did he provide him with the opportunity for a redemptive conversion? Again, the evidence is somewhat mixed. In response to an interviewer's comment that Humbert "retains a touching and insistent quality," Nabokov declared: "I would put it differently: Humbert Humbert is a vain and cruel wretch who only manages to appear 'touching.' That epithet, in its true, tear-iridized sense, can only apply to my poor little girl" (*SO* 94). He also asserted that Humbert's double name was "a hateful name for a hateful person" (*SO* 26). On the other side of the ledger, however, is Nabokov's comment on Humbert's fate in his foreword to his English-language translation of *Despair*. Contrasting the eternal judgment awaiting the murderer Hermann from *Despair* with the sentence conferred upon Humbert, Nabokov wrote: "Both are neurotic scoundrels, yet there is a green lane in Paradise where Humbert is permitted to wander at dusk once a year; but Hell shall never parole Hermann" (*Des* xiii). Both men are murderers, and Humbert is guilty of child abuse as well, but presumably it was his recognition of his crime against Dolly and his desire to atone for it through the medium of authentic art that earns Humbert one day's reprieve per year. In yet another interview, Nabokov specifically addressed the issue of whether Humbert underwent some kind of change or not: "I don't think *Lolita* is a religious book [...] but I do think it is a moral one. And I do think that Humbert Humbert in his last stage is a moral man because he realizes that he loves *Lolita* [sic] like any woman should be loved. But it is too late; he has destroyed her childhood. There is certainly this kind of morality in it."[24]

In addition to affirming that Humbert underwent some change in *Lolita*, Nabokov here declares that his novel is a "moral" book. And he made a similar claim in a letter to Edmund Wilson in 1956: "When you do read LOLITA, please mark that it is a highly moral affair" (*NWL*, 331). These claims may strike some readers as odd, given the fact that Nabokov wrote in his essay "On a Book Entitled *Lolita*" (first published in 1957) that "despite John Ray's assertion, *Lolita* has no moral in tow" (*L* 314). How can we reconcile these two statements? Alfred Appel, Jr. made an early stab at this when he wrote: "when Nabokov says that there is 'No moral in tow' in *Lolita*, he is not denying it any moral resonance, but simply asserting that his intentions are not didactic."[25] This is an important point. Nabokov himself stated in his essay on *Lolita* that he was "neither a reader nor a writer of *didactic* fiction" (*L* 314, emphasis added), and what he rejects here is the idea that his work would set forth some moral prescription that can easily be extracted from the text and identified as the work's "message." In his view, morality is an essential element of an authentic work of art. He articulated this position forcefully in a 1945 letter to a reader of his monograph on Nikolai Gogol: "I never meant to deny the moral impact of art which is certainly inherent in every genuine work of art. What I do deny and am prepared to fight to the last drop of my ink is the deliberate moralizing which to me kills every vestige of art in a work however skillfully written" (*SL* 56).

Thus, in writing *Lolita*, Nabokov did not seek simply to inform his readers that pedophilia is evil. Although there have been some readers who wish that Nabokov *had* provided a simple, didactic message (Elizabeth Dipple writes that "Nabokov *should* perhaps [...] have a more exacting moral in tow"[26]), his method was more subtle. Leland de la Durantaye has eloquently argued that *Lolita* is "a moral book in the simple sense that from its first page to its last it explicitly treats moral questions [...] Morality, moral choices, moral falterings, faults, failings, and failures make up the matter of the work."[27] Every decision that Humbert makes in his dealings with others carries ethical implications. What is more, as readers who must contend with Humbert's rhetoric and his artistic pretensions, we become aware of what kinds of art, or approaches to art, are themselves morally questionable. And then, even our own response to the text — to its humor, charm, and pathos — may provide a stimulus for ethical self-examination. As Marilyn Edelstein puts it: "*Lolita* encourages its readers to examine their own ethical responses to the text and its relation to our world."[28]

Nabokov wants us to recognize Humbert's crimes in their every dimension. It should be self-evident that child abuse is evil, but the author would like us to be alert to all the ways in which the human spirit can be manipulated, controlled, and crushed. The human capacity for language is a miracle, but it can be used to manipulate and dominate as well as to entertain and to edify. Nabokov would have had no trouble in depicting a pedophile as a foul creature from whom we would all recoil at first sight, but that would not present a very interesting challenge to him as a writer. A much more interesting challenge is what he undertook in *Lolita*: to depict the monster as someone who can perhaps be engaging, humorous, intelligent, etc., and then to have us pay sufficient attention to see the "cesspool of rotting monsters behind his slow boyish smile" (*L* 44).[29]

As several commentators have pointed out, Nabokov makes the challenge even more interesting by giving Humbert some of his, Nabokov's, own talents and tastes (such as an aversion to Freudian theory, "progressive" education, etc.). Vladimir Alexandrov states: "Nabokov grants his character's document a range of cunning narrative strategies, and numerous passages of great beauty, pathos, and humor [...] In other words, Nabokov can be understood as having intentionally shared part of his own genius as a writer with a first-person narrator who in most other respects is deplorable."[30] But of course, Humbert is *not* Nabokov, and although one might find some areas of agreement, they diverge completely in one crucial area: their understanding of art and of the relationship between oneself and others. Immediately after stating that *Lolita* "has no moral in tow," Nabokov declares: "For me a work of fiction exists only insofar as it affords me what I shall bluntly call aesthetic bliss, that is a sense of being somehow, somewhere, connected with other states of being where art (curiosity, tenderness, kindness, ecstasy) is the norm" (*L* 314–15). What is particularly important about this remark is the list of qualities Nabokov attributes to his conception of art. With the possible exception of "ecstasy," each of the traits involves attention to the world beyond the self, and the middle two — tenderness and kindness — imply a particular attitude that we find sorely lacking in Humbert Humbert: a sensitive regard for other people. Indeed, Humbert lacks a fundamental empathy for others. He repeatedly demonstrates an unwillingness or inability to imagine himself in another's position, and even at the end of his memoir, he seems to express regret for this only in regard to Dolly; his attitude toward Quilty shows nothing but contempt and anger. What is more, Nabokov, unlike Humbert, valued freedom above all: not just freedom for one person to pursue his or her selfish visions at the expense of other people, but freedom for all in society to pursue their goals and to strive to attain their potential.[31] What then *is* the relationship between Humbert Humbert and Nabokov? Humbert may be one of those characters described by Nabokov in an interview as comparable to the "mournful monsters of a cathedral facade — demons placed there merely to show that they have been booted out." He then continues: "Actually, I'm a mild old gentleman who loathes cruelty" (*SO* 19).

Ultimately, I think, Nabokov's aspiration for readers of *Lolita* was the same as in all of his novels: to have them become sharper, more observant, and more sensitive readers — of literary texts, of words and worlds alike. Through his novel, Nabokov strives to develop our own capacity for empathy, curiosity, kindness, and ecstasy. As magnificent as the verbal texture of *Lolita* is, what makes it exceptional is its vivid evocation of characters and situations that we can imagine and respond to, whether in sympathy, horror, shock, or sheer wonder. *Lolita*'s vitality, complexity, and human depth continue to entrance its readers, both those who are approaching it for the first time and those whose copies of the novel are well-worn from repeated rereadings. *Lolita* will undoubtedly exert a compelling appeal to readers for some time to come.

Notes

1. Pekka Tammi neatly outlines the various reading audiences that are alluded to in Nabokov's novel in his *Problems of Nabokov's Poetics: A Narratological Analysis* (Helsinki: Suomalainen Tiedeakatemia, 1985), 272–76.
2. See Tamir-Ghez, "The Art of Persuasion in *Lolita*," *Poetics Today* 1:1–2 (1979): 77–80.
3. Leslie Fiedler, "The Profanation of the Child," *The New Leader*, 23 June 1958, 29.
4. Lionel Trilling, "The Last Lover: Vladimir Nabokov's *Lolita*," *Encounter* 11.4 (1958): 14. Trilling also admits that Humbert's "unrelenting self-reference" and his "impious greediness [...] seduce us into kinship with him" (11).
5. Martin Green, "The Morality of *Lolita*," *The Kenyon Review*, 28.3 (1966): 365, 369–70.
6. Ellen Pifer, "Introduction," *Vladimir Nabokov's* Lolita*: A Casebook,* ed. Ellen Pifer (Oxford: Oxford University Press, 2003), 10. Even Trilling experienced this reaction. Speaking of the "outrage" one feels at the violation of the prohibition against adult men having sex with twelve-year-old girls, Trilling writes that one feels this "all the more because we have been seduced into conniving in the violation, because we have permitted our fantasies to accept what we know to be revolting" (Trilling, "The Last Lover," 14).
7. Stephen Butler, "*Lolita* and the Modern Experience of Beauty," *Studies in the Novel* 18 (1986): 434.
8. Tamir-Ghez, "The Art of Persuasion in *Lolita*," 75.
9. Ellen Pifer, *Nabokov and the Novel* (Cambridge, MA: Harvard University Press, 1980), 164.
10. Tamir-Ghez, "The Art of Persuasion in *Lolita*," 76.
11. The situation Humbert bemoans here is quite similar to that depicted in Fedor Dostoevsky's story, "The Gentle Creature." See Julian Connolly, "Nabokov's Dialogue with Dostoevsky: *Lolita* and 'The Gentle Creature,'" *Nabokov Studies* 4 (1997): 15–36.
12. Michael Wood, "Revisiting *Lolita*," in *Vladimir Nabokov's* Lolita*: A Casebook*, ed. Ellen Pifer, 193.
13. Martin Amis, "*Lolita* Reconsidered." *Atlantic* (September 1992): 119.
14. David Rampton, *Vladimir Nabokov: A Critical Study of the Novels* (Cambridge: Cambridge University Press, 1984), 110.

15. Tamir-Ghez, "The Art of Persuasion in *Lolita*," 79.
16. Green, "Tolstoy and Nabokov: The Morality of *Lolita*," 370.
17. Michael Wood, *The Magician's Doubts* (London: Pimlico, 1995), 139.
18. Alfred Appel, Jr., "*Lolita*: The Springboard of Parody," *Wisconsin Studies in Contemporary Literature* 8.2 (1967): 226.
19. James Phelan, "Estranging Unreliability, Bonding Unreliability, and the Ethics of *Lolita*," *Narrative* 15.2 (2007): 236.
20. Lucy Maddox, *Nabokov's Novels in English* (Athens, GA: University of Georgia Press, 1983), 65.
21. David Rampton, *Vladimir Nabokov* (New York: St. Martin's Press, 1993), 99.
22. Brian Boyd, "'Even Homais Nods': Nabokov's Fallibility or How to Revise *Lolita*," *Nabokov Studies* 2 (1995): 84–85.
23. Pifer, *Nabokov and the Novel*, 167.
24. Douglas M. Davis, "On the Banks of Lake Leman: Mr. Nabokov Reflects on 'Lolita' and 'Onegin,'" *National Observer*, 29 June 1964, 17.
25. Appel, "*Lolita*: The Springboard of Parody," 224–25.
26. Elizabeth Dipple, *The Unresolvable Plot: Reading Contemporary Fiction* (New York: Routledge, 1988), 74.
27. Leland de la Durantaye, *Style is Matter: The Moral art of Vladimir Nabokov* (Ithaca: Cornell University Press, 2007), 190.
28. Marilyn Edelstein, "Teaching *Lolita* in a Course on Ethics and Literature," in *Approaches to Teaching Nabokov's* Lolita, ed. Zoran Kuzmanovich and Galya Diment (New York: The Modern Language Association, 2008), 47.
29. In an interview in 1962, Nabokov spoke about the difficulty he faced in creating this novel: "It was my most difficult book—the book that treated of a theme which is so distant, so remote, from my own emotional life that it gave me a special pleasure to use my combinational talent to make it real" (*SO* 15).
30. Vladimir Alexandrov, *Nabokov's Otherworld* (Princeton: Princeton University Press, 1991), 162. Additionally, Leland de la Durantaye points out the specific ways that Humbert's "spinal sensitivity" to beauty echoes Nabokov's own pronouncements on the subject. See his *Style is Matter*, 58–60.
31. Nabokov told an interviewer that his "political creed" was "classical to the point of triteness. Freedom of speech, freedom of thought, freedom of art" (*SO* 34–35).

Chapter Four

WHO WAS DOLLY HAZE?

"Wanted, wanted: Dolores Haze" (*L* 255)

The title of this chapter is prompted by an observation made by Michael Wood in his book, *The Magician's Doubts*. After noting that Humbert's narrative is not really about a child named Lolita, but about "the obsessive dream of Lolita which captured the actual child and took her away," Wood argues that if Humbert had not faintly evoked a Lolita (the authentic child) as well as a "Lolita" (his fantasy obsession), then there is "no novel here that matters, only the brilliant, vain spinning of a mind hooked on nothing but its own figments."[1] In this chapter I will go looking for that authentic child who has been "faintly evoked" by Humbert, and to see if she can be brought out of Humbert's shadows to be viewed on her own terms.

We can begin by quoting two of Humbert's characterizations of his beloved "Lolita." Recalling his experiences on his first cross-country trip with her, he declared: "Mentally, I found her to be a disgustingly conventional little girl" (*L* 148). Later, after he has lost her, and then met with her again in Coalmont, he reevaluates his attitude toward her and concludes: "quite possibly, behind the awful juvenile clichés, there was in her a garden and a twilight, and a palace gate — dim and adorable regions which happened to be lucidly and absolutely forbidden to me" (*L* 284). What are we to make of these two very different opinions? On the one hand, her mental world is described as being "disgustingly conventional." On the other hand, behind "the awful juvenile clichés," there is perhaps "a garden and a twilight, and a palace gate" — a state of mind that is by no means "disgustingly conventional." On the contrary, it is rather exotic and unusual; this is Dolly as royal princess. Which evaluation is the more accurate? The first, the second, or neither? Or both together? This is the conundrum I would like to explore here.

If we turn to the critics' and scholars' responses to the novel, we find a similarly mixed picture. The early reviewers tended to take a rather jaundiced view of young Dolly. For example, Dorothy Parker wrote that Dolly was "a dreadful little creature, selfish, hard, vulgar, and foul-tempered."[2] J.K. Hutchens chimed in, exclaiming that she was "singularly experienced, vulgar, and depraved."[3] Perhaps the most strident voice belonged to Thomas Molnar, who wrote that the "central question the reader ought to ask of himself is whether he feels pity for the girl" (one notes the use of the masculine pronoun here). He continues: "Our ethical ideal would require that we look at Lolita as a sacrificial lamb," but, he says, this is impossible for two reasons. First, "before yielding to Humbert, the girl had had a nasty little affair with a nasty little thirteen-year-old in an expensive summer camp. Besides, she is a spoiled sub-teenager with a foul mouth, a self-offered target for lechers, movie-magazine editors, and corrupt classmates."[4]

Later critics were more sympathetic toward and protective of young Dolly. Linda Kauffman emphasizes Dolly's status as a suffering victim, graphically describing her as "enslaved" and "bleeding" on the morning after she and Humbert have spent the night together at the Enchanted Hunters Hotel.[5] More recently, the evaluations have taken on greater complexity: contemporary readers see Dolly as more protean, spirited, and nuanced than the early readers and reviewers did.

In general, I would say that the evolution in critical opinion of Dolly roughly matches up with developments in Nabokov criticism as a whole. The early reviewers of Nabokov's work in English tended to see the writer as a cunning creator of aesthetic puzzles. Later, particularly in the 1980s, critics began to focus on the ethical dimensions of his work. Since then, critical evaluation of Nabokov has grown more complex and wide-ranging.

This broad evolution in the critical response to Nabokov finds reflection in the critical response to Dolly Haze. Indeed, those who view *Lolita* the novel primarily as a verbal performance or aesthetic tour de force have tended to regard Lolita the character in a less than complimentary light, while those who have been focused on the ethical dimension in Nabokov's work have tended to regard Dolly as an innocent child, a victim of vicious sexual abuse. As a side note, it's worth pointing out that Nabokov himself may have anticipated this kind of dual reading. In having Humbert name Dolly "Lolita" (and playing up the sound qualities of this name: "Lo-lee-ta: the tip of the tongue taking a trip of three steps down the palate to tap, at three, on the teeth. Lo. Lee. Ta." [L 9]), Nabokov underscores the aesthetic impulse that Humbert believes is informing his attitude to Dolly, while her real name, "Dolores," reminds the reader of the genuine pain and suffering this child must endure at the hands of her supposed protector.

How, then, is the reader supposed to know who the *real* Dolly Haze is: is she the "disgustingly conventional" vamp, or a fairy-tale princess imprisoned by an evil wizard? Unfortunately, she is not given much of a voice of her own. We are entirely dependent on an unreliable and self-absorbed narrator for all of our information about Dolly. He does not really tell us much of what she says herself, and he often delivers his own (harsh) judgments of her tastes and her morals. Frequently, a summary judgment of her speech is substituted for her actual words. For example, he denigrates her "intense and vehement griping" (*L* 148) without telling the reader precisely what she said. Although Humbert is very good at observing her *physical* attributes — height, weight, skin color, body odor, etc. — he is much less interested in her inner world. His rapt attention to her physical appearance begins when he first sees her: "It was the same child — the same frail, honey-hued shoulders, the same silky supple bare back, the same chestnut head of hair," (*L* 39), and it continues throughout the narrative (see, e.g., *L* 41, 42, 48, 51). At one point he writes that he has a thousand eyes "wide open in my eyed blood" and with these eyes he sees "her slightly raised shoulder blades, and the bloom along the incurvation of her spine, and the swellings of her tense narrow nates clothed in black, and the seaside of her schoolgirl thighs" (*L* 42). We can contrast the precision of the measurements he provides when he goes shopping for Dolly ("hip girth, twenty-nine inches; thigh girth [just below the gluteal sulcus], seventeen [...] waist, twenty-three; stature, fifty-seven inches; weight, seventy-eight pounds" [*L* 107]) with the lack of information he provides about her emotional or mental life: "I simply did not know a thing about my darling's mind" (*L* 284). Nor does he really want to know what's she's thinking or feeling: "it was always my habit and method to ignore Lolita's states of mind while comforting my own base self" (*L* 287).

Given this lack of information about what Dolly is thinking and feeling, the character becomes a figure upon whom the reader can make his or her own projections. Indeed, Todd Bayma and Gary Allen Fine have argued that the negative evaluation of Dolly Haze's character found in the early reviews of *Lolita* may be attributed to the projection of the reviewers' own "personal and cultural knowledge" about teenage girls onto the figure of Dolly. Reacting to a widespread cultural anxiety about wayward teenagers in the 1950s, these reviewers "drew upon stereotypes of the bad girl to understand and then defame Lolita, portraying her as sexually depraved, manipulative, rude, and obnoxious."[6] Bayma and Fine provide a catalogue of such evaluations: Howard Nemerov judged Dolly to be "thoroughly corrupted already"; John Hollander called her "completely corrupt"; and Charles Rolo proclaimed her to be "utterly depraved."[7] To this catalogue they could have added Leslie Fiedler's astonishing critique: "Annabel Lee as nymphomaniac, demonic rapist of the soul — such is the lithe, brown Campfire Girl."[8]

To a certain degree, these types of evaluations suggest not only that the reviewers may have been reflecting widespread cultural stereotypes about "bad girls," but that they themselves have been taken in by Humbert's pronounced anxiety about the loose morals he perceives in Dolly and the teenagers who surround her. Nabokov, however, surely wished us to be better "readers" than Humbert, and not approach either Dolly or his novel with ready-made preconceptions that look only for friendly data to reinforce and support those preconceptions. As he proclaimed to his students at Cornell and to others, "In reading, one should notice and fondle details" (LL 1).[9] And when we do so with Lolita, we find that Dolly, when Humbert enters her life, is probably a fairly normal twelve-year-old girl. Conventional, perhaps, but "disgustingly" so? Hardly. That adverb tells us more about Humbert than about Dolly. What do we know about Dolly's tastes? Although he chooses not to inquire into her inner world, Humbert does record many of her external pursuits. So, the attentive reader learns that Dolly likes comic books (L 42), "[s]weet hot jazz, square dancing, gooey fudge sundaes, musicals, movie magazines" (L 148), popular music, "novelties and souvenirs" (L 148), films, tennis, roller skating, and, occasionally, boys. She can be rude and defiant to her mother, prankish around Humbert, and mesmerized by the glittering allure of Hollywood stardom. She can be very funny, and her mockery (especially of Humbert) can be lethal. At one point Humbert's diary sums up the wide range of her moods as "[c]hangeful, bad-tempered, cheerful, awkward, graceful with the tart grace of her coltish subteens" (L 49). In short, she appears to be a typical young adolescent. Michael Wood expresses this beautifully: "She is, in short, an entirely ordinary child, unbearable, lovable, funny, moody, and soon trapped in the circle of Humbert's obsession."[10]

One of Dolly's traits that Humbert repeatedly mentions is her susceptibility to the blandishments of the marketplace. As he puts it, "She believed, with a kind of celestial trust, any advertisement or advice that appeared in *Movie Love* or *Screen Land*," and he summarizes her state by saying: "She it was to whom ads were dedicated: the ideal consumer, the subject and object of every foul poster" (*L* 148). Humbert's evaluation here might indeed be accurate, but we should note that Nabokov has surrounded this statement with abundant irony. Humbert himself once had a job "thinking up and editing perfume ads" (*L* 32), and he works just as hard as any Madison Avenue advertising agent in trying to sell his personal vision to Dolly and, we should note, to the reader as well. He tries to mesmerize us with witty comments and pithy observations, and, as part of his sales pitch, he tries to flatter the reader by belittling Dolly's attachments, thereby setting up an implicit contrast between her conventional tastes and the reader's undoubtedly more discriminating and refined ones. In other words, by putting down Dolly's tastes, he tries to promote his own.

What is more, Humbert is just as much of a dreamer as Dolly. But while her dreams are indeed ordinary and conventional (and thank goodness for that), his own dreams are perverse and destructive. Finally, as Susan Mizruchi has pointed out, Dolly's "consumptive habits" may reflect a desperate desire to compensate for the losses she has endured under Humbert's control. In Mizruchi's formulation, Dolly's consumptive hunger "is a sign of desire, for the desires of children who live in homes with other children and parents. She consumes [...] to be normal—the most pathetic kind of consumption in the world."[11] Even Humbert provides a most poignant example of this desperate desire for normalcy when he observes that "she was curiously fascinated by the photographs of local brides, some in full wedding apparel, holding bouquets and wearing glasses" (*L* 165).

If Dolly is essentially an ordinary young adolescent, what is the degree of her involvement or complicity with Humbert's sexual obsession? Is she the "utterly depraved" or "completely corrupt" figure that the early reviewers discovered? Or is she an unsuspecting victim raped by a vicious pedophile, as later readers have suggested?[12] Or is the truth somewhere in between? Again, we are forced to read between Humbert's lines, and to draw inferences from the ambiguous clues he has left behind. I think that the evidence suggests that when Humbert moved into the Haze household and began to pay attention to Dolly, she was flattered by the attention and, in her own way, displayed a reciprocal interest. We know that she tended to idolize certain adults. When Humbert took up residence, he is "said to resemble some crooner or actor chap on whom Lo has a crush" (*L* 43). In her bedroom, Dolly has posted an advertisement featuring a "distinguished playwright [...] solemnly smoking a Drome" above her bed (*L* 69). Unbeknownst to Humbert, the figure in the ad is Clare Quilty, who had once visited Ramsdale and had pulled ten-year-old Dolly into his lap and kissed her face (*L* 272). When she tells Humbert about this incident years later, she says that she was furious about Quilty's action at the time, but, the fact that she has posted his picture on her wall indicates that the fury had perhaps been replaced with another kind of intense feeling. Observing the poster, Humbert states that the resemblance between himself and the man in the ad was "slight," but the fact that there was *any* resemblance may have sparked Dolly's interest in him. Then too, perhaps Dolly's interest in Humbert was heightened by a subtle rivalry with her mother. At one point, Charlotte warns Humbert not to grow a moustache, or else "somebody" would go "absolutely dotty" (*L* 48). Dolly reacts indignantly to this comment, and later, according to Humbert, the two "rivals" had a "ripping row" (*L* 48).

Dolly tries on several occasions to engage Humbert's attention, and may even indulge in a kind of awkward flirtation. On one occasion, she squeezes herself between Humbert and her mother and keeps shoving a "ballerina of wool and gauze" into his lap (*L* 45); on another, she jumps into the Haze car next to Humbert and slips her hand into his (*L* 51). On a third occasion, she comes into his room and begins to study the notes Humbert had made of his observations in the Haze household, "the hideous hieroglyphics" of his "fatal lust" (*L* 48). He claims that she cannot decipher them, but whether this is true or not, we cannot tell. What we do know is that as she studies the notes, Humbert puts his arm around her and she sinks to a "half-sitting position" on his knee. He asserts that she was waiting "with curiosity and composure" for him to kiss her, but before he could do this, they were interrupted by the maid disclosing the discovery of a "dead something" in the basement, and Dolly rushed off to investigate (*L* 48–49). Again, we cannot be sure that Humbert's assessment of Dolly's mood is accurate, but it is certainly not out of the realm of possibility. Indeed, a week later, after Dolly has rebuffed a physical advance by Humbert made while she was talking with the paper boy through the window, she steals up to him and puts her hands over his eyes; later she tosses a tennis ball his way (*L* 55).

This flirtatious or attention-getting behavior culminates in the notorious couch scene in Chapter Thirteen, when Humbert manages to have an orgasm by rubbing himself against Dolly's legs. In his narrative,

Humbert gloats over the fact that Dolly "had noticed nothing" (*L* 61) and "knew nothing" (*L* 62) about what had occurred, but a careful reading of the evidence suggests otherwise. When Humbert describes the moment of his climax, he also describes Dolly's movements and expressions: "'Oh it's nothing at all,' she cried with a sudden shrill note in her voice, and she wiggled, and squirmed, and threw her head back, and her teeth rested on her glistening underlip as she half-turned away [...] Immediately afterward (as if we had been struggling and now my grip had eased) she rolled off the sofa and jumped to her feet." Answering the phone, she stood and blinked, "cheeks aflame" (*L* 61). Several specific details in this description suggest that Dolly is not as unsuspecting as Humbert wishes to believe. In fact, on the morning when she and Humbert wake up in the Enchanted Hunters Hotel, she attempts to teach Humbert how to kiss, and his description of her contains some of the same images he had used when describing her reaction to his orgasm. The description "her full underlip glistened" can be compared with "her glistening underlip" in the couch scene (*L* 61), and the observation "[h]er cheekbones were flushed" (*L* 133) can be compared with the earlier "cheeks aflame" (*L* 61), as well as with a later description of her reaction to the sight of Quilty's car following them on their second cross-country trip: "her joyful eye, her flaming cheek" (*L* 219).

Analyzing this scene, Sarah Herbold goes so far as to state that Dolly herself may be having an orgasm, and indeed, she may have been orchestrating their "mutual stimulation."[13] I, however, am not confident that the evidence provided in the description justifies such a conclusion. It's more likely, in my view, that Dolly is aware of Humbert's excitement. She may be intrigued and curious, but it's not clear that she's orchestrating the entire episode. In fact, she may be alluding to this moment nearly two years later when she defends herself against Humbert's harsh interrogation about what she had been doing when she skipped her piano lessons in Beardsley. Humbert reports: "She said I had attempted to violate her several times when I was her mother's roomer" (*L* 205). This suggests to me that Dolly was more a passive (if curious) participant in the scene than an active orchestrator of it.

Her somewhat erratic interest in Humbert shows up again on the day of her departure for summer camp, when she runs into the house one last time to kiss Humbert farewell. And it resumes again on the day he picks her up from camp when she tells him she's been "revoltingly unfaithful" to Humbert but that this is all right, because he's "stopped caring for [her]."

When he asks her why she thinks this, she tells him its because he hasn't kissed her yet. Then, after he stops the car, "Lolita positively flowed" into his arms (*L* 112–13). Clearly, Dolly still has some interest in Humbert, but her degree of interest, and her responsibility for their subsequent sexual encounter at the Enchanted Hunters Hotel is very much up for debate.

The key question here is "Did Dolly 'seduce' Humbert?" as he himself alleges in his memoir (*L* 132). Or was she an innocent victim of his rapacious lust? Or again, does the truth lie somewhere between? To try to shed light into this question, I think we have to begin with the odd hints Dolly makes to Humbert as they drive toward the hotel. Here are a few excerpts from her conversation: "Fact I've been revoltingly unfaithful to you" (*L* 112); then, referring to herself: "Bad, bad girl [...] Juvenile delickwent, but frank and fetching" (*L* 113) (aside: we can pause here and consider why she changes the word "delinquent" to "delickwent"). A bit later she says: "I am a friend to male animals [...] I am thrifty and I am absolutely filthy in thought, word and deed" (*L* 114). When Humbert asks her if she has finished telling him all that she did at camp, she says yes, "Except for one little thing, something I simply can't tell you without blushing all over" (*L* 115). She makes one final attempt to let Humbert know what's on her mind just before she falls asleep: "If I tell you — if I tell you, will you promise [...] promise you won't make complaints? [...] Oh, I've been such a disgusting girl [...] Lemme tell you — " (*L* 123).

During the same period of time, her reactions to Humbert's attempts to kiss her send a mixed message. After "positively flow[ing]" into his arms in the car for a firm kiss (*L* 113), she rebuffs a later attempt he makes to kiss her on the neck ("'*Don't* do that,' she said looking at me with unfeigned surprise. 'Don't drool on me. You dirty man'" [*L* 115]). In the hotel room, she again rebuffs his attempt to kiss her by saying "Look, let's cut out the kissing game and get something to eat" (*L* 120). But when she sees the suitcase of new clothes he had bought for her, she creeps into his arms, "radiant" and "relaxed" and indicating that she will show him the right way to kiss.

What are we to make of all this evidence? Are her sardonic comments about being a "juvenile delickwent," "absolutely filthy in thought, word and deed," and "such a disgusting girl" meant to show that she's a cool kid, experienced and wise in the ways of the world? Or, can we detect behind the bravado an element of insecurity or anxiety. Might she not be trying to find out what Humbert, a trusted adult, thinks of something she's done at camp? Leona Toker interprets Dolly's words this way when she writes that it is "only in a repeated reading of the Enchanted Hunters episode that we become aware of the intensely troubled emotional life behind Dolly's brash facade."[14] Humbert, however, is absolutely tone deaf to the possibility that something is gnawing at Dolly's conscience. Although at one point he does say: "What have you been up to? I insist you tell me?" (and the tone of this injunction is hardly conducive to inspiring candor or confidence in an anxious child), for the most part he is focused on his own personal goal: to get Dolly to the hotel and into bed as quickly as possible. Let us not forget that he is withholding from her the most crucial piece of information that could affect her emotional state at this point: the news of the death of her mother!

In his subsequent commentary on what he imagined Dolly's sexual experience to have been, he admits that he gave it little thought, assuming at the most that her "purity" might have been "slightly damaged through some juvenile erotic experience, no doubt homosexual, at that accursed camp of hers" (L 124). In a typical example of Humbertian duplicity, he asserts: "the moralist in me by-passed the issue by clinging to conventional notions of what twelve-year-old girls should be" (L 124). This comment rings with a double irony. First of all, Humbert himself had been sexually active at the age of thirteen with a girl who was "a few months [his] junior" and therefore was about Dolly's age. In other words, as he well knew, twelve-year-old girls could easily have had some sexual experience.[15] More significantly, his claim that he was "clinging" to conventional notions about the ostensible innocence or purity of twelve-year-old girls is completely discredited by his ensuing behavior: he aggressively participates in the sexual abuse of this very child!

It is on the following morning that, according to Humbert, Dolly "seduced" him. Yet he is surprisingly reticent about providing a clear indication of just what went on. He writes that Dolly whispered something in his ear, apparently telling him about a "game" that she had played with Charlie Holmes at camp. When he feigns ignorance about this game, she asks him: "You mean [...] you never did it when you were a kid?" He responds "Never," and she says: "Okay [...] here is where we start" (L 133). Because Humbert does not provide details about the "game" that Dolly has mentioned, or what she specifically attempts to "start" with him, readers are left to speculate on what precisely transpired between the two. According to Humbert, Dolly showed "not a trace of modesty" and revealed herself to be "utterly and hopelessly depraved" (*L* 133). Some readers, including many of the earlier reviewers mentioned above, have accepted Humbert's perspective and pronounced Dolly "completely corrupt" (Hollander) or "utterly depraved" (Rolo). Others, such as Elizabeth Patnoe, argue that the game Dolly played with Charlie was simply a kissing game, "or, at the very most, some kind of fondling activity."[16] Again, I think that a close examination of the details may help here. When Dolly tells Humbert the story of her activities with Charlie Holmes, she states that when she, Charlie, and Barbara Burke would carry a canoe through the woods at camp, she would serve as sentinel "while Barabara and the boy copulated behind a bush" (*L* 137). At first, she says, she refused to "try what it was like," but "curiosity and camaraderie prevailed," and soon, "she and Barbara were doing it by turns with [...] Charlie, who [...] sported a fascinating collection of contraceptives" retrieved from a nearby lake (*L* 137). It seems to me that the pronoun "it" here can only refer to "copulation," and that it is quite plausible that when Dolly ask Humbert "You mean [...] you never did it when you were a kid?" she is referring to intercourse. What were Dolly's motives in suggesting the she and Humbert play this "game" together? Is she a depraved and corrupt youth who cannot restrain her carnal desires? It is more likely that she simply wants to share her secret with a man she has had a crush on, and to enlist him in the furtive sport she had discovered during the summer. Not only would she show him how sophisticated she was, but she could also enjoy a little victory in her rivalry with her mother.

Nonetheless, as Humbert himself points out, Dolly was "not quite prepared for certain discrepancies between a kid's life and mine" (*L* 134), with the word "life" probably meaning not only life experiences but "penis" as well ("My life was handled by little Lo in an energetic, matter-of-fact manner as if it were an insensate gadget unconnected with me" [*L* 133–34]). Again, in another characteristic bit of rhetorical legerdemain, Humbert declines to tell us what he did to or with Dolly, but the very words he uses tend to give him away. First he says that he "feigned stupidity and had her have her way," but he then adds the revealing note: "at least while I could still bear it" (*L* 134). The clear implication here is that he could not bear her inexperienced maneuvers, and took charge himself, turning her now into the subordinate object of his desires. Secondly, he tries to indicate that what transpired next was of little significance: "But really these are irrelevant matters; I am not concerned with so-called 'sex' at all" (*L* 134).

Here again he tries to pull the wool over the reader's eyes: he is indeed concerned with sex, but he does not want the reader to know what kind of physical abuse he inflicted upon Dolly. Nabokov, however, does not want to let Humbert off the hook here, and so he has Humbert acknowledge what has transpired as they drive away from the hotel: "This was a lone child, an absolute waif, with whom a heavy-limbed, foul-smelling adult had had strenuous intercourse three times that very morning" (*L* 140). He aptly conveys his sensation that he is sitting "with the small ghost of somebody I had just killed" (*L* 140). As he himself now seems to recognize, even if Dolly had engaged in some kind of sexual activity at summer camp, she is still a twelve-year-old girl, whereas he is a thirty-seven-year-old man who ought to know better. She is also an orphan, and he is supposed to be her guardian and protector. This is a monstrous betrayal on many levels.

Once they have had this sexual encounter, any fantasies about Humbert that Dolly may have had have been utterly exhausted. She cries that night, and every night, during their aimless cross-country travels. He ceases to be someone she might have a romantic interest in; his constant sexual demands become increasingly tiresome and tyrannical. She cannot yet leave him ("she had absolutely nowhere else to go" [*L* 142]), so she tries to soothe herself through her pursuit of entertainment, distractions, rich food, etc. Although Humbert may see Dolly as vulgar and "disgustingly conventional" (*L* 148), Ellen Pifer offers an insightful explanation of Dolly's behavior: "Against the powerful force of [Humbert's] animated imagination, Lolita wields her trite toughness like a weapon. It is the shield she raises, with small success, to defend that besieged kingdom — her personal identity."[17]

After moving to Beardsley, Dolly begins to learn how to carve out some life of her own. Taking on a role in a play, she learns how to be an actress, and she develops some of the same skills of deception and prevarication that Humbert had utilized during their time together when he presented himself to the world as a caring stepfather and nothing more. As Humbert later puts it, she had learned to "cultivate deceit" (*L* 229). Finally, she seizes the moment and manages to escape, although sadly, she turns to another adult male about whom she has developed an unrealistic romantic fantasy. Unlike Humbert, however, this man, Clare Quilty, has the added attraction of being a celebrity, and indeed, it appears that Dolly's fascination with him not only preceded her passing interest in Humbert, but may have played a role in developing this interest in the first place (we have already noted that Humbert remarks on the "slight" resemblance between the picture of Quilty in the Dromes ad and himself). Tragically, Quilty does not really care for Dolly as an individual, and he loses interest in her when she refuses to participate in his porn films. Twice now she has been let down by adult males for whom she felt affection and trust.

Perhaps then it is no surprise that she seems to have lowered her sights when she settles on Dick Schiller, and her marriage to him can be seen as a modest attempt to achieve a "normal" life as wife and mother. When Humbert sees her again in Coalmont, she is wearing glasses, just like the brides in the photographs she had studied with such interest years earlier. For many readers, the scene between Humbert and this new, more mature Dolly, is one of the most moving episodes in the novel. There are so many fine things in Nabokov's portrait of the seventeen-year-old pregnant Dolly that it is hard to single them all out. One striking feature is her refusal to condemn either Quilty (whom she still admires) or Humbert (whose time with her is dismissed "like a bit of dry mud caking her childhood" [L 272]). Harold Bloom has called this a "wonderful freedom from bitterness,"[18] and Michael Wood explains: "This dazed tolerance is more terrible than resentment or rage because it belongs to a person who is past surprise, who has lived with more human strangeness — Humbert's obsession — than anyone should have to."[19] Another feature is her refusal either to comply with Quilty's demands for her participation in his porn films or to accede to Humbert's plea that she leave Coalmont with him at that very moment. She has developed the internal resources necessary to resist the coercive pressures (whether they be romantic or financial) of the men in her life, and to make independent decisions for herself and for her unborn child. And she is so protective of the latter, that she refuses to talk about Quilty's kinky films "with that baby inside her" (L 277). This is no corrupt or depraved child, but a woman who has had to grow up too quickly, and has managed despite all odds to retain a sense of decency, integrity, and hope. As Elizabeth Janeway, one of the first reviewers of Lolita put it, Dolly Schiller is a "triumph for the vital force that has managed to make a life out of the rubble that Humbert's passion created."[20]

Nabokov's depiction of this new, more subdued and mature Dolly is so striking that at least one critic, Sarah Herbold, finds it overly mawkish and sentimental. Dolly Schiller, as Herbold sees her, "is no longer the elusive and sassy nymphet who has eluded Humbert for years. Instead, she has become a white-trash married mother-to-be [...] In effect, Lolita has been transformed into a latter-day Virgin Mary of Coalmont."[21] But surely this is just as misguided as the earlier view of Dolly as corrupt or depraved. In Dolly Schiller, Nabokov has drawn a portrait of of an ordinary girl who has gone through extraordinary hardship, not to become a saint, or much less the mother of a god, but simply to become a woman who clings to a small hope that she can have a stable relationship, have a child, and raise a family.

By this point, the reader is rooting for Dolly to find some happiness with Dick in Alaska, and yet, if the reader has understood what John Ray, Jr. has written in the foreword, the reader is painfully aware that this happiness will never arrive, for Dolly will die in childbirth in Gray Star just three months later on Christmas Day. The death of Dolly's child is emblematic of the death of the child that Dolly herself once was. The damage inflicted by Humbert spirals on, unchecked, leaving death and destruction in its wake. Both Vladimir and Véra Nabokov were appalled by the reaction of those reviewers who saw only corruption and depravity in Dolly. Nabokov found himself on more than one occasion reminding interviewers of Dolly's genuine distress: "Humbert Humbert is a vain and cruel wretch who manages to appear 'touching.' That epithet, in its true, tear-iridized sense, can only apply to my poor little girl" (SO 94). His wife was even more eloquent in her defense of Dolly: "I wish, though, somebody would notice the tender description of the child's helplessness, her pathetic dependence on monstrous HH, and her heartrending courage all along culminating in that squalid but essentially pure and healthy marriage [...] They all miss the fact that 'the horrid little brat' Lolita, is essentially very good indeed — or she would not have straightened out after being crushed so terribly, and found a decent life with poor Dick more to her liking than the other kind."[22]

Over the last fifty years, Dolly Schiller, née Haze, has been subjected to a broad range of critical opinions, ranging from the extremely negative to the defiantly protective. I believe that a close reading of Nabokov's novel reveals a vibrant figure who is more complex and multi-faceted than the simplistic epithets that have been attached to her would have one believe. Though it may be difficult to discern the genuine Dolly from behind the veil of Humbert's fantasies, I think that it is the rich, multi-dimensional personality sensed within that gives this novel much of its fascination and enduring appeal.

Notes

1. Michael Wood, *The Magician's Doubts: Nabokov and the Risks of Fiction* (London: Pimlico, 1995), 115.
2. Dorothy Parker, "Sex — without the asterisks," *Esquire*, October 1958, 103.
3. John K. Hutchens, "Lolita," *New York Herald Tribune*, 18 August 1958, 13.
4. Thomas Molnar, "Matter-of-Fact Confession of a Non-Penitent," *Commonweal*, 24 October 1958, 69.
5. Linda Kauffman, "Framing *Lolita*: Is There a Woman in the Text?", in *Refiguring the Father: New Feminist Readings of Patriarchy*, ed. Patricia Yaeger and Beth Kowalski-Wallace (Carbondale and Edwardsville: Southern Illinois University Press, 1989), 142.
6. Todd Bayma and Gary Alan Fine, "Fictional Figures and Imaginary Relations: The Transformation of Lolita from Victim to Vixen," *Studies in Symbolic Interaction* 20 (1996): 170.
7. Cited in Bayma and Fine, 170–71.
8. Leslie A. Fiedler, *Love and Death in the American Novel* (New York: Criterion Books, 1960), 327.
9. Vladimir Nabokov, "Good Readers and Good Writers," *Lectures on Literature*, ed. Fredson Bowers (New York: Harcourt Brace Jovanovich / Bruccoli Clark, 1980), 1.
10. Michael Wood, *The Magician's Doubts*, 116.
11. Susan Mizruchi, "*Lolita* in History," *American Literature* 75.3 (2003): 648.
12. See, e.g., Elizabeth Patnoe, "Lolita Misrepresented, Lolita Reclaimed, Disclosing the Doubles," *College Literature* 22.2 (1995): 95.
13. Sarah Herbold, "'(I have camouflaged everything, my love)': *Lolita* and the Woman Reader," *Nabokov Studies* 5 (1998/1999): 82.
14. Leona Toker, *Nabokov: The Mystery of Literary Structures* (Ithaca: Cornell University Press, 1989), 204.
15. Frederick Whiting speculates that Humbert's attitude here may reflect his own reluctance to admit that Dolly may have her own desire and will, her own "agency." Whiting, "'The Strange Particularlity of the Lover's Preference': Pedophilia, Pornography, and the Anatomy of Monstrosity in *Lolita*," *American Literature* 70.4 (1998): 846.
16. Elizabeth Patnoe, "Lolita Misrepresented," 93.
17. Ellen Pifer, *Nabokov and the Novel* (Cambridge, MA: Harvard University Press, 1980), 170.
18. Harold Bloom, "Introduction," *Lolita* (Major Literary Characters), ed. Harold Bloom (New York: Chelsea House 1993), 2.
19. Wood, *The Magician's Doubts*, 136.
20. Elizabeth Janeway, "The Tragedy of Man Driven by Desire," *New York Times Book Review*, 17 August 1958, 5.
21. Herbold, "'(I have camouflaged everything, my love),'" 83.
22. Quoted by Stacy Schiff in *Véra (Mrs. Vladimir Nabokov)* (New York: Modern Library, 2000), 236.

Chapter Five

HUMBERT'S MEMOIR, NABOKOV'S NOVEL: A READER'S ANALYSIS

FOREWORD

Nabokov's celebrated novel begins innocuously enough, with a foreword by one John Ray, Jr., who informs the reader of the origin of the ensuing narrative and provides some details about its author, "Humbert Humbert." The conceit of the "found" manuscript has a long lineage in literature, and even Nabokov's beloved predecessor, Alexander Pushkin, created a special introduction for his short story collection, *The Tales of Belkin* (1831). The figure about whom Pushkin's foreword is written, however, is a meek and mild Russian landowner who is described as "as bashful as a girl" and marked by "lack of imagination."[1] Nabokov's Humbert is cut from entirely different cloth, and one of the very first things we learn about him is that he died in "legal captivity" a few days before his "trial" was scheduled to start. Curiously, we are not told what he was on trial for. Ray later tells us that references to Humbert's crime can be looked up in the daily newspapers of September–October, 1952, but again, the specific nature of this crime is not disclosed. *Lolita* plays with some of the conventions of detective fiction, but unlike the traditional detective story, the question facing the first-time reader of this novel is not *"who* dunnit," but *what* was done, and *to whom*?

Having created some mystery in his ostensible effort to provide explanatory information, Ray goes on to offer several other pieces of information about the people mentioned in Humbert's manuscript. Again, the way Ray presents this information conceals as much as it reveals. He states that "Mrs. 'Richard F. Schiller' died in childbed, giving birth to a stillborn child on Christmas Day 1952" (*L* 4). At this point, however, the first-time reader does not know who Mrs. Richard F. Schiller is, or what it means that she died giving birth to a stillborn child. To one who has reread the novel, though, this is shattering news. Mrs. Richard F. Schiller is the married name of Dolores Haze, Humbert's "Lolita." Her death on the verge of motherhood represents the final blow in the life of hardship that began when she fell under Humbert's control. The date of her death of course resonates with grim irony: her story carries no message of hope or salvation; it is a bitter testament to the end of possibility, not the beginning. The fact that Nabokov inserts the news of the death of the title character of his novel in such a subtle way points to his own conviction that "one cannot *read* a book, one can only reread it" (*LL* 3). In creating his novels, Nabokov weaves together themes, images, and events in such a way that their full significance can only be appreciated when one stands back and looks at the whole, remembering and piecing together scattered clues that create a dazzling whole to arrive a moment of bracing discovery.

Another character mentioned here is "Vivian Darkbloom" who, we are told, has written a biography entitled "My Cue." Again, the meaning of this information is not entirely clear to the first-time reader. One might perceive that "Vivian Darkbloom" is an anagram of Vladimir Nabokov, and Nabokov was fond of inserting his name in his texts in this way (see also "Vivian Badlook" and "Blavdak Vinomori" in the English-language version of *King, Queen, Knave*; "Baron Klim Avidov" in *Ada*; and "Adam von Librikov" in *Transparent Things*). But the significance of "My Cue" is a mystery for the first-time reader. We will learn in good time that "Cue" is a nickname for Clare Quilty, the playwright who will become Humbert's nemesis and rival for Dolly's attention, and that Vivian Darkbloom was Quilty's collaborator. The fact that Nabokov has provided this collaborator with an anagram of his own name has raised speculation about the author's own involvement in the unfolding story, and we shall discuss this subject later in our analysis. For the moment, we might take note of Alfred Appel's suggestion that Nabokov inserted an anagram of his name here as a marker of his authorship at a time when he thought he might be publishing the novel anonymously (*AnL* 323).

Beyond providing some crucial information about the fate of the main characters in Humbert's narrative, John Ray tries to shape the reader's attitude toward the narrative itself. Many commentators have pointed out that John Ray was the name of a famous seventeenth-century British naturalist who focused on structural characteristics in the classification of plants. Nabokov's use of this name is ironic, for *this* John Ray is a specialist in the classification of certain "morbid" psychological states. Ray argues that if Humbert had gone to a competent psychologist, there would have been no disaster, and no book. Nabokov here parodies the Freudian idea that art springs from the artist's neurosis. Nabokov further parodies the reductive nature of Freudian theory when he has Ray refer to a doctor named "Blanche Schwarzmann" who conducts research on sexuality. The name contains the French word for "white" and the German word for "black"; the intellectual palette of such figures pales in comparison to the rainbow spectrum preferred by Nabokov.

The style of Ray's commentary alternates between the prosaic and the poetic. Of Humbert he writes: "He is abnormal. He is not a gentleman. But how magically his singing violin can conjure up a *tendresse*" (*L* 5). "*Tendresse*" is a word that Humbert himself uses (*L* 204), and the very quirkiness of Ray's style has led some readers to speculate whether Ray might be another mask for Humbert Humbert. Such an interpretation, however, radically changes the reader's understanding of the book, and there seems to be little to recommend its adoption. More traditionally, Ray's foreword is seen a model for how *not* to read Humbert's text. Ray celebrates the work's usefulness in psychiatric circles as a "case history," and though he acknowledges its artistic merits, he claims that the work's greatest value lies in its "ethical impact" (*L* 5). He then reduces the story to a few hyperbolic stereotypes: "the wayward child, the egotistic mother, the panting maniac" and finds in their story "a general lesson" which should make "all of us — parents, social workers, educators" redouble our efforts to raise our children in a "safer world" (*L* 5–6). Nabokov viewed this very notion of a "general lesson" with high skepticism, and as he makes quite clear in his essay "On a Book Entitled *Lolita*," he did not wish to have his readers view the novel primarily as a lesson in morality: "despite John Ray's assertion, *Lolita* has no moral in tow" (*L* 314). Such a reading, in his view, absolutely leaches out all the color and spirit from his artistic creation. Nabokov would not want his readers to view his works through a monochromatic filter. Instead, he encourages the reader to be alert to all the sensations that his multidimensional art might evoke.

PART ONE

Humbert's Introduction

Humbert's text begins with one of the most memorable opening lines in literature: "Lolita. Light of my life, fire of my loins. My sin. My soul." The harmonious sound play, the parallel constructions, the rhythmic repetitions, and the depth of feeling suggested here make these lines ring as exemplars of poetic prose. But, even in this poetry there are signs of Humbert's fundamental obsession. While the phrase "fire of my loins" explicitly points to Humbert's sexual desire for his Lolita, the preceding phrase — "Light of my life" — carries the same message, albeit in cryptic form. The attentive reader will learn later in the text that Humbert uses the word "life" as a euphemism for "penis" (as in "My life was handled by little Lo in an energetic, matter-of-fact manner as if it were an insensate gadget unconnected with me" [*L* 134]). Thus, the two disparate phrases end up repeating the same concept, and this kind of mirroring repetition will become a hallmark of Humbert's personality as he reveals it over the course of his memoir: he is an incredibly self-absorbed, narcissistic individual, and he tends to view the world as a reflection of his own desires, fears, and fantasies.

The sound play continues in the rest of the first paragraph as Humbert describes how the name "Lolita" is pronounced, with each syllable distinctly articulated: "Lo. Lee. Ta." This emphasis on sounds is itself significant, for Humbert's treatment of the name here has the effect of dissecting it, and reducing it to its constituent parts. Whatever human figure the name might refer to nearly disappears (although an echo can be detected in the syllable "Lo," which is how Charlotte Haze sometimes refers to her daughter). What is left are arbitrary sounds, and this perhaps points Humbert's tendency to indulge in poetic flights of fantasy, leaving the "real" world behind in pursuit of his artistic dreams. As he laments later, "I have only words to play with!" (*L* 32).

In the next paragraph, Humbert lists the various names that Dolores Haze has borne, depending on the social, cultural, and legal situation in which her name is evoked. We should that Humbert establishes a subtle tension here between Dolly's legal name ("She was Dolores on the dotted line") and the nickname he gives to her ("But in my arms she was always Lolita"; *L* 9). In calling Dolly "Lolita," Humbert not only creates a pet name of his own for her (and one that has an exotic Spanish lilt), but he sweeps away her legal name, "Dolores," which comes from *dolor*, the Latin word for sorrow. He would perhaps like to block out any reminders of sorrow and pain, but both Dolly and the reader will recognize how apt her legal name is for her life with Humbert.

Humbert eventually moves beyond his preoccupation with the sounds of Dolly's name and introduces a new figure into the text. He states that

Dolly had a "precursor" and suggests that it was his earlier experience with this precursor that led to his obsession with Dolly. In mentioning this, Humbert makes his first clear allusion to the work of Edgar Allan Poe. He writes that this experience occurred "[i]n a princedom by the sea," and follows this up in the next paragraph by referring to "noble-winged seraphs" (*L* 9). These references point to Poe's famous poem "Annabel Lee," which serves as an important subtext for the first part of the novel. In Poe's poem, the speaker describes his love for a young girl who died while still young and whom the speaker continues to love and to mourn up to the present day. Humbert associates himself with this poetic experience by calling his youthful love "Annabel Leigh." In making this association Humbert perhaps seeks to add a poetic patina to his own story, and connect his personal sorrow with a haunting creation of Romantic poetry.

At the same time, however, he may also be disclosing that the way he frames his personal experience rests to a certain degree on literary models. That is, although his interference in Dolly's life will have real effects on a real child, he may tend to overlook this because he is obsessed with a fictitious figure generated by his creative imagination, which in turn has received inspiration from the work of an earlier poet. Thus, while Humbert may seek to establish some sense of legitimacy by connecting his personal experience with that commemorated in a famous poem, he may also be showing that there is something derivative in his attitudes, not only toward Dolly, but toward Annabel herself.

In the concluding paragraph to his opening chapter, Humbert makes his first reference to a jury and a trial. Addressing the ladies and gentlemen of the jury, he asks them to consider "exhibit number one," which will turn out to be the story of his relationship with Annabel Leigh. With these words and images, Humbert seems to validate the claims he makes at the end of his memoir: that when he began writing the manuscript, he thought he would use his notes at his trial, not to save his head, but his soul (*L* 308). What he is trying to do here is to garner some sympathy on the part of his "jury" and to prove that his obsession with Dolly was something beyond his control because it had originated in an earlier life experience. In a final plea for compassion he writes: "Look at this tangle of thorns" (*L* 9). In referring to thorns, Humbert is not simply trying to convey how much pain he experienced, but also to suggest a link between his situation and that of Christ, who wore a crown of thorns at his crucifixion. Humbert's suggestion is, of course, preposterous, and it seems especially out of place since the rereader knows that Dolly Schiller herself died on Christmas Day. She is the one whose torments are to be pitied, not Humbert.

Humbert's Childhood. Annabel Leigh

Humbert provides just a brief sketch of his childhood. Born in Paris in 1910 to a Swiss father and English mother, he was raised at his father's "luxurious" hotel on the Riviera. In one of the strangest passages in the novel Humbert tells the reader how his mother died: "in a freak accident (picnic, lightning) when I was three" (*L* 10). Nabokov is known for his rich use of parenthetical expressions to clarify or modify a statement, but Humbert's two-word pronouncement here is truly surprising. The slightly dismissive tone of the statement may be an indicator of Humbert's high degree of self-absorption. This seems to be borne out shortly when Humbert declares: "everybody liked me, everybody petted me" (*L* 10). Humbert's account of his early childhood ends with a discussion of his first sexual stirrings, which sets up his account of his relationship with Annabel Leigh.

Humbert's description of this relationship emphasizes the mental and emotional compatibility of the two. Viewing Annabel and himself as "intelligent European preadolescents," he states that among their interests were "infinity, solipsism, and so on" (*L* 12). This reference to solipsism is surely relevant, since Humbert tends not to be very interested in the internal worlds of others, and evaluates others primarily in terms of how well they meet his own preconceptions and desires. Another statement of shared interests also merits notice. Humbert claims that the "softness and fragility" of baby animals caused the two of them "the same intense pain" (*L* 12). Considering that he once was moved by the vulnerability of baby animals, one is struck by how unmoved he seems to be by Dolly's own vulnerability. It is she who will regularly experience intense pain, not he.

Humbert's initial description of his relationship with Annabel ends with an account of the last time they tried to make love in a cave at the beach. He was at the point of possessing her when two men came out of the water making ribald comments, and Humbert concludes his sentence with the sudden comment that four months later "she died of typhus in Corfu" (*L* 13). The stark reality of premature death has now been illuminated three times in the opening pages of *Lolita*, affecting Dolly Schiller, Humbert's mother, and Annabel Leigh (not to mention Humbert himself). Humbert's narrative is permeated with a sense of loss, or, as Martin Amis put it, "the sweat of death trickles through *Lolita*."[2] It is noteworthy that Humbert informs the reader of Annabel's death before describing their relationship in more detail. It is as if he wishes the reader to feel the sense of absence that he himself feels as he recalls their relationship. This, of course, resonates with the larger sense of loss he feels in regard to Dolly.

In his comments on his relationship with Annabel, Humbert underscores the affinity he felt with her. In glowing terms he writes that "the spiritual and the physical" had been blended in the two of them with a "perfection" that would seem incomprehensible "to the matter-of-fact, crude, standard-brained youngsters of today" (*L* 14), and that they shared the same thoughts and dreams. Humbert's valorization of his own youth is accompanied by a contemptuous attitude toward the youth of the present day. It is little wonder that he fails to appreciate Dolly when he gets to know her. However, it is a characteristic example of Humbert's limited ability to consider any perspective other than his own that he fails to see that he is comparing apples and oranges here. His sense that he and Annabel were somehow specially attuned to each other is typical of people who are infatuated with each other, and this may be particularly true of young people who are in love for the first time. It is unrealistic for an adult to expect that a twelve-year-old girl would have the same maturity and depth of thought as he, an adult, might have, but this is precisely what Humbert laments about Dolly during their time together.

Nonetheless, Humbert insists that in some "magic" and "fateful" way "Lolita" began with Annabel (*L* 14). It is significant that Humbert invokes the realm of the supernatural here to help explain his subsequent obsession with Dolly. He tries to make it appear that he had no control in the matter, and that all this was somehow arranged by otherworldly powers. He returns to this theme as he concludes his description of his relationship with Annabel. He states that twenty-four years later, he broke Annabel's "spell" by "incarnating her in another" (*L* 15). Here the word "spell" again implies that something beyond Humbert's control has tamed his will. What is more, the image of "incarnating" Annabel in Dolly again suggests that his interest in Dolly is somehow derivative and he does not perceive or appreciate her (at least initially) as an original and independent being in her own right.

"Nymphets"

In providing a brief précis of his life, Humbert states that he at first planned to obtain a degree in psychiatry, but then switched to English literature, "where so many frustrated poets end as pipe-smoking teachers in tweeds" (*L* 15). This disclosure not only provides an explanation for Humbert's interest in psychology (which he goes on to mock throughout his narrative), but it also helps to explain his frequent recourse to literary allusion. Even more important, though, is his comment about "frustrated poets," for in a very real sense, this could be an apt description of Humbert himself. He often compares himself to a poet or an artist, and he provides several samples of poems he created. He does not pursue poetry as a profession, however, and the evidence suggests that he views Dolly somewhat like the way poets might view words at their disposal: manipulated and arranged properly, they can provide great satisfaction. It is only when Humbert stops treating Dolly in this way, and uses words actual words to construct his artistic edifice that he comes near to understanding what authentic art truly is.

At this point in his biographical sketch Humbert pauses to define his concept of the "nymphet." The language he uses is very significant: "Between the age limits of nine and fourteen there occur maidens who, to certain bewitched travelers, twice or many times older than they, reveal their true nature which is not human, but nymphic (that is, demoniac); and these chosen creatures I propose to designate as 'nymphets'" (*L* 16). There are several important points to be made here. First, Humbert's terminology underscores the exotic nature of what he is attempting to define. These are not ordinary "girls," but "maidens" and even "creatures." More significantly, their essential nature, he tells us, is not "human" but "nymphic," which he glosses as "demoniac." He subsequently refers to the nymphet as a "little deadly demon among the wholesome children" (*L* 17). Through this language and imagery, Humbert lifts these children out of the realm of the human, and he does not place them in the ranks of angels, but rather puts a dark, disturbing spin on their character.

The word "nymph," from which the diminutive "nymphet" is formed, carries several connotations. Its primary meaning, according to the *Compact Edition of The Oxford English Dictionary* (1971), derives from mythology, where it refers to "one of a numerous class of semi-divine beings, imagined as beautiful maidens, inhabiting the sea, rivers, fountains, hills, woods, or trees, and frequently introduced by the poets as attending on a superior being." This is the meaning that Humbert presumably has in mind as he casts Dolly and girls like her into this supra-human category. An additional meaning, which Humbert may not have known about (although his creator certainly did) is an "insect in that stage of development which intervenes between the larva and the imago; a pupa." Dieter Zimmer explicates how this entomological term would relate to Dolly, as Humbert sees her: "if Lolita is a little nymph, she is a young individual on the very verge of turning into an adult, already showing the adult's wings, but not yet sexually mature."[3] This accords with Humbert's view of Dolly and the other "nymphets" he describes.

Uppermost in Humbert's mind, it would seem, is the mythological connotations of the word "nymph." In his comment about finding the "little deadly demon among the wholesome children" he implies that nymphets are *un*wholesome. Significantly, however, he states that this little demon may not be aware herself of her "fantastic power" (*L* 17). This is the second aspect of Humbert's conception that bears analysis. In describing the relationship between the nymphet and the men who are captivated by them, he indicates that it is the nymphets who have power, and it is the men who are "bewitched." Humbert would like to persuade his readers that he is the vulnerable one in the pair, not the child. In essence, Humbert's claim is just a loftier version of a frequent defense that child molesters employ: they insist that it was the child that led them on; they themselves were not really responsible for what occurred.

Yet Humbert's assertions that there must be a "gap of several years, never less than ten [...] generally thirty or forty" between the "maiden and man" for the man to fall under the maiden's "spell" (*L* 17) serve to remind the reader that Humbert is describing the sexual attraction a grown man feels for a young girl, and in doing so, he reminds one of those characters in Dostoevsky who chortle over this very gap. In *Crime and Punishment*, Arkady Svidrigailov relishes the idea that he is fifty and a girl he has proposed to is not yet sixteen: "I don't know how you feel about women's faces, but to my mind, those sixteen years, those still childish eyes, that timidity, those bashful little tears — to my mind they're better than beauty."[4] Svidrigailov, however, enthuses over the charm of a sixteen-year-old; Dolly Haze is only twelve when Humbert first sees her.

Age, and the fact that the child has not yet turned into an adult, are key here, and Humbert resorts to an interesting image to communicate his vision most effectively. He tells his readers that he would like them to envision the ages of nine and fourteen as physical boundaries of "an enchanted island" haunted by nymphets and surrounded by a sea (*L* 16). He repeats the image of an island twice: "that intangible island of entranced time" (*L* 17) and "that same enchanted island of time" (*L* 18). In Humbert's fantasy, time is enchanted; it does not pass, and the children do not grow older. This is a crucial point for Humbert. As his narrative unfolds, we see clearly how troubled Humbert is by the thought that Dolly will inevitably grow older, and will lose those prepubescent features he cherishes in the nymphet. His desire to stop time, to arrest the natural processes of life, represents an important theme in the novel as a whole. Humbert's creator, Vladimir Nabokov, had himself suffered major losses in his life, including the loss of Russia and the shocking death of his father, and he pondered the best way to preserve those things that slip away. Realizing that there was no way to prevent physical loss, he turned to memory, the imagination, and art as means to retain and enshrine the precious, evanescent experiences of life. This is a lesson that Humbert himself may come to learn only at the end of his life.

Humbert is already thinking of art at this point in his narrative, but characteristically, his concerns are self-centered. In finishing up his description of the nymphet he asserts that not every man is able to identify one. As he puts it: "You have to be an artist and a madman, a creature of infinite melancholy" to discern the "deadly demon" among the other children (*L* 17). Here, Humbert stakes his claim to being one of a select group, one of the elite, as it were, and in stating that one must be an "artist," he attempts to place his carnal desires on a loftier plane. The fallacy of this claim will reveal itself in due time.

Humbert also asserts that he was capable of having sex with adult women, but that his real interest remained focused on the young. After discussing with resentment the legal and social constraints that prevent adult males from having sex with children, Humbert sums up his dilemma by declaring: "Humbert Humbert tried hard to be good. Really and truly, he did" (*L* 19). We note here Humbert's reference to himself in the third person. This is a common occurrence in the first part of the novel. This type of reference reminds the reader that the Humbert who is writing this memoir is not precisely the same Humbert who underwent the experiences being described. This distinction between the narrating Humbert and the experiencing Humbert has significant implications for the reader's understanding of whether Humbert has indeed undergone some internal change since the time of his original experiences.

Continuing to distinguish between two types of females, Humbert writes that he "was perfectly capable of intercourse with Eve, but it was Lilith he longed for" (L 20). The reference to Eve and Lilith has a double significance. Humbert will later treat his relationship with Dolly as an attempt to dwell in Paradise, and he associates Dolly with the figure of Eve as temptress through the image of an apple. Yet the mention of Lilith here adds to the notion that nymphets are dangerous figures for mortals. Lilith, according to Talmudic legends, was Adam's first wife, and after their separation (due, in some accounts, to her insistence on equality with him), she became a demon. As noted in Chapter Two, Nabokov had written a poem about the treachery of a demonic child named Lilith in 1928. Humbert concludes his chapter on the nymphet with an account of watching girls playing in a park, and he writes: "Let them play around me forever. Never grow up" (L 21). Significantly, Humbert's last sentence has no subject noun or pronoun. While logic would suggest that Humbert is referring to "them" — the girls — it is perhaps more appropriate to consider the phrase as referring to Humbert himself. *He* does not wish to grow up, and conduct himself responsibly as other adults do.

Monique and Valeria

Humbert devotes a chapter to his encounters with a Parisian prostitute named Monique and his first marriage to a woman named Valeria. These episodes are often overlooked in criticism of the novel, as readers and scholars tend to focus on the Humbert-Dolly relationship. Humbert includes the two episodes to show how he tried to deal with his pedophiliac impulses: he looked for adult women who might bear enough resemblance to a younger girl to satisfy his erotic imagination. As it turns out, however, the women ultimately fail to fulfill his carnal desires over time, and the episodes testify to the futility of his attempts to make others conform to the roles his fantasies ascribe to them.

Humbert's encounter with Monique follows the basic arc of initial anticipation, signs of discontent, and ultimate disappointment that his marriage to Valeria, and for different reasons, his relationship with Dolly will follow. In his second meeting with Monique, Humbert observes himself in the mirror "reflecting our small Eden — the dreadful grimace of clenched-teeth tenderness that distorted my mouth" (*L* 22). The mirror image here points to Humbert's essential narcissism and it will resurface prominently when he takes Dolly to the Enchanted Hunters Hotel. The image of Eden, as noted above, represents an important theme in the novel. Humbert's quest for bliss with an enchanting nymphet is a quest for a Paradise that cannot be sustained. Corruption and an inevitable fall must follow.

After the failure of a grotesque and farcical attempt to buy the sexual favors of a girl who turns out to be a teenager, not a nymphet, Humbert decides he must marry to keep his desires under control. He declares to the reader that he could have had any woman he wanted because of his "striking" good looks (*L* 24). This is just one of many comments Humbert makes in praise of his appearance. He is the consummate narcissist, and he cannot resist informing the reader that he was "an exceptionally hand-some male" (*L* 25). Despite this lady-killing charm, though, Humbert settles on the daughter of a Polish doctor, and in a typical appeal to the reader's sympathy he writes that this simply went to show "how dreadfully stupid poor Humbert always was in matters of sex" (*L* 25).

Humbert's account of his marriage to Valeria provides abundant opportunity for him to make jokes at her (and his own) expense. He states that Valeria "mislaid her virginity under circumstances that changed with her reminiscent moods" (*L* 25). Here Humbert revitalizes th dead idiom of "losing" one's virginity by substituting the word "mislaid" for "lost." The substitution both suggests a comical absentmindedness on Valeria's part and allows Humbert to sneak in a vulgar pun related to sexual intercourse (to "lay" someone or to "get laid"). At the same time, he insists again on his own vulnerability: "I [...] was as naive as only a pervert can be" (*L* 25). It may come as a surprise to Humbert's readers that perverts are naive; one might think just the opposite.

Humbert's relationship with Valeria is one of several instances in the novel when Humbert's determined belief that he can control events and others founders on the rocky shoals of reality itself. He had hoped to marry a woman who could pass for a little girl, but he soon discovered that he was stuck with a "big-breasted and practically brainless *baba*" (*L* 26; note the neat concatenation of "b"s). More surprising than her physical appearance, however, was her conduct. Humbert remarks that she exhibited signs of restlessness and discomfort that were "quite out of keeping with the stock character she was supposed to impersonate" (*L* 27). This is an extremely important image, for it conveys Humbert's fundamental conviction that other people are supposed to behave according to the roles he provides for them (he later labels Valeria "the comedy wife" [*L* 28]). Eventually, he discovers the cause of her discontent: she is having an affair. This infuriates Humbert, not because he loves her, but because it indicates that she was arranging her own future without regard to his wishes. Again one sees that Humbert resents the attempts of others to demonstrate a spirit of independence and self-determination.

Humbert's intentions of punishing Valeria for her audacity are quite cruel: he imagines himself "hurting her very horribly" as soon as he could be alone with her. Once more, though, his plans are foiled, for they are never alone. The taxi driver who had picked them up turns out to be her lover, and he accompanies the couple to their apartment so she can pack her belongings. Humbert's description of this ride contains a marvelous play on words. He writes that the taxi driver "drove the Humberts to their residence, and all the way Valeria talked, and Humbert the Terrible deliberated with Humbert the Small whether Humbert Humbert should kill her or her lover, or both, or neither" (*L* 29). Normally one would think that the phrase "the Humberts" would refer to the couple, Humbert and Valeria, but the ensuing comment on the debate between Humbert the Terrible and Humbert the Small leads to another possibility, that the phrase refers solely to Humbert and his warring impulses. This would be consistent with his fundamental self-absorption.

Although Humbert cannot punish Valeria when he discovers her infidelity, he reports with satisfaction that he had his "little revenge" years later when he learned that she had died in childbirth, and that before her death, she had taken part in an anthropological study in which she and her husband had to crawl around on all fours and eat fruit. Not only is it to Humbert's discredit that he considers Valeria's untimely death to be revenge, but to the rereader of *Lolita*, Valeria's death in childbirth links her with Dolly Schiller. Nabokov thus urges the reader to reconsider their response to Humbert's own satisfaction. Valeria may have been a "brainless *baba*" to Humbert (though she was smart enough to keep her affair from him secret), but association with Dolly in the manner of her death ought to engender some sympathy on the part of the reader. Both women were struck down at the moment of what should have been their greatest joy.

Having described his marriage to Valeria, Humbert pauses in his narration to comment on the books found in his prison library. He even provides excerpts from one of the books, *Who's Who in the Limelight*, and tells us that in glancing through the book he was treated to "one of those dazzling coincidences that logicians loathe and poets love" (*L* 31; once more he allies himself with the ranks of poets). Humbert's comment here should alert the reader to be on the lookout for this dazzling coincidence, but the first-time reader of *Lolita* might be hard-pressed to identify it. The key entry excerpted by Humbert is, of course, "Quilty, Clare," and the titles of the works that Quilty had written have suggestive relevance for the events in *Lolita*. They include *The Little Nymph*, *The Strange Mushroom*, and *Fatherly Love*. *The Little Nymph*, we learn, "traveled 14,000 miles and played 280 performances on the road" (*L* 31). Humbert would see in this an echo of his own travels with Dolly. He later tells us that his first trip with Dolly totaled 27,000 miles and some 350 days (*L* 175). Quilty's hobbies are reported as "fast cars, photography," and "pets." All these figure in Humbert's narrative as well, but the word "pet" stands out as one of the terms Humbert applies to Dolly herself. The entry informs us that a "Vivian Darkbloom" collaborated with Quilty in writing *The Lady Who Loved Lightning*. The reader will remember that Vivian Darkbloom had written a biography called *My Cue*. "Cue," it turns out, is Quilty's nickname (Q = cue). But all this still lurks in obscurity for the first-time reader.

For Humbert, though, the coincidences continue in the next entry: "Quine, Dolores." Here is Dolly's Haze's legal name, and we learn that this Dolores is an actress who made her debut in a play entitled *Never Talk to Strangers*. This foreshadows the advice that Humbert gives to Dolly at the Enchanted Hunters Hotel, and he will repeat the injunction in the very last lines of his text. Humbert's anguished awareness of Dolly's absence from his life causes him to make an error in transcribing one line from the entry. He writes "Has disappeared since in [...]" rather than "Has appeared in [...]" but he instructs his first reader, his lawyer Clarence, not to correct it. This series of dazzling coincidences — the entry on Quilty, the mention of the traveling nymph, the reminder of Dolly's name — causes Humbert to vent his emotion. Making up a continuation of the last entry he recorded he writes "Appeared [...] in *The Murdered Playwright*. Quine the Swine. Guilty of killing Quilty" (*L* 32). To the rereader of the novel, these comments are perfectly clear. Humbert is ruminating on his murder of Quilty, whom he blames for taking Dolly away from him. The first-time reader, however, might have a harder time in putting all the clues together: Humbert died in legal captivity while awaiting trial; he has called himself a "murderer"

(*L* 9); and he has come up with the phrase "Guilty of killing Quilty." If the reader concludes that Humbert is on trial for killing Quilty, the reader still does not have a clear idea of the motive. At the very least, however, the reader should now be alerted to look for further references to Quilty and his possible role in Humbert's life.

In Chapter Nine, Humbert provides a brief synopsis of his activities from the end of his marriage to Valeria to the summer when he entered the Haze household. He lists an odd set of pursuits: writing and editing ads for a perfume business, working on a study of French literature for English students, participating in a scientific expedition to the Arctic whose purpose was never clear to him, and enduring three periods of confinement in mental institutions. Although the reader might be curious to know precisely what led Humbert to seek such treatment, Humbert himself is fairly casual in his account of this experience, and he confides merrily to the reader that he became so proficient in the ways of psychiatry that he could manipulate the doctors themselves. One wonders about the accuracy of his claims in this regard.

The Haze Household

Once discharged from the hospital, Humbert begins to look for a quiet place to work on his study, and he arranges to become a lodger with a family named McCoo who have a twelve-year-old daughter in the house; the child immediately becomes the object of Humbert's fantasy, though he has not yet seen her. In one of the extraordinary coincidences that stud the story (and remind us that this is not real life, but a novel), Humbert arrives in the town of Ramsdale to find that the McCoo house has just burned down (an event that Humbert jokingly attributes to the "conflagration" that had been raging all night in his veins [*L* 35]). Humbert is ready to ascribe fantastic powers to himself (even if in a facetious spirit), but he is not yet aware that there is another, greater creative power arranging his destiny for him.

Concerned that Humbert has arrived with no place to live, Mr. McCoo has found someone else willing to take him in — Charlotte Haze. On the way to the Haze house, Humbert notes a "meddlesome" dog that runs out into the street chasing after the car (*L* 36). Here, the rereader will note, is the first appearance of the dog that will play such a fateful role in Charlotte's life (or, more properly, her death) later in the novel. Once at the Haze house,

Humbert observes with great disdain signs of what he would perceive to be middle-class pretentiousness, and when he meets the owner of the house, he immediately consigns her to the same category. Physically, he describes the "poor lady" as having features that suggest a "weak solution of Marlene Dietrich" (*L* 37). His evaluation of her intellectual capacities is even more severe: "She was, obviously, one of those women whose polished words may reflect a book club or bridge club, or any other deadly conventionality, but never her soul" (*L* 37).

What is striking about this characterization is the rapidity with which Humbert is ready to pronounce his judgment. Without having spoken to Charlotte, he declares that she was "obviously" one of "those" women, and he immediately begins to criticize her personality. Interestingly enough, many readers have been quick to accept Humbert's opinion about Charlotte. Their readiness to see her as a shallow, middle-class housewife mindlessly aping the tastes of others perhaps stems in part from these readers' own preconceptions. It may easy for them to imagine the living rooms of America filled with middle-brow, conventional figures such as Humbert perceives in Charlotte. But perhaps Humbert is not being quite fair to Charlotte here, or throughout most of his narrative. We must recall that he is not an unbiased commentator. From his point of view, Charlotte primarily serves as an obstacle between him and the object of his desire, Dolly Haze. He is, as he himself acknowledges later, quick to find fault with her, and not entirely with cause. He consistently lampoons her with terms such as "bland Mrs. Haze" (*L* 41), "phocine mamma" (*L* 42), "fat Haze" (*L* 43), "the old cat" (*L* 47), "the obnoxious lady" (*L* 55), and "big cold Haze" (*L* 57). It is only later that he weakly acknowledges his catty attitude and writes: "Fortunately, my story has reached a point where I can cease mocking poor Charlotte for the sake of retrospective verisimilitude" (*L* 71). Charlotte does belong to a book club, and she does look to home design magazines for ideas on home decorating, but she also expresses strong opinions of her own — especially in regard to Dolly — and she seems quite devoted to Humbert. Perhaps the problem stems less from the fact that her words never reflect her "soul" than from the fact that Humbert himself is not the least interested in her soul, or even interested to find out whether she even *has* a soul.[5]

Charlotte aside, Humbert's entire impression of the Haze household is unfavorable, and he is ready to flee the premises. He refers to Charlotte as a "doomed dear" (*L* 38), which the first-time reader may interpret as meaning that Charlotte is doomed to lose Humbert as a lodger, but which the rereader will recognize as one of several markers that the narrating Humbert inserts into his memoir to foreshadow the misfortune that will later strike Charlotte. Such markers add to the aura of loss and misfortune that permeates Humbert's narrative to the core.

Humbert remains determined to leave the Haze house until he is taken into the garden and suddenly sees "my Riviera love peering at me over dark glasses" (L 39). He continues: "It was the same child—the same, frail, honey-hued shoulders," etc. Of course it is not the same child, as Humbert himself acknowledges when he says that this *"nouvelle"* Lolita would completely eclipse her "prototype" (L 40). But in having Humbert leap to this kind of identification, Nabokov subtly foreshadows a great flaw in his attitude toward Dolly—his failure to see her as truly a unique individual in her own right, rather than as the desired object of an internal fantasy. What is more, his relentless focus on her body parts—her "indrawn abdomen" and "puerile hips"—underscores that fact that Humbert's primary interest is in her body, not her mind or soul.

Earlier in his narrative Humbert had invoked images from mythology to characterize the "nymphet." Now he invokes the world of the fairytale, comparing himself to the "fairy-tale nurse of some little princess (lost, kidnaped, discovered in gypsy rags through which her nakedness smiled at the king [...])" (L 39). As several commentators have pointed out, *Lolita* makes rich use of fairy tale motifs.[6] Humbert would like to see his encounter with Dolly as a kind of fairy tale, something like "Sleeping Beauty," for example, where he awakens the dormant maiden with a kiss and the two live happily ever after. But, his fairy tale is dreadfully corrupt, and there will be no happy ending for his would-be little princess. A second set of literary or mythological associations is triggered when Humbert observes the "brown core of an apple" (L 37) in the house. In Humbert's narrative, Dolly functions somewhat like Eve, leading her helpless Adam into sin. Yet the nature of the apple Humbert sees—already eaten and turning brown—again suggests that there may be something rotten in his dreams.

Over the next four chapters Humbert recounts the rapt attention he payed to Dolly, and her intermittent responses to this attention. The form in which he presents this account is that of a diary. In an earlier novel, Nabokov had his protagonist declare that the diary is "the lowest form of literature" (*Des* 208). Humbert tells the reader that he destroyed the diary five years ago, but that he has reconstructed it due to his "photographic memory" (*L* 40). This is another one of Humbert's exaggerated or misleading remarks, as he himself will acknowledge just a few pages later, when he interrupts a stream of recorded thoughts with the parenthetical corrective "(all this amended, perhaps)" (*L* 47). The fact is that Humbert's awareness of the outcome of his story in the Haze household has shaded his current account of it. Humbert's diary does record some noteworthy moments. Most important, of course, is his account of his attempts to get close to Dolly; these maneuvers have been outlined in the previous chapter.

Describing his attempts to find Dolly's location in the house one day, Humbert characterizes himself as a spider sending out mental feelers from his room. The scene provides a wonderful evocation of how sounds (or the lack of them) can be interpreted by the listener for potential content. Humbert hears Charlotte speaking softly on the phone, denying those "amusing rumors, rumor, roomer" — a nice play on words which concisely summarizes Humbert's perception of Charlotte's amorous interest in him. Humbert, however, proves to be a very poor detective indeed. Just as he concludes that Dolly is not in the house, he hears her informing him through his door that she's eaten all the bacon from his breakfast tray. When Humbert emerges from his room, he finds that the tray "leers" at him "toothlessly" (*L* 50). Here Humbert's erotic preoccupation transform the sight of a breakfast tray missing the oblong shapes of bacon strips into a leering face. What is more, the spider image is itself significant, for the two most notorious perpetrators of child abuse in Dostoevsky's work are associated with spiders. Arkady Svidrigailov in *Crime and Punishment* imagines that the afterlife is a small room, like a village bathhouse, with spiders in all the corners, while Nikolai Stavrogin in *The Devils* recalls staring a tiny spider on a geranium plant while he waits for the young girl he has abused to kill herself out of mortal shame. Humbert himself later returns to this image and calls himself "Humbert the Wounded Spider" (*L* 54).

Humbert's imagination is on further display when he comments on a list of names of the children in Dolly's class at school. Calling the list a "poem," Humbert projects identities for Dolly's classmates, and it is troubling to see that most of the identities he imagines are either unflattering or grotesquely eroticized (e.g. "Grace and her ripe pimples," "Gordon, the haggard masturbator," "Stella, who has let strangers touch her"). The only note of compassion sounded in Humbert's roll call concerns "Irving, for whom I am sorry" (*L* 53). Irving Flashman appears to be the only Jewish name in the list, and Humbert reveals here a sensitivity to anti-semitism that will recur throughout the text.[7] This is one trait that Humbert shares with his creator, who, having married a Jewish woman Germany and watching Hitler's rise to power, was well aware of the pernicious effects of antisemitism, whether overt or covert. One final name on the list will take on a life of its own. Humbert will seize upon the name of "Aubrey McFate" and assign it to the force of fate that he feels at work in his life. Just a few pages earlier he had wondered "Is Fate scheming" (L 50), and over the course of his narrative, he anthropormophizes fate and attributes to it both cunning and will. Initially he believes that "Aubrey McFate" may be on his side, but later in his narrative, he feels the forces of fate moving against him.

The incident that Humbert describes in greatest detail is the scene in which he succeeds in having an orgasm while Dolly's legs are stretched across his lap. It is a Sunday morning, Charlotte has gone to church, and Dolly is left alone with Humbert. Humbert describes the scene in detail, but the reader will note that he introduces a significant change in his expository technique here. First, he urges his readers to "participate" in the "scene" that he is about to "replay," and then he describes the setting as if it were a play itself: "Main character: Humbert the Hummer. Time: Sunday morning in June. Place: sunlit living room." (L 57). What is the point of this shift in Humbert's technique? He is about to describe his sexual encounter with a twelve-year-old child, and he desperately wants to transform the experience into an *aesthetic* moment, to move it, as it were, out of the realm of quotidian reality and into the realm of art. What is more, he would like this readers to adopt his perspective too and view what occurs as a theatrical performance with no consequences in "real" life.

He notes that Dolly is holding an apple, which he describes as "banal, Eden-red" (L 58). Humbert evokes the image of Eden as the site of temptation and fall, even though he tries to undercut it with humor by adding the epithet "banal." Later he will refer to Dolly's apple as the "immemorial fruit" (L 59). Humbert uses the apple to begin his flirtation with her. Instead of her offering it to him, as occurred with Eve and Adam, Humbert snatches the apple from Dolly, and she takes it back. In her turn, she takes away the magazine Humbert had been looking at, and Humbert laments that it was a pity that no film recorded their overlapping moves. Humbert will later express similar regrets about not having taken pictures of Dolly, and this concern serves as a link between him and Quilty, who wanted to film Dolly in obscene movies.

As they tussle over the magazine, Dolly puts her legs across Humbert's lap, and he begins to use their contact to work toward an orgasm. He tries to distract Dolly from what he's doing by distorting the words of a popular song. He characterizes this as "holding her under its special spell" (*L* 59), a further echo of the fairy tale theme he had introduced earlier. For her part, Dolly sings along, shifting her legs occasionally.

Humbert sinks deeper into his erotic trance, and the language of his narrative conveys the hypnotic rhythm of the moment: "I lost myself in the pungent but healthy heat which like summer haze hung about little Haze" (*L* 59; note the repetition of the "h" sounds). When Dolly shifts position once more, Humbert reaches a state of "absolute security," and he feels that he can slow down to prolong the pleasure. He declares: "Lo had been safely solipsized" (*L* 60). This is a key image, and it conveys the extent to which the living, autonomous Dolly has been dismissed, to be replaced by the fantasy figure "Lolita," which is a product of Humbert's erotic imagination. His subsequent description further reveals the depth of his narcissism and self-absorption. He feels that he has left behind his pathetic persona as "Humbert the Hound, the sad-eyed degenerate cur" and turned into "a radiant and robust Turk" about to enjoy "the youngest and frailest of his slaves" (*L* 60). This transformation of his relationship to Dolly, even if in fantasy, is unsettling. He has reduced Dolly not only to the status of a slave, but of "the youngest and frailest" slave at that. Humbert seems to have forgotten his earlier claim that the "softness and fragility of young animals" once caused him "intense pain" (*L* 12). Having introduced this image of imminent violence, Humbert quickly shifts the reader's away from that and says that the state of equipoise he had achieved is "comparable to certain techniques in the arts" (*L* 60). Once again, Humbert asserts a connection between his erotic world and art. Finally, Humbert moves his hand up along Dolly's thigh, and as she "wiggled and squirmed" he attains his orgasm.

Immediately afterwards, according to Humbert, Dolly rolled off the sofa "as if we had been struggling and now my grip had eased" (*L* 61). Humbert's qualifying phrase "as if" does not entirely erase the possibility that they *had* been struggling; certainly, his "grip" has now eased. Although he asserts with relief that "she had noticed nothing!" (*L* 61), a careful examination of his description suggests that this may not be the case. For one thing, as he grasps her thigh and asks her about a bruise there, she cries out "'it's nothing at all' [...] with a sudden shrill note in her voice"

(*L* 61). What is the cause of this sudden shrillness? As she wiggles and squirm, she throws her head back, and her teeth rested "on her glistening underlip." This image, coupled with the subsequent description of her standing with "cheeks aflame," can be compared with the description of Dolly on the morning when she wakes up in bed with Humbert at the Enchanted Hunters Hotel and kisses him. Humbert's description at that time reads: "Her cheekbones were flushed, her full underlip glistened" (*L* 133). Humbert's description of Dolly's reactions during the sofa scene has led at least one reader to speculate whether Dolly herself may not only have had an orgasm, but may have "orchestrated their mutual stimulation."[8] While many readers not agree with this conclusion, I think it is safe to say that Humbert's perception that she had noticed "nothing" may well be inaccurate. It is quite possible that Dolly was aware that something was going on, although the full extent of her knowledge is not clear. After all, the fact that she jumped up "as if we had been struggling and now my grip had eased" seems to indicate that Humbert was literally keeping her under his thumb at that moment.

In the following chapter Humbert reviews his experience. He feels "proud" that he achieved his orgasm without Dolly being aware of it. "Absolutely no harm done," he writes (*L* 62). We have already seen that Humbert's opinion on this is probably flawed, and as he continues his review, he further reveals his self-absorption and lack of regard for what Dolly might have experienced. He compares his actions to that of a "conjurer" who pours "milk, molasses, foaming champagne into a young lady's new white purse, and lo, the purse was intact" (*L* 62). The word "purse," as many commentators have noted, is an Elizabethan euphemism for "vagina." By putting the word "lo," which is a nickname for Dolly, in apposition to the word "purse," he punningly suggests that Dolly's virginity remains intact after his conjuring trick.

Continuing to maintain that Dolly was "safe," he explains: "What I had madly possessed was not she, but *my own creation*, another, fanciful Lolita — perhaps, more real than Lolita; overlapping, encasing her, floating between me and her, and *having no will, no consciousness — indeed, no life of her own*" (*L* 62; emphasis added). There could be no clearer expression of Humbert's solipsistic attitude toward Dolly than this. In his "ignoble" dream, the real child Dolly Haze disappears. All that matters is the fantasy figure he thinks he's dealing with, a fantasy figure who has no life or will of her own. However, Humbert's belief that he can treat Dolly in this way with no consequences is tragically flawed. The child *does* have a will, a consciousness, and a life of her own. It is Humbert's continual disregard for that life that has such devastating consequences for the young girl.

As Humbert's narrative makes clear, moments of excitement and fulfillment are inevitably decline into periods of disappointment and frustration. In this case, Humbert's satisfaction with his stolen bliss and his anticipation of its repetition of the experience are soon dashed by Charlotte's announcement that she is sending Dolly to a summer camp run by Shirley Holmes (a reference to Arthur Conan Doyle's famous detective and a reminder of the detective motif that runs throughout the novel). Humbert is distraught because of the thought that Dolly would soon lose her prepubescent form and would eventually become that "horror of horrors"—a "college girl" (*L* 65). Running through a list of her physical features, he laments that he would lose forever "*that* Lolita, *my* Lolita" (*L* 65). We should remember this concern when Humbert sees Dolly Schiller in Coalmont years later. By the way, we should note that Humbert calls the camp "Camp Q" (*L* 64). This is surely Humbert's invention, and it probably reflects the narrating Humbert's relentless awareness of the fact that Clare Quilty ("Q") was the one who ultimately took Dolly away for him for good.

After Charlotte has left for camp with Dolly, Louise hands Humbert a letter to him written by Charlotte in which she declares her love for him and expresses her willingness to marry him if he so chooses. Humbert does not merely summarize the letter; he provides a large portion of the text, because, he claims, he remembers it "verbatim" (*L* 68). The language and wording of the letter, however, give one reason to doubt Humbert's claim. For example, a phrase in which Charlotte speculates that Humbert, in his "dark romantic European way," might find her attractive seems to this reader, at least, the kind of flattering compliment that the narcissistic Humbert might insert the text while maintaining that these are Charlotte's words, not his own. Indeed, Humbert himself admits that there is "just a chance" that another phrase in the letter is his own contribution (*L* 69). Humbert's comments on the letter afford the reader another opportunity to see just how insensitive he can be to the emotional worlds of others. He states that the letter was at least twice as long, but that he left out a "lyrical passage" which he "more or less skipped at the time" about Dolly's brother who died at the age of two when she was four. Humbert is simply not interested about how that loss may have affected Charlotte or even Dolly.

Humbert's first reaction upon reading the letter is to recoil with repulsion, but he quickly reconsiders. Moving into Dolly's room, he sees
an advertising poster featuring a "distinguished playwright" smoking
a "Drome" (read "Camel") cigarette. Humbert does not acknowledge it,
but this is Clare Quilty. Earlier, Humbert had asserted that he was said
to resemble "some crooner or actor chap on whom Lo has a crush" (L 43).
This was probably Clare Quilty, but Humbert characteristically fails to
pay attention and register the identification properly. Looking at the
poster, he comments: "The resemblance was slight" (L 69). Humbert is thus
not aware, nor would his vanity permit him such awareness, that Dolly's
interest in him may have been conditioned by her "crush" on Quilty. From
Dolly's perspective, then, Humbert is the follower, not the original. He is
not the primary center of attraction he would surely like to be.

As he reconsiders Charlotte's proposal, Humbert realizes that as her
lawful husband, he would presumably have easy access to Dolly, and such
a prospect makes the marriage idea palatable. At this point in the narrative,
Humbert pauses to make a comment about the style of his memoir itself.
Claiming that the "artist" in him has been given the upper hand over the
"gentleman," he states that he has thus far been preserving the intonations
of his journal, "no matter how false and brutal" they may seem to him
now. He then makes an important observation: "Fortunately, my story has
reached a point where I can cease insulting poor Charlotte for the sake
of retrospective verisimilitude" (L 71). This is one of the few moments
when Humbert reminds the reader of the distinction between the Humbert
who experienced the events being described, and the Humbert who is
remembering and recording those experiences years later. The narrating
Humbert would like his readers to believe that he has had a change of
heart toward Charlotte, and that his subsequent experiences have softened
his opinion of her.

Why would he now announce a change in approach and "cease insulting"
Charlotte? Why has he kept the insulting language in his narrative until
this point? Humbert's answer to the latter question is that he is an "artist"
and that it is his artistic duty to reveal the tenor and tone of his original
view of Charlotte. Yet this may not be the entire story. Up until this point,
Charlotte's main function from Humbert's point of view was as someone
who stood between him and the object of his desire, Dolly. Now, Dolly
has gone off to summer camp, so the tension created by her presence has
dissipated. What is more, Charlotte has taken on a new function as well:

she is to be his wife, and as he will note, she turns out to be surprisingly "touching" and "gentle" in that role (*L* 77). However, despite Humbert's seeming relief that he no longer has to insult Charlotte, he continues to do just that. Trying to stir some erotic feeling toward her, he states that he tried not to visualize her "too realistically" with her "heavy hips [...] coarse pink skin of her neck [...] and all the rest of that sorry and dull thing: a handsome woman" (*L* 72). Later he refers to her as "she of the noble nipple and massive thigh" (*L* 76).

In Humbert's description of his brief marriage to Charlotte ("fifty days of cohabitation" he states [*L* 77]), he emphasizes the essentially middle-brow nature of Charlotte's tastes. Inspired by books on interior decorating, she makes great plans to renovate their home. In reacting to this renovation, Humbert unwittingly echoes that of a character in one of Dostoevsky's works who witnesses a similar transformation. Humbert states that because he had been so intimately interested in every corner of the house due to his constant quest for Dolly's whereabouts, he had "long entered into a sort of emotional relationship with it," and he now could "almost feel the wretched thing cower in its reluctance to endure the bath of ecru and ocher and putty-buff-and-snuff that Charlotte planned to give it" (*L* 77). This can be compared to the experience of the first-person narrator in Dostoevsky's "White Nights." Asserting that the houses in St. Petersburg were "familiar" to him, the narrator writes that some of them were "good friends." Thus it was with dismay that he heard one house call out to him "with a most plaintive cry" one day: "They are going to paint me yellow!" The narrator responds: "Fiends! Savages!"[9]

Interspersed among Humbert's account of Charlotte's activities one finds several prefigurations of her impending fate, although the references are not clear to the first-time reader. "A bad accident is to happen quite soon," he writes (*L* 79); and later he refers to Charlotte as "the logical doomed dear" (*L* 82). This last comment is included in Humbert's account of a visit the couple made to a body of water named Hourglass Lake. Before this point, Humbert had mistakenly believed that the name of the lake was "Our Glass Lake." His misunderstanding is significant, for in hearing the name as "our glass," Humbert indicates his narcissistic orientation: the hourglass becomes a mirror. Now, however, he learns the proper name, and the revelation of the true name "Hourglass" introduces the theme of passing time and mortality, issues that come to the fore in Humbert's account of this visit.

This episode itself contains several important elements. First of all, it is upon their arrival at the lake that Charlotte surprises Humbert with the news that she plans to send Dolly directly from camp to boarding school. This revelation send Humbert into a tailspin. He recognizes that he cannot intimidate Charlotte as he could Valeria, and so he fantasizes about drowning her during their swim. He thinks that he could do this without fear of detection because the only two observers are two men on the far shore. But although he can visualize the act, he cannot bring himself to carry it out because "her ghost would haunt me all my life" (*L* 87). This statement may strike the reader as odd, for Humbert has shown no signs of a superstitious nature up to this point. But the concept of Charlotte's ghost may not be so far-fetched in Nabokov's fictive universe. The spirits of dead women in "The Vane Sisters" send cryptic messages to the living narrator of the story, while the narrator of the novel *Transparent Things* is a dead writer's ghost. Here too it has been suggested that Charlotte lingers over the story as an incorporeal shade after her death.[10] Humbert characterizes Charlotte as a "mediocre mermaid" (*L* 86), and this image may be telling. Humbert uses it again later in Part One when describing his fitful dreams at the Enchanted Hunters Hotel ("Charlotte was a mermaid in a greenish tank" [*L* 132]). When Nabokov translated *Lolita* into Russian, the word he chose to use for this second reference was *rusalka*, and the *rusalka* in Russian folklore was often thought to be the spirit of a woman who suffered an untimely death, perhaps committing suicide because of unrequited love.[11] Charlotte, Humbert's rejected lover, may indeed become a spectral presence later in the novel.

Explaining to the reader why he could not kill Charlotte, Humbert places himself in the category of sex offenders who are "innocuous, inadequate, passive, timid strangers" who merely seek to pursue their "practically harmless, so-called aberrant behavior" in peace (*L* 88). Of course, the modifier "practically" here expresses a characteristic Humbertian qualification that nearly nullifies the assertion itself. He continues: "Emphatically, no killers are we. Poets never kill" (*L* 88). This last claim calls for further scrutiny. In its immediate context, which deals with Humbert's inability to kill Charlotte, the statement implies that Humbert is a poet, and therefore cannot kill. Later in the novel, though, he *does* commit murder, thus signifying either that he is *not* a poet, or that poets *do* in fact kill after all. Though he himself would like to deny the "seriousness" of Quilty's murder (see *L* 47), the fact remains that it *is* murder, and it appears likely that he is not the poet he might fancy himself to be at the time of the Hourglass Lake episode. Humbert then goes on to beseech Charlotte not to hate him in her "eternal heaven" among an "eternal alchemy of asphalt and rubber and metal and stone" (*L* 88). This comment will surely appear cryptic to the first-time reader, but the rereader recognizes it as one more prefiguration of Charlotte's upcoming death, planted there by the narrator who is anticipating the event he will soon describe.

Humbert then suggests that the whole point of his discussion of his vision of murder and his inability to go through with it is that it testifies to the genius of fate, because unbeknownst to him, there *was* a spectator on the scene, Charlotte's friend Jean Farlow, who now comes to join the couple on the beach. Jean Farlow (whose name rhymes with Harlow, to complement Charlotte's "weak solution of Marlene Dietrich" [37]) is a frisky married woman with artistic aspirations. She comments that as she observed the two swimming, she noticed something that Humbert had overlooked — his wrist watch. Charlottes replies that the watch is "Waterproof" (much as she herself had been). This detail about the watch is noteworthy, for it may indicate that as much as Humbert would like to stop the passage of time (and live on an island of "entranced time" with a nymphet), he cannot. The sands in the hourglass continue to run, and his watch will not be slowed down by immersion in water. At this point, the conversation turns to gossip, and Jean is about to tell a "completely indecent story" about the nephew of Ivor Quilty, the local dentist, but the arrival of her husband John interrupts the anecdote. As it turns out, this nephew is none other than Clare Quilty, and the rereader may speculate that if Joan's story had gone on uninterrupted, Humbert might have learned something that would have alerted him to the potential danger Quilty posed to his obsessive designs on Dolly. This scene will come back to Humbert years later when Dolly finally tells him the name of the man for whom she left Humbert.

Now resigned to the fact that he is not able to get rid of Charlotte, Humbert hopes to persuade her to let Dolly return to Ramsdale instead of going off to boarding school. And he remains hopeful that he can find a way to drug both mother and daughter so that he can gain access to the latter. For this purpose Humbert visits a doctor who gives him a vial of pills that he assures Humbert would work even on "great sleepless artists" (*L* 94). Like many of Humbert's schemes, this pill fails to work as planned. Perhaps the fantasy of being associated with great artists makes Humbert more vulnerable to the suggestion that this pill will meet his needs.

Returning home from the doctor's office, Humbert finds Charlotte writing a letter. She turns to him and spits out a list of pejorative terms that he had applied to her in his journal (although some of them, such as "the big bitch" (*L* 95) are even stronger than what he has included in his memoir, which makes one wonder whether he had toned down his language in the version he presented to the reader earlier). It is clear that she now knows what his intentions toward Dolly are. She tells him that she is leaving that night and that he will never see her daughter again. In the eyes of some commentators, Charlotte's determination to keep Dolly away from Humbert provides the motivation for her ghostly presence later in the novel. Taken aback, Humbert tries to maintain his poise and think of a way to calm Charlotte down. He decides to make them both a drink, and his description of the process introduces imagery that is both strikingly original and fitting for the context in which they appear. He opens the refrigerator, which roars at him viciously while he "removed the ice from its heart." The ice cubes themselves emit "rasping, crackling, tortured sounds" as the warm water loosens them "in their cells" (*L* 97). These images of pain and entrapment accord well with Humbert's panicky feelings.

At this point, Humbert's creator intervenes like a deus ex machina and effortlessly removes Charlotte from the scene. Humbert answers the telephone and hears that his wife has been run over. Dismissing such a preposterous idea, he looks into the living room, but Charlotte has vanished. She had indeed been run over on her way to mail the letters she had been writing. The car that hit her had swerved to avoid that neighbor's dog who was so fond of chasing cars down the street. In an instant, the main roadblock standing between Humbert and Dolly has been removed, and ironically, it was the exposure of his lustful designs on Dolly that precipitated this unexpected removal.

The following day, Humbert, in his role of the distraught widower, intimates to the Farlows that he had known Charlotte years earlier, and that they had had a romantic fling. Jean leaps to the (desired) conclusion that Dolly is really Humbert's daughter, and that therefore he should naturally become her guardian and caretaker. He fakes a telephone conversation with Shirley Holmes at Dolly's camp, and tells the Farlows that Dolly is away on a hiking trip and cannot be reached. Therefore, he will drive over to the camp himself and pick her up. Humbert's cold-hearted cunning is evident: he intends to keep Dolly away from prying busybodies, and he wants to keep her in the dark about her mother's death as long as possible.

To the Enchanted Hunters Hotel

Now free to retrieve (and possess) Dolly on his own, Humbert leaves Ramsdale to pick her up at her camp. On the way there, he stops to buy Dolly some new clothes: he had told the reader earlier that "any wearable purchase worked wonders with Lo" (*L* 64). A devoted observer of Dolly's physique, Humbert has no trouble in finding the right sized clothing for Dolly, but his account of the shopping expedition takes on an air of the otherworldy. Stating that there is something of the "mythological and the enchanted" about a large department store, he compares his experience to being in a large aquarium, where the belts and bracelets he selects seem to fall from "siren hands into transparent water" (*L* 108). On the one hand, these images recall Humbert's reveries about "an enchanted island" where he imagined his nymphets at play (*L* 16–17). Perhaps his mind turns to such imagery because he is anticipating being alone with Dolly on just such a metaphoric island. But the references to the aquarium, and to "siren hands" (or the hands of *rusalki* in the Russian version) may also bring to mind the image of Charlotte as mermaid, and this may lend support to those who believe that Charlotte may be exercising a spectral influence on Humbert from beyond the grave.

Humbert's account of his arrival at Dolly's camp exhibits the same contemptuous attitude toward those around him that he has shown up to this point. He labels the camp director "hag Holmes" and he makes a passing reference to "some gaudy moth or butterfly, still alive, safely pinned to the wall" (*L* 110). Many commentators have point out that Humbert's ignorance about whether the insect is a moth or a butterfly stands in conspicuous contrast to his creator's expertise in this area.[12] Moreover, the image of a creature pined to the wall while still alive may strike some readers as emblematic of Humbert's imminent dominion over Dolly. Although Humbert's first glimpse of Dolly leads him to feel an impulse to shelter and protect the "little orphan," the instant passes, the "angelic line of conduct was erased," and he returns to his predator mode, even referring to Dolly as his "prey" (*L* 111).

The ensuing drive, which culminates in their arrival at the Enchanted Hunters Hotel, is marked by some curious, faltering attempts on Dolly's part to communicate something imporant to an impatient and scarcely attentive Humbert. She alternates between affection ("you haven't kissed me yet, have you?" [*L* 112]) and recoil (*"Don't* do that [...] Don't drool on me. You dirty man" [*L* 115]). She seems curious about Humbert's relationship with her mother, but not overly concerned one way or the other. Regarding her time at camp, she makes several enigmatic references to some kind of bad behavior: "Bad, bad girl [...] Juvenile delickwent" (with a meaningful distortion of the middle syllable of the last word [*L* 113]); and "I am absolutely filthy in thought, word and deed" (*L* 114). She seems to want to tell Humbert what's she's done, presumably to get it off her chest and see what his reaction might be. After all, she may perceive him as a trusted adult with whom she could discuss things in a way she would not be able to do with a more judgmental mother. Humbert, however, is raging with desire to get to the hotel, and he pays scant attention to her need to talk.

At last they arrive at the hotel, and Humbert's account of the scene conveys the impression that he has entered a kind of dream space where things are happening around him, but he is only dimly aware of their significance, if at all: he has truly become an "enchanted hunter." For example, he finds cars lined up in the parking lot "like pigs at a trough" (*L* 117). The pig motif will be carried over into the hotel lobby, and one should note that pigs are associated with the demonic in several folk traditions, including Russian.[13] There seems to be no room for their car, but then, "by magic," a "rubious" car pulls out, and Humbert drives into the empty space. This incidental event is actually quite significant. The driver of the car is, as the rereader will surmise, none other than Clare Quilty. He has left the space to move to a more advantageous spot, thus one-upping Humbert, and he will eventually do this again with Dolly later in the novel. Then too, the fact that Quilty has first occupied a spot taken by Humbert repeats the pattern of priority involving these two men and Dolly: she had met (and developed a crush on) Quilty before she met Humbert. Humbert, as it were, occupies the spot in Dolly's life she had imagined for Quilty, and she will eventually leave Humbert for the man she considers more glamorous.

At the reception desk, the clerk examines both Humbert's features and the telegram he had sent requesting a reservation. After wrestling with "some dark doubts," he declares that the hotel is full. The meaning of this behavior may not be readily apparent to the contemporary reader, but for Nabokov, the episode reflects the atmosphere of anti-Semitism that made its way through certain segments of American society in the post-war period.[14] This is confirmed when an anxious Humbert tries to tell the clerk that his name is not the potentially Jewish-sounding "Humberg," but "Herbert," which has more of a British feel to it. Only then does he come up with his correct name, Humbert. He will ultimately sign the hotel register as "Dr. Edgar H. Humbert," assigning himself E. A. Poe's first name, just as he had done when giving his name to a reporter in Ramsdale before his wedding.

The pig motif introduced in Humbert's account of parking the car resurfaces here. Humbert describes the clerk as "porcine," and the motif is further developed in the dialogue between this clerk and his colleague. The latter calls the first clerk "Mr. Swine," and asks him if there are any cots left. "Swine" replies: "I think it went to the Swoons" (L 118). The entire exchange sounds like an old comedy routine, and Humbert refers to "Swine" as an "old clown." Of course, the real name of the clerk may not be Swine at all; the cognomen may have been generated by Humbert's agitated mind at the time: when he reports that one clerk says that three ladies and a child once shared a cot, and that one of the ladies was a disguised man, Humbert characterizes all this as "*my* static" (L 118). Or, it could be a name that the narrating Humbert invents because of the Quilty association. After Humbert had described the entries in *Who's Who in the Limelight*, he writes: "Quine the Swine. Guilty of killing Quilty" (L 32).

Humbert is given the key to his room, which, by one of those dazzling coincidences in Nabokov's work that point to the creative control of the maker behind the text, bears the number 342 — the same number as the Haze house in Ramsdale. The utter significance of the moment is underscored by a long sentence that presents several discrete actions that occur in rapid sequence: "Lo, leaving the dog as she would leave me some day, rose from her haunches; a raindrop fell on Charlotte's grave; a handsome young Negress slipped open the elevator door, and the doomed child went in [...]" (L 119). Two things about this sentence merit comment. First, this kind of multi-leveled description often occurs in Nabokov's work at moments of high significance. It is as if the author stands back and surveys the entire scene from an elevated perspective. He (and the reader) can see what is going on in a larger context, while the lowly protagonist remains focused on whatever preoccupies him at that moment. In this case, the narrating Humbert is aware of the losses that will issue from this moment: the "doomed" girl will lose her childhood innocence, and ultimately, Humbert will lose the doomed child. The reference to a raindrop falling on Charlotte's grave is intriguing. At the very least, it is a reminder of Charlotte's untimely death, which has made her daughter vulnerable to Humbert's predation.

This is something that the narrating Humbert may well be reflecting on, if not the experiencing Humbert. For those who think that Charlotte's spirit survives her death, this image may evoke her continued presence at such a crucial moment in her daughter's life.

Once inside their hotel room, Humbert takes stock of the furnishings: "There was a double bed, a mirror, a double bed in the mirror, a closet door with mirror, a bathroom door ditto" and so on (*L* 119). This emphasis on mirrors and doubling conveys in compelling fashion the hermetic drive of the narcissistic protagonist: the entire room is an enclosed, self-reflecting space with no exits or apertures to the outside world. Dolly is initially taken aback by the thought of sharing the room with Humbert, but she quickly accustoms herself to the fact. When Humbert tries to provide a rambling explanation about how their travels will necessitate them spending a lot of time in close proximity, he struggles to find the right word to describe the relationship, and Dolly breezily supplies an apt name for it: "Incest" (*L* 119). She is trying to show Humbert what a savvy girl she is, and he becomes utterly confused by the entire situation. His attempt to kiss her is rebuffed, but when she catches sight of the fabulous purchases he had made for her (and the description of the slow, stalking way she approaches the suitcase is a marvelous piece of description), she returns to his embrace. Dolly's words and behaviors continue to leave Humbert perplexed.

The pair now moves on to the dining room. Dolly carries her "old white purse," which recalls the episode of Humbert sexual arousal in the Haze living room, where he imagined himself a conjurer pouring milk and champagne into a young lady's "new white purse" (*L* 62). Does this change in epithet reflect a change in the narrating Humbert's evaluation of Dolly's innocence? In the dining room Dolly sees a lone diner who looks to her "exactly like Quilty." Humbert can only think of the dentist, Ivor Quilty, but Dolly informs him that she has in mind "the writer fellow in the Dromes ad" (*L* 121) which, the reader recalls, she had posted above her bed. Characteristically, Humbert pays no attention to this important piece of news. Instead, he tricks her into taking one of his sleeping pills, telling her that it is a special vitamin pill. Returning to the hotel room, Dolly makes one last attempt to tell Humbert what is on her mind, but he rebuffs her and leaves her to got to bed while he waits downstairs.

The stage is now set for Humbert to execute his plan to derive sexual satisfaction from the body of a drugged and therefore defenseless Dolly. At this point, the narrating Humbert works assiduously to recreate the mind set and mood of the experiencing Humbert, and signs of a penitent and chastened Humbert soon fade away. However, the beginning of Chapter Twenty-Eight contains both perspectives. He tells the reader of his immense joy at the prospect of returning to the room and finding his "nymphet," his "beauty and bride, emprisoned in her crystal sleep" (*L* 123). This phrase interestingly combines both an image of Sleeping Beauty, to be awakened by him as the charming prince, and an image of someone whom he himself has made captive. The narrating Humbert then takes over and provides an extended reflection on the subsequent consequences of his encounter with Dolly: "And my only regret today is that I did not quietly deposit key '342' at the office, and leave the town, the country, the continent, the hemisphere, — indeed, the globe — that very night" (*L* 123). Some readers will find a certain ambiguity in this claim. On the one hand, Humbert seems to be expressing sincere regret that he had not left Dolly alone and thus spared her the terrible damage he would ultimately inflict upon her. But those who are skeptical of Humbert's reformation might argue that he is merely sorry that the entire experience proved so much more difficult for them both than he had anticipated at the time. Humbert's explanation of his statement does not entirely settle the matter. He claims that when he first met Dolly he took it for granted that she was as "unravished as the stereotypical notion of 'normal child'" would encompass. He further claims to have been under the impression that whatever sexual activity might occur among American schoolchildren — "brash brats" he calls them — it would have occurred at a later age than twelve. However, Humbert seems to forget here that he and Annabel were engaged in sexual activity when he was thirteen and she was a few months younger, so the fact that he clings to a belief that Dolly had had no sexual experiences may reflect his desire to see her as perfectly preserved for his own private delectation, and not someone who has a romantic or erotic life of her own.

Indeed, in the next part of his reflection on the topic he seems perturbed that she as not as "innocent" as his fantasies of her would have it. "I should have understood that Lolita had *already* proved to be something quite different from innocent Annabel," he begins (overlooking the fact that he and Annabel had been sexually active at a young age). His agitation increases as he states that there was "nymphean evil breathing through every pore of the fey child" (*L* 124–5). It seems clear that he is blaming Dolly for not being the passive, dependent, virginal doll he had envisioned her to be. He concludes: "I should have known [...] that nothing but pain and horror would result from the expected rapture" (L 125). Again, the reader might will ask at this point whose pain and horror is he concerned about here — Dolly's, or his own? The fact is, though, that whomever Humbert had in mind as he penned these lines, there can be no doubt that pain and horror *did* emerge from this encounter, and that Dolly bore the brunt of it. From this point on, notes of remorse from the narrating Humbert fade away, and he cedes the floor to the perspective of the experiencing Humbert: "she was mine, she was mine [...] she was mine" (L 125).

The ensuing events consist of three distinct episodes: Humbert's meeting with Quilty, Humbert's frustrated attempts to approach the sleeping Dolly during the night (when he tries to enlist the reader's sympathy), and the morning encounter with Dolly (where Humbert strives to get his readers to adopt his point of view). The first of these — Humbert's meeting with Quilty — is noteworthy for several reasons. First of all, Humbert is unaware of the identity of his interlocutor, yet this shadowy figure will become ever more prominent in Humbert's consciousness, moving from a disembodied voice to a terrifying (from Humbert's perspective) figure of pursuit and persecution. Secondly, the entire encounter between the two has something of a dream-like or hallucinatory quality, and this very quality becomes a recurring element in the subsequent interactions between the two characters. The scene begins when Humbert goes out onto the hotel porch, and he "suddenly" becomes aware of a figure in the darkness next to him. He does not see the figure, but only hears his voice. The sudden appearance of a disembodied figure recalls the scene in Dostoevsky's *The Double* when the distraught Golyadkin suddenly senses the presence of a figure next to him on a bridge. When he looks, there is no one, but Golyadkin has the impression that the figure had "said something of intimate concern to him."[15] The figure will turn out to be Golyadkin's double, and he serves as Golyadkin's nemesis, ultimately taking his place in the social order. Quilty's role in Humbert's life has affinities with that of Golyadkin's double in Golyadkin's life, and several commentators on *Lolita* have flatly declared that Quilty is Humbert's "double."

The conversation between the two is more than a little hallucinatory. The unseen figure asks — "Where the devil did you get her?" — and this mention of the devil reminds one of the demonic leitmotif introduced upon Humbert's arrival at the hotel. When Humbert asks for clarification, the voice offers an entirely revised utterance: "I said: the weather is getting better" (L 127). The question arises: did Quilty actually ask the first question Humbert heard? Is he toying with Humbert? Or is this simply more of Humbert's "static"? The penetrating questions that Quilty poses work like suppressed accusations swimming to the surface of Humbert's consciousness. When Quilty asks "Who's the lassie?" and Humbert responds "My daughter," Quilty pointedly declares: "You lie — she's not," thereby giving voice to Humbert's own sense of deception and guilt. This unsettling episode will eventually lead to Humbert's loss of Dolly to Quilty. To the rereader it serves as a reminder that as much as Humbert would like to feel that he is in control of his destiny, or that McFate is on his side, larger forces are arrayed against him.

The second episode involves Humbert's fumbling attempts to gain some sexual pleasure from his proximity to Dolly's body, and here, the reader will take note of his fervent attempts to disarm what he (rightly) anticipates might be a hostile or indignant response on the part of his readers. He does this by depicting himself as helpless or pitiable. Observing that Dolly periodically seemed to jolt awake, he realizes that the doctor who had prescribed the sleeping pills had deceived him; they may have been nothing more than placebo. He admits that he was now afraid that Dolly might "explode in screams" if he touched her with any part of what he calls his "wretchedness" (*L* 129). This, of course, is precisely what transpired in the precursor to *Lolita*, Nabokov's *The Enchanter*. So, Humbert turns to the reader with a direct appeal for sympathy, trying to cast himself in the most favorable light: "Please, reader, no matter your exasperation with the *tenderhearted, morbidly sensitive, infinitely circumspect* hero of my book, do not skip these essential pages" (*L* 129; emphasis added). All the epithets Humbert applies to himself stress his sensitivity and tenderness, which may not be the qualities that come to mind when one sits back and thinks about just what Humbert is trying to do. By referring to himself as the "hero of my book," Humbert casts himself as a literary character, and by doing so he perhaps hopes to deflect the reader from seeing not only him, but Dolly too, as real people to whom real harm can come.

Humbert goes on to evoke the existential quandary facing any literary character, and tries to engage the reader's imaginative sensibilities: "Imagine me; I shall not exist if you do not imagine me" (*L* 129). He then returns to his pleas for sympathy from the reader: "try to discern the doe in me, trembling in the forest of my own iniquity" (*L* 129). With this image, Humbert reverses the "hunter" setup implicit in the name of the hotel and in his plans for getting pleasure from Dolly's body. According to his self-description, he is no longer an enchanted hunter, he identifies himself with the target of the hunt! We should note that in associating himself with a doe, rather than a buck or a stag, Humbert wishes to underscore his supposed vulnerability and weakness. As his description of the fitful night moves on, he comments on the incessant racket that surrounds him — flushing toilets, clanking elevator — and he gives special attention to the sound of a neighbor who was "extravagantly sick" and whose toilet sounded like a "veritable Niagara" (L 130). This figure, one may assume, is Clare Quilty. The theme of the noisy neighbor will recur in Humbert's accounts of his cross-country trips.

Humbert continues to emphasize his timorousness and reserve. "Mists of tenderness enfolded mountains of longing," he writes (L 131), and he tries one more time to convince the reader not only that he was essentially harmless, but even that he was engaged in something lofty and poetic: "I insist on proving that I am not, and never was, and never could have been, a brutal scoundrel. The gentle and dreamy regions through which I crept were the patrimonies of poets — not crime's prowling ground" (L 131). This, it seems to me, is the perspective of the experiencing Humbert, or more precisely, an effort by the narrating Humbert to convey the desired self-image of the experiencing Humbert. Thus we note the return to the notion that he is a poet and not a criminal, and the claim that he never was and never could have been a brutal scoundrel. Not only are these claims refuted by the narrating Humbert near the end of his text (see, in particular, Chapters Thirty-Two and Thirty-Three of Part Two), but even here, within a very few pages, he will acknowledge his lack of gentleness with Dolly (see pp. 140–41). All of this is a key element in Humbert's rhetorical strategy to prevent the reader from instantly recoiling in discomfort or indignation. As this section of the memoir grades into the next — the account of Humbert's actual sexual encounter with Dolly — the urgency of this rhetorical strategy becomes even clearer.

When dawn breaks, Dolly wakes up, and Humbert makes one final attempt to shape the reader's reaction to what he is about to describe: "Frigid gentlewomen of the jury!" he begins. "I am going to tell you something very strange. It was she who seduced me" (L 132). Humbert had begun Chapter Twenty-Eight with the neutral address — "Gentlewomen of the jury!" — perhaps realizing that the toughest audience he would have to win over would be a female one. Here, however, he adds the epithet "frigid," which would surely be off-putting to women sitting on an actual jury. It is likely, then, that Humbert's real addressee here is not any imagined members of a jury, but his unknown readers of the future. By invoking that imaginary audience of "frigid gentlewomen," he hopes to trigger a defensive response from the future reader who will think, "Well, *I'm* not like that. I'm not frigid; I can be open-minded." Such a reader might be more willing to listen to and go along with Humbert's version of events.

Indeed, Humbert works hard to demonstrate that what is about to transpire is all engineered by Dolly, whom he calls a "sportive lassie" with "laughing" eyes. After a kiss, she whispers something about a "game" that she and Charlie Holmes had played at camp, and Humbert feigns ignorance. According to Humbert, Dolly asks him: "You mean you never did it when you were a kid?"and he answers "Never" quite "truthfully" (*L* 133). It is not clear precisely what activity the pronoun "it" refers to here. If, as appears likely from her subsequent description of her activities with Charlie (see page 137), she is referring to intercourse, then Humbert can truthfully say that he never did "it" as a child, although he had every intention of doing so with Annabel until they were interrupted by the ribald bathers from the sea.

Hearing Humbert's reply and, presumably, believing in error that he may be naive in matters of sex, Dolly says: "Okay [...] here is where we start." Significantly, Humbert does not tell the reader what Dolly "starts." What he does say is that he found "not a trace of modesty" in her and he declares that her entire upbringing had "utterly and hopelessly depraved" her (*L* 133). Humbert is surely exaggerating the degree of Dolly's "depravity" here, for as he would shortly note, she was not prepared "for certain discrepancies between a kid's life and my own" (*L* 134). He uses the word "life" here as a euphemism for "penis" (as in: "My life was handled by little Lo in an energetic, matter-of-fact manner as if it were an insensate gadget unconnected with me" [*L* 133–34]). Dolly had had very limited experience with sexuality, and her only previous partner was a thirteen-year-old. Humbert, however, is only willing to remain passive and let her take the lead for so long. As he puts it: "I feigned supreme stupidity and had her have her way — at least while I could still bear it" (*L* 134). Here again is one of those meaningful qualifying phrases in Humbert's discourse. The clear implication is that he could only "bear" it for a limited amount of time, and then he took the initiative and had *his* way. Significantly, it is at just this point that Humbert turns away from the scene and states: "But really these are irrelevant matters; I am not concerned with so-called 'sex' at all" (*L* 134).

This is an extraordinary claim, even from Humbert. He is, of course, intensely concerned with sex. That is all he has been dreaming and talking about for the last few pages. But once he assumes control of the sexual encounter with Dolly, he turns away, for he would not want the reader to know just how much pain and discomfort he might have inflicted upon the child. In fact, he reintroduces the image of the "nymphet" as dangerous, stating that his real endeavor is to "fix once and for all the *perilous magic*" of nymphets (*L* 134; emphasis added). Once more he suggests that Dolly is a fantastic creature who has powers of enchantment over the vulnerable mortal.

In place of any explicit description of his sexual activity with Dolly, Humbert tries to conjure up a fanciful "mural" that evokes sexual initiation, once more shifting focus from real life, with its attendant possibilities of real distress and real pain, onto an aesthetic project ("There would have been a lake. There would have been an arbor in flame-flower."). Nevertheless, even in this aestheticized creation, intimations of pain and distress seep through. For example, in the midst of his mural he imagines a "sultan" helping a "slave child" to climb a column of onyx. Here we remember the image Humbert created of himself when he was with Dolly on the living room sofa as a "robust Turk" enjoying "the youngest and frailest of his slaves" (*L* 60). And at the end of the passage, after evoking summer camp, and "poplars, apples, a suburban Sunday" (bringing to mind again that sexual experience on the sofa), he imagines "a last throb [...] a sigh, a wincing child" (*L* 135). Behind Humbert stands Nabokov, and by having Humbert include this last image of a wincing child, Nabokov makes sure that the reader does not become entirely carried away by Humbert's rhetorical escape into aesthetics.

Reflecting the ebb of lust itself, Humbert's narrative returns from this fanciful canvas to a more sober narrative tone and point of view. He again declares that he has only been following "nature" (*L* 135), or, in other words, that he has not done anything abnormal in pursuing sexual pleasure with a child. But already he is haunted by doubt: "Why then this horror that I cannot shake off?" (*L* 135). In an interesting rhetorical move, he now addresses his audience as "*Sensitive* gentlewomen of the jury" (*L* 135; emphasis added). What has prompted this change in epithet from "frigid" to "sensitive"? Humbert has satisfied his sexual desire and can now afford to be generous. What is more, he would like to enlist the reader's endorsement of his position when he asserts that he was not Dolly's first lover and launches into an account of her previous sexual experimentation.

As Humbert prepares to leave the hotel, he sends Dolly ahead to the lobby, where he soon finds her being stared at by a man of his age "over his dead cigar and stale newspaper" (*L* 138). The man is Clare Quilty, and the images "dead" and "stale" foreshadow both the end of his relationship with Dolly and the ultimate fate of all the main characters themselves. Humbert now provides an extended description of Dolly's appearance, thus conveying both *his* concentration on Dolly's figure and that of the "lecherous fellow" who, Humbert tells us, resembles Humbert's Swiss uncle Gustave, a resemblance that Humbert will invoke later in the tale as a marker of Quilty's presence. Humbert takes great satisfaction in knowing that although the other man may be looking with desire at Dolly, it was he, Humbert, who had enjoyed her body that morning, a body that he characterizes as "the body of some immortal daemon disguised as a female child" (*L* 139). Even here, Humbert continues to regard Dolly not as an ordinary human being, but as some kind of supernatural creature.

As Humbert checks out of the hotel he continues to maintain the pretense that he has a wife, and he tells the clerk that if she should call, the clerk should inform her that Humbert and Dolly "had gone on to Aunt Clare's place" (*L* 139). "Clare" is Quilty's first name, and one wonders whether the experiencing Humbert actually uttered this name at this very moment. If so, it would be a wondrous coincidence or an example of extraordinary prescience. It is more likely, however, that the narrating Humbert slips the name in at this point to suggest the covert presence of his nemesis on the scene, even if he was ignorant of the fact at the time. For the first-time reader, however, the name "Clare" lacks meaning here. It may seem as insignificant to the reader as the actual presence of Clare Quilty was to Humbert when he was staying in the hotel in the first place.

This evocation of Quilty's figure perhaps paves the way for a dramatic change in mood in Humbert's narrative, and between Dolly and Humbert themselves as they resume their car trip. From Humbert's perspective, Dolly becomes ominously uncommunicative and sullen, and Humbert begins to feel an uncomfortable sensation "as if I were sitting with the small ghost of somebody I had just killed" (*L* 140). This impression is highly significant, for Humbert has in essence taken a life: he has forever changed the destiny of this twelve-year-old child. When she gets out of the car, Dolly winces with pain, and in response to Humbert's query, she calls him a "brute." Now he begins to feel a sense of panic and for a moment, he has a lucid understanding of Dolly's situation and his relationship to her: "This was an orphan. This was a lone child, an absolute waif, with whom a heavy-limbed, foul-smelling adult had had strenuous intercourse three times that very morning" (*L* 140). Gone is the fanciful evocation of a "lake," an "arbor," and a "suburban Sunday" (*L* 134). As Humbert now perceives it, his "lifelong dream" had "overshot its mark — and plunged into a nightmare" (*L* 140). He acknowledges that he has been "careless, stupid, and ignoble" (*L* 140), yet despite this acknowledgment, he also recognizes that he's already feeling new pangs of desire for Dolly. In an astonishing display of his innate selfishness, Humbert writes: "In other words, poor Humbert Humbert was dreadfully unhappy" (*L* 140). In the space of just a few sentences, Humbert has moved from seeming compassion for the lone child, the "orphan," to a concern only for his own unfulfilled cravings!

In his subsequent interaction with Dolly, Humbert cannot gauge precisely what she is feeling. When she calls him a "revolting creature" and says that she should tell the police that he had raped her, he cannot tell whether she's joking or not. He detects an "ominous hysterical note" in her words (*L* 141). The rising tension of the moment, however, comes to an abrupt end when she demands to call her mother and Humbert finally tells her the awful truth that he has been concealing from her all this time simply so that he could have access to her while she was in a relatively tranquil state of mind. Without even attempting to soften the blow, Humbert reveals the truth in words that could not be simpler or more austere: "your mother is dead" (*L* 141).

The final chapter in Part One is extremely short. Humbert describes how he bought Dolly a long list of items from sanitary pads to a tennis racket and, of course, more clothes. The reader will recall Humbert's declaration that "any wearable purchase worked wonders with Lo" (*L* 64). This is Humbert's attempt to pacify a stunned and distraught child. At their next hotel, they had separate rooms, but Humbert tells the reader that Dolly came sobbing into his room in the middle of the night and they "made it up very gently" (*L* 142). Then Humbert concludes Part One with a sentence that is chilling in its simplicity and finality: "You see, she had absolutely nowhere else to go" (*L* 142). The very position of this sentence adds to its austere meaning. Not only does Dolly have nowhere to go, but we as readers have reached the end of a major section of the text. There is nowhere else to go in this part of the narrative. Only when one turns the page will the narrative resume again, and this time, things will be forever changed.

PART TWO

On the Road

Readers of *Lolita* might notice a compression of time through much of
Part Two. That is, unlike the latter sections of Part One, where a relatively
small number of days (and even hours) took up many pages, in Part Two the
opposite situation prevails: large passages of time take up a smaller number
of pages. Perhaps this reflects the "Hourglass" phenomenon: Humbert feels
his precious time with Dolly slipping away at an increasing rate.

Part Two begins with Humbert's description of the first cross-country
automobile trip he took with Dolly after leaving the Enchanted Hunters
Hotel. The theme of the road has a long and rich literary and cultural
history, with deep roots in American as well as world literature. Although
Mark Twain's *Adventures of Huckleberry Finn* may be the most widely-read
American travel novel, by the end of World War II, cars had supplanted
boats and trains as the vehicle of choice among Americans, and Jack
Kerouac's *On the Road*, which was published in 1957, just a year before
Lolita was published in the United States, became an iconic text for
a restless generation. Humbert's road trip, however, was predicated on
his need to keep Dolly moving, in part because he wanted to keep her
entertained and in a decent mood for his sexual urges, and in part because
he wanted to keep her away from others who might begin prying into his
relationship with her. The very rootlessness suggested by their incessant
travels recalls the role played by train travel in *Anna Karenina*: shunned by
society, the two lovers had no fixed abode, no place to call their "home."
But this is America, not Russia, and Humbert makes it clear that he, as
a European, is discovering new territory as he travels around the country.
Humbert's travels with Dolly afford Nabokov an opportunity to demonstrate his own keen powers of observation, and he offers an original
perspective on the local customs and sights of his adopted land. The
detailed catalogues of cultural phenomena provided by Humbert range
from the names of popular singers that Dolly liked ("Sammy and Jo and
Eddy and Tony and Peggy" [*L* 148]) to the various types of lodging that
car travelers have at their disposal, including an endless series of places
with similar names (e.g., "Mountain View Courts, Skyline Courts" [*L* 146]).
Of course, Humbert is wryly aware that these "courts" are far different
from royal courts of his European past, and he is especially quick to skewer
what he sees as the pretentiousness of American consumerism. Playing

with the name of an early promoter of restaurant ratings, Duncan Hines, Humbert writes that Dolly wanted to go only to those restaurants "where the holy spirit of Huncan Dines had descended upon the cute paper napkins and cottage-cheese-crested salads" (*L* 148)[16].

Some early commentators conflated Humbert's condescending attitude toward the realia of the American road with Nabokov's own views, and they concluded that Nabokov himself was mocking America and its customs. This precipitated a vigorous defense from Nabokov in his essay on *Lolita*. Acknowledging that a few readers have charged the novel with being "anti-American," Nabokov wrote: "This is something that pains me considerably more than the idiotic accusation of immorality." While maintaining that there is nothing "more exhilarating than philistine vulgarity," Nabokov argued that when it came to such vulgarity, there is no "intrinsic difference between Palearctic manners and Nearctic manners" (that is, between Europe and America). He underscored the fundamental distinction between Humbert and himself: "my creature Humbert is a foreigner and an anarchist, and there are many things, besides nymphets, in which I disagree with him" (*L* 315). Indeed, I think that there is a certain amount of affectionate amusement in the catalogue of sights that Humbert records, from the "trochaic lilt" of the phrase "novelties and souvenirs" that so mesmerized Dolly (*L* 148) to the variety of names that proprietors would apply to the men's and women's rest rooms: "Guys–Gals, John–Jane, Jack–Jill and even Buck's–Doe's (*L* 153). The entire list of specific sites that Humbert and Dolly visited reflects a genuine interest in America and its richly diverse landscape, from Western ghost towns to the Corn Palace in South Dakota.

Even Humbert, who at first expresses extreme skepticism about what he encounters, eventually comes to a greater appreciation of the country's subtle beauty. Although initially he views the landscape through the prism of art works he had seen in Europe (see page 152), he gradually discovers that the land around him had an original beauty all its own, which he describes in lyrical tones: "Beyond the tilled plain [...] there would be a slow suffusion of inutile loveliness, a low sun in a platinum haze with a warm, peeled-peach tinge pervading the upper edge of a [...] cloud fusing with the distant amorous mist" (*L* 152). Humbert's perspective is, of course, informed by his obsession with Dolly, which finds expression in this sentence in the words "low" (Lo) and "haze" (Haze), as well as the epithet "amorous." Nonetheless, Humbert's gradual realization that the American landscape has a beauty of its own, independent of the artist's attempts to render it in oil paintings, may be analogous to his eventual realization that Dolly has a personality and spirit of her own that is independent of the projections Humbert imposes upon her. One of Humbert's observations of the surrounding landscape evokes well Dolly's essential condition: "I would stare at the honest brightness of the gasoline paraphernalia against the splendid green of oaks, or at a distant hill scrambling out — scarred but still untamed — from the wilderness of agriculture that was trying to swallow it" (*L* 153). The phrase set off by dashes — "scarred but still untamed" — provides a marvelous metaphor of Dolly's own struggle to break free from Humbert and establish a life of her own. And a second phrase "the wilderness of agriculture" provides an apt image for Humbert himself. Normally, one would not think of agriculture as "wilderness"; generally, it would seem to be just the opposite. But perhaps Humbert is signaling that things which seem to have a veneer of civilization or refinement about them may actually work to overwhelm and obliterate other entities they encounter, much like he does with Dolly. Sadly, full recognition of the extent of his domination of Dolly does not come until years later.

As is evident in the quotation above, Humbert's initial impressions of America are deeply affected by his relentless desire for Dolly's body, and by his fear that his illicit conduct will be discovered. He tends to see everything through a filter of lechery, anxiety, and mistrust. Thus he sees the "Functional Motel" as an ideal place for "sleep, argument, reconciliation, insatiable *illicit* love" (*L* 145; emphasis added), and the double units in such places he perceives as conducive to "young couples merrily swapping mates" (*L* 145). Presumably he is generalizing his consciousness of what he is doing with Dolly to everyone else around him: why couldn't "licit" love occur in these places? On the other side of the coin, he makes his own contribution to the list of things that the signs posted above the toilet beseech the patrons not to throw into the toilet: "garbage, beer cans, cartons, *stillborn babies* (*L* 146; emphasis added). Similarly, he wryly regards "Tourist Homes" as "country cousins of Funeral ones" (*L* 146). For Humbert, the notion of illicit love conjures up images of mortality as well.

Throughout his account of the journey he reminds the reader of his awareness of Dolly's age, and of her relationship to him. Thus, when he sees a sign that reads "Children welcome, pets allowed," he mentally addresses Dolly: "*You* are welcome, *you* are allowed" (*L* 146). Dolly is not only a child, she is, in Humbert's eyes, his "pet." He also revises admissions signs to reflect his own concerns: "adults one dollar, pubescents sixty cents" (*L* 155); or even more ominously: "children under 12 free, Lo a young captive" (*L* 157). This last image points to Dolly's real situation. Although Humbert needs her to be as compliant as possible so that he can take his pleasure from her whenever he wants, he must resort to a variety of measures to ensure her compliance, or as he puts it, to keep her "in *passable* humor from kiss to kiss" (*L* 154; emphasis added). The bar Humbert sets for Dolly's mood is quite low. Still, he laments that it would "take hours of blandishments, threats and promises to make her lend me for a few seconds her brown limbs [...] before undertaking anything she might prefer to my poor joy" (*L* 147). We note how Humbert continues to feel sorry for himself and his troubles, not for Dolly and her plight. We also note how Humbert slips the word "threats" into the passage between the more positive "blandishments" and "promises," but "threats" may initially be uppermost in Humbert's arsenal of coercive weapons. As Humbert tells us, he succeeded in "terrorizing" Dolly (*L* 151) with a series of gloomy scenarios if she did not cooperate with him, from a life of isolation under the supervision of the spinster Miss Phalen to a stay in a reform school or juvenile detention home. He also tries to keep her isolated from others, refusing to let her talk with friends she sees during their travels and attempting (with somewhat less success) to keep her away from boys her own age.

Humbert's focus on satisfying his sexual desires is unremitting during this trip. Sitting by a swimming pool, he would go over in his mind his morning sexual encounter with Dolly, and start planning an afternoon one (*L* 161). These encounters were, apparently, not always gentle, as he indicates when he remarks that "after a particularly violent morning in bed," he would allow Dolly to go outside and play with other children (*L* 159–60). And the object of his sexual fantasies was not always Dolly, even if he included her in his schemes. He describes how he would have Dolly "caress" him while he watched other children emerge from school. Again, he speaks disparagingly of Dolly for not appreciating his desires, and he characterizes her attitude as "a childish lack of sympathy for other people's whims" (*L* 161). Of course, it is not only children who might find this "whim" less than sympathetic. Humbert's account of his relationship with Dolly indicate that there is a certain amount of physical coercion involved in his attainment of sexual favors. In one particularly unsettling scene, Humbert recalls interrupting Dolly while she was teaching another girl how to jump rope: "thrusting" his "fatherly fingers" deep into Dolly's hair from behind, "and then gently but firmly clasping them around the nape of her neck," he led his "reluctant pet" into their room for a "quick connection before dinner" (*L* 164). It is hard to know what is more chilling in this sentence, the epithet "fatherly" or the grip on her neck that he describes as both "gentle and firm."

Even when Humbert resorts to less physical means of persuasion, and actually promises Dolly a treat in return for her sexual favors, he would often renege on the promise as soon as he had satisfied his desire. See, for example, the scene where he describes Dolly sobbing and pinching him while he is "laughing happily" after retracting "some silly promise" he had made earlier "in a moment of blind impatient passion" (*L* 169). There is something very troubling in the satisfaction Humbert seems to take in his cruelty toward Dolly. At one point he writes "how sweet it was to bring that coffee to her, and then deny it until she had done her morning duty" (*L* 164–65)." But what is even more disturbing is the claim he makes immediately afterwards: "And I was such a thoughtful friend, such a passionate father, such a good pediatrician attending to all the wants of my little auburn brunette's body!" (*L* 165). Notice that his attention is entirely directed to her "body." There is no mention of her feelings or her spirit. Humbert's hypocrisy here is stunning. Despite his protestations, he is anything *but* a thoughtful friend, and when he registers Dolly's own desires and needs, he does so disparagingly. He complains: "Lolita, when she chose, could be a most exasperating brat" and "Mentally, I found her to be a disgustingly conventional girl" (*L* 148). Readers will perhaps see irony in the fact that Humbert seeks sexual ecstasy with the body of his "nymphet," but the real girl — a being with a "will," "consciousness," and "life" of her own (see *L* 62) — gets in the way. Humbert remarks on the contradiction he experiences in his dealings with Dolly. He writes that he dwelled in his "elected paradise [...] whose skies were the color of hell-flames — but still a paradise" (*L* 166). The Edenic apple that Doly had held earlier in the novel shows clear signs of rot. Nevertheless, Humbert is reluctant to let go of his find. When he speculates about the future, he alternates between anxiety over the prospect of getting rid of a "difficult adolescent" who has outgrown her "magic nymphage," and fantasies of having sex with a daughter produced by Dolly, and even with a granddaughter produced by the first child (*L* 174). This incestuous nightmare boggles the mind.[17]

Despite his obsession with possessing Dolly, or, more probably, *because* of the obsession, Humbert is also paranoid about losing her, and at one point in their travels he has a prophetic vision. Commenting on her love for tennis (an activity that he would wax eloquently upon during his description of their second cross-country trip), Humbert recalls her playing with another girl when he suddenly has a bizarre vision. He sees "Charlotte's face in death," and he looks around, only to see Dolly leaving the court in the company of a tall man carrying two tennis rackets (*L* 163). The association of Charlotte with this vision of loss may add support to those who think that Charlotte's spirit may have some role in helping Dolly get away from Humbert. At the very least, the association suggests that Humbert is haunted by guilt, and that he correctly suspects that Dolly will leave him for another man someday in the future.

Although he offers relatively little information about what Dolly is thinking and feeling during their travels together (in contrast to his exhaustive account of his own emotions), the bits of information he does let out indicate how desperate Dolly is for a different kind of life. Thus, he records her being "curiously fascinated by the photographs of local brides, some in full wedding apparel, holding bouquets and wearing glasses" (*L* 165), and he notes that her favorite genre of movies was the musical, where the characters had "unreal stage careers in an essentially grief-proof sphere of existence wherefrom death and truth were banned" (*L* 170). Dolly's fascination with brides, of course, reveals her own longing for what she perceives to be a normal romantic life, even if Humbert might find it "disgustingly conventional." And, given the endless abuse she suffers from Humbert, why wouldn't she long for a "grief-proof sphere of existence" as well?[18]

Dolly's attitude toward what is most important to Humbert — his sexual appetite — seems to range from repulsion to indifference, at best. He records holding her in her lap and seeing her "engrossed in the lighter sections of a newspaper, as indifferent to my ecstasy as if it were something she had sat upon, a shoe, a doll [...] and was too indolent to remove" (*L* 165). Even more telling, he declares: "Never did she vibrate under my touch" (*L* 166). In other words, she did not derive any erotic pleasure from their sexual activity. Yet Dolly actually feels more than mere indifference or even disgust. In one of the most profound and most haunting passages in his memoir, Humbert sums up his months of travel with Dolly. He begins: "We had been everywhere. We had really seen nothing." And he goes on to say that he feels that they had "defiled" the country with a "sinuous trail of slime." As for that country itself, he says that in retrospect it was nothing more to them than "a collection of dog-eared maps, ruined tour books, old tires, and her sobs in the night — every night, every night — the moment I feigned sleep" (*L* 176). This is an extraordinary passage. First we have a series of inanimate objects — maps, tour books, tires — whose epithets convey an air of use and abuse ("dog-eared," "ruined"). Then, we come to a reminder that there's a living person involved, and yet, the only feature reported to us is her profound sadness, her "sobs in the night." Finally, we have the repetition "every night, every night" set off by dashes. Not only the words, but the repetition itself underscores the permanent nature of this sadness. Capping the entire picture is the comment that Dolly hid her misery until she thought Humbert was asleep: her distrust of and distaste for him was so deep that she did not wish him to know what was tearing her apart.

Beardsley

After their months of aimless traveling, Humbert and Dolly settle in Beardsley, where he enrolls Dolly in an expensive private school for girls and where he tries to establish a sense of normalcy in their lives. But since their relationship is anything *but* normal, such a state is beyond reach, and it is here that Dolly begins to develop a semblance of an independent life and to learn how to develop skills of cunning and deception of her own. She is assisted in this by the entire philosophy of the Beardsley School. Headmistress Pratt explains the school philosophy to Humbert, thus offering Nabokov the opportunity to poke fun at so-called "progressive education," where the emphasis lies, as Miss Pratt puts it, on the four "D's" — "Dramatics, Dance, Debating, and Dating" (*L* 177). Miss Pratt returns to the last item to make a simple pun: for the "modern pre-adolescent child," she says, "medieval dates are of less vital value than weekend ones [twinkle]" (*L* 178). What's worse, she has appropriated the pun from the Beardsley college psychoanalyst, and given Humbert's (and Nabokov's) views on psychoanalysis, the pun falls flat indeed. The utter foolishness of Miss Pratt's harangue is underscored by her careless inattention to Humbert's name. In the course of her monologue, she calls him "Mr. Humbird," "Dr. Humburg," "Mr. Humberson," and "Dr. Hummer" (*L* 178–79). The last name, one might recall, is how Humbert referred to himself as he introduced his sexual encounter with Dolly on the Haze sofa ("Humbert the Hummer"), and one wonders whether this name has not come back to the narrating Humbert as he reports Miss Pratt's pun on the concept of dates: it was on a weekend that Humbert achieved his first (and most blissful?) sexual experience with Dolly's body.

Humbert's attempt to blend into his bland suburban surroundings falls comically short, and one of the ways that Nabokov signals this is to have Humbert mangle the verbs associated with the ordinary maintenance of the suburban lifestyle. Humbert reports that one of his neighbors would occasionally speak to him "as he barbered some late garden blooms or watered his car, or, at a later date, defrosted his driveway" (*L* 179). He then remarks, "I don't mind if these verbs are all wrong." Humbert has one so-called friend in Beardsley, an overweight, gay professor named Gaston Godin, but his disdainful attitude toward Godin just reinforces our impression of Humbert as a self-absorbed narcissist, concerned not about other people's joys or woes, but only his own. He sums up his supposed friend with a few devastating strokes: "a mediocre teacher, a worthless scholar, a glum repulsive fat old invert," and notes with resentment that this figure is adored by others, while he himself remains unloved and alone (*L* 183). Humbert apparently does not register the fact that it is his own disdain for others that promotes his isolation. Peering more closely at the Godin figure, however, the reader may detect some likeness between Godin and Humbert. Whereas Humbert is interested in little girls, Godin is interested in little boys (although, as far as we can tell, Godin has no young captives in his house, unlike Humbert). Perhaps in Humbert's disdain for Godin there is some (unconscious?) aversion to what he may see as an unkindly mirror for his own character.

Humbert bemoans a "definite drop" in Dolly's "morals" while they are in Beardsley (*L* 183). What he has in mind is that Dolly has learned to capitalize on the system of monetary bribes he had instituted to ensure his access to "a fancy embrace" and other sexual favors. Again, as is his wont, Humbert depicts himself as the victim here: "I was weak, I was not wise, my schoolgirl nymphet had me in thrall" (*L* 183). But equally characteristic is his subsequent description of a typical interaction be-tween the two that demonstrates that *he* is in control and that she is still vulnerable. He tells the reader how he would dole out coins to Dolly during a sexual act, but then, as Dolly clutched the coins in her fist, he would pry that fist open and get the money back, unless she escaped first. Anxious lest she save up enough money to run away, he burgled her room and confiscated whatever funds he could find.

Given her home situation, Dolly is of course desperate to have a life of her own, or, to be more specific, to have life like that of other kids. One of her ambitions is to be in the school play. Here Miss Pratt comes to the rescue when she summons Humbert to a meeting in which she expresses concern about Dolly's emotional development. In language that parodies Freudian theory, Miss Pratt declares that Dolly is "shuttling [...] between the anal and genital zones of development" (*L* 194). She calls upon Humbert to allow Dolly to take part in the play that she mistitles as *The Hunted Enchanters*. Relieved that Miss Pratt does not know anything more damaging about his relationship to Dolly, Humbert agrees to this, albeit with the promise that "male parts are taken by female parts" (*L* 196), creating the kind of pun on genitalia that Miss Pratt cannot help but notice. Humbert believes that he has made an enormous concession, and to extract payment for this from Dolly, he has her fondle him in a near-empty classroom while he looks at a young girl sitting at a desk and reading a book in front of him. To add to the grotesque atmosphere of the scene, Humbert notes that a copy of Joshua Reynold's "Age of Innocence" hangs over the chalkboard. Humbert thoroughly enjoys his violation of this innocence.

Humbert's decision to let Dolly participate in the play has decisive consequences both for her and for him. It turns out that the play (the actual title of which is *The Enchanted Hunters*) was written by Clare Quilty, who named it after the site where he had seen Dolly with Humbert. What is more, Quilty himself attends some of the rehearsals, and it is during this visit in May that he becomes reacquainted with Humbert's young charge. Dolly is immediately smitten with Quilty (one recalls that she had posted over her bed in Ramsdale an advertisement featuring him), and in an echo of Flaubert's *Madame Bovary*, she skips her piano lessons to meet with her new admirer. Humbert signals the Flaubert connection by naming the piano teacher "Miss Emperor" after Mlle Lempereur in the Flaubert novel. Although Humbert considers himself too busy to bother reading the play or to consider its origins (here his self-absorption works against him), he mistakenly assumes that the plot reflects some bit of New England folklore, and that both the hotel and the play are named after the same story. If he had known the true origin of the name, he might have been more on his guard.

The plot of the play actually has broad relevance to central themes in *Lolita*. The play revolves around a farmer's daughter (played by Dolly) who imagines herself to be a "woodland witch" and who hypnotizes a series of men who have entered the woods and fallen under her spell (*L* 200). The seventh hunter, however, is a poet who insists that both the maiden and her milieu are *his*, the poet's, invention. At the end of the play, the maiden will lead the poet back to her father's house and there a "last-minute kiss" would reveal the play's message "that mirage and reality merge in love" (*L* 201). What is significant about this is the dueling vision of who is the inventor or creator, and who is the invention or object of creation. As the subsequent events of *Lolita* unfold, Humbert gradually becomes less and less sure that he is in control of his destiny, and he begins to suspect that someone else might be in charge; this suspicion culminates in the final scene involving Humbert's murderous attack on Quilty. What is more, the optimistic vision of mirage and reality merging in love is something that will never be attained by Humbert himself. He only gains a glimpse of it when it's too late, and too much damage has been done.

When Humbert learns that Dolly has been skipping her piano lessons, he demands an explanation. Concealing her meetings with Quilty, she tells him that she was rehearsing her part with her friend, Mona Dahl. Mona happily provides corroboration. Humbert is furious, however, and he begins a vicious assault on Dolly. She manages to escape, and when Humbert finally tracks her down, she is just finishing up a phone conversation. Although she tells him that she had just been trying to reach him, the reader comes to understand that she was really on the phone with Quilty. She now expresses great contrition and tells Humbert that she is ready to leave the play, the school, and the town behind. Humbert is overjoyed, of course, never suspecting that this is all part of a plan concocted by Quilty to begin the process of removing Dolly from Humbert's clutches. For the first time since the Enchanted Hunters Hotel, Dolly initiates a sexual encounter: she asks Humbert to carry her upstairs, for she feels "sort of romantic" at that moment (*L* 207). Dolly has begun to shape her own future, and the freedom she senses is empowering.

On the Road Again

From the very outset of the second journey, Dolly displays more confidence and ease than in her first cross-country trip. *She* determines the itinerary, and insists on going to "Wace," supposedly to see some special "ceremonial dances," but as it turns out, she is really eager to see a performance of a play by Clare Quilty and Vivian Darkbloom in that town. Unaware of this,

Humbert remarks on how "bravely" Dolly took the news when they arrived in Wace and found that the ceremonial dances were over. He describes the theatrical performance they attended instead, and from this description the attentive reader might conclude that they had seen *The Lady Who Loved Lightning*, which is listed in the prison volume of *Who's Who in the Limelight* under the Clare Quilty entry (see page 31). In fact, during a thunderstorm they passed through on their way to Wace, Dolly herself had declared: "I am not a lady and do not like lightning" (*L* 220), thus indicating that had she already had this theatrical performance in mind even before they had arrived in Wace. Humbert, however, has not yet heard about the play, and although he notes that Dolly seems to linger after the play is over, staring at the co-authors on stage, Dolly shows her quickness of mind by telling Humbert that Vivian Darkbloom is the male author and Clare Quilty is the female author, and not the other way around as he had assumed (*L* 221).

While Dolly rides high, Humbert becomes increasingly anxious during their drive West. As he states at the outset, "it is easy" for the reader and him to "decipher *now* a past destiny; but a destiny in the making is [...] not one of those honest mystery stories where all you have to do is to keep an eye on the clues" (*L* 211). Humbert's reference to a "mystery story" is apt, for he finds himself in the middle of a mystery that he cannot fathom, pursued by a figure whose identity and intentions are unknown. The rereader and the narrating Humbert know well that this figure is Quilty, but the first-time reader and the experiencing Humbert remain in the dark.

The first significant sign of trouble comes in a town named Kasbeam, at a place called Chestnut Court. Dolly tells Humbert she wishes to stay in bed on the morning after their arrival, and Humbert sets off to town to get groceries and a haircut. The ensuing scene at the barber shop is one of just a few scenes that Nabokov would later single out and identify as the "nerves of the novel"; the Kasbeam barber cost him "a month of work" (*L* 316). What is significant in this scene is that the barber talks incessantly about his son while cutting Humbert's hair, and it's only well into the barber's monologue that Humbert realizes that the son had been dead for thirty years. Humbert acknowledges that he had been "inattentive" to the man's words (*L* 213), and the scene illustrates once again Humbert's deafness to the cares of other. Returning to his lodging, Humbert notices the "red hood" of a car protruding from a garage in a "somewhat cod-piece fashion" (*L* 213). This image is appropriate not only because it displays Humbert's sexualized imagination, but because the car presumably belongs to Clare Quilty, who had been driving a "rubious" convertible at the Enchanted Hunters Hotel (see page 117). It appears that Quilty has just been with Dolly, for when Humbert enters the cabin, he sees Dolly sitting on the bed and dreamily brimming with a "diabolical" glow. The word "diabolical" provides an echo of the theme of the demonic that had been evoked at the Enchanted Hunters Hotel in the reference to pigs and in Quilty's question: "Where the devil did you get her?" (*L* 127).

Humbert is now on the lookout for an Aztec Red Convertible that begins following his car like a "red ghost" (*L* 217) or an "imperious red shadow" (*L* 219). The image of the shadow becomes a haunting refrain in Humbert's psyche. When he finds Dolly glowing at the Chestnut Court, he tears at her clothing to pursue the "shadow of her infidelity" (*L* 215), and he later writes that the problem of the red convertible "overshadowed" the theme of Dolly's lovers (*L* 217). Humbert does not know who is driving this red car. His initial thought is that it is a detective who resembles Humbert's uncle, Gustave Trapp. It has not yet occurred to Humbert that he might have a serious rival for Dolly's attention, or as he puts it, that "another Humbert was avidly following Humbert and Humbert's nymphet" (*L* 217). This notion, however, will grow in significance, for Humbert himself will later come to perceive Quilty as a kind of double or alter ego, as we shall see below.

At this point, however, the entire affair so baffles Humbert that it takes on a dreamlike or hallucinatory quality in his mind. Ever aware of the pursuit of his unknown nemesis, Humbert becomes mesmerized by the absolute precision of the distance between his car and the trailing car. He resorts to such images as "spell," "zone of evil mirth and magic," and "enchanted interspace" (*L* 219). Humbert's fantasy of an "enchanted island" haunted by nymphets has turned into a nightmare of entrapment and pursuit. Even though Quilty eventually changes tactics, turning to different cars so that Humbert becomes even more befuddled as he tries to keep track of his pursuer, Quilty is never far away. In an episode that unnerves Humbert, he finds Dolly frolicking madly in an "Aztec Red" bathing suit (the same color as Quilty's first car) with a puppy by a swimming pool while being watched by a man a short distance away. Humbert can tell by Dolly's antics that she is putting on a lascivious display for the man, who leans against a tree "in which a multitude of dappled Priaps shivered" (*L* 237). This is an intriguing image, for in addition to the obvious figure of licentiousness — Priapus,

117

a minor god associated with fertility and often depicted with an enormous penis — the word "dappled" contains the word "apple," that fruit which was associated with Dolly from the moment of Humbert's arrival at the Haze household. Humbert's private paradise has given way to a kind of pagan bacchanalia to which he has not been invited. This will be the last time that Humbert sees Dolly in such a mood, for they now arrive in the town of Elphinstone, and it is there that Dolly will abandon Humbert for good.

Elphinstone

The owner of the motor court where Humbert and Dolly stop in Elphinstone is a widow named Mrs. Hays. Humbert originally found Dolly in the care of a widow named Mrs. Haze, and he would now lose Dolly while staying at a place run by a widow with a name that is phonetically identical. This is the kind of coincidence that indicates that Humbert's life is in the hands of a higher force who surrounds the protagonist with distinctive patterns against which the protagonist's own designs seem pale and insignificant. Dolly is running a fever, and following Mrs. Hays's advice, Humbert takes her to see a local doctor, and this leads to her hospitalization. This is, Humbert realizes, the first time in two years that he has been separated from her.

Anxious that his pursuer, whom Humbert variously labels as "that secret agent, or secret lover, or prankster, or hallucination" (L 241) may be lurking nearby, Humbert tries to visit Dolly as often as he can, and he suspects that she is now in league with her nurse, the daughter of a Basque shepherd. The Basque association leads Humbert to return to the Carmen theme introduced earlier, and he refers to Dolly as "Carmencita," "Carmen," and "the gitanilla." This association in turn leads Humbert to allude to Alexander Pushkin's narrative poem *The Gypsies* (which some scholars believe influenced Mérimée's novella *Carmen*). He writes that Dolly and the nurse were plotting "in Basque, in Zemfirian, against my hopeless love" (L 243; Zemfira is name of the gypsy woman whose infidelity leads Aleko to kill her).

Humbert is unable to influence matters, however, because he himself falls ill, and cannot go to the hospital for two days. On the second day of his illness he hears the sounds of firecrackers, and he assumes that there is "some great national celebration" going on in town. It is the Fourth of July, and it is on this day that Dolly achieves her own independence from Humbert, for when Humbert phones the hospital on the following day, he learns that Dolly "had checked out the day before" and had been picked up by "her uncle, Mr. Gustave" and were going to go to "Grandpa's ranch as agreed" (*L* 246). Humbert races to the hospital still wearing his pajamas and robes, and raises a furor there, but he quickly comes to his senses when he realizes that he could be arrested. He leaves the hospital telling himself that he was "still a free man — free to trace the fugitive, free to destroy my brother" (*L* 247). Humbert's adoption of the term "brother" here is significant, and the nurse will repeat it when Humbert confronts her later (see page 249), trying to learn the identity of the man who spirited Dolly away. As Humbert's subsequent discussion of his attempts to track the man down make clear, Quilty's interests, education, and sense of humor are not unlike Humbert's own. One might even say there's a family resemblance.

Humbert now undertakes a frantic, but ultimately futile, attempt to track his nemesis down. By his account, he visits 342 different lodging establishment to see if the man had left any clues in the hotel and motel registers (*L* 248). This is the third time that the number 342 has turned up in regard to location: it was the street number of the Haze home as well as the number of Humbert and Dolly's room at the Enchanted Hunters Hotel. While it may seem improbable that Humbert actually visited no more or no less than 342 establishments, his citation of this number may indicate his sense of being caught in a circular web with no exit at hand. At the very least, the number serves as one more marker of Nabokov's presence as the controlling spirit of the novel.

What Humbert finds as he examines these numerous registers is that Quilty has invented a rich variety of pseudonyms ranging from simple literary allusions to complex puns and anagrams. While in some cases, it is easy for Humbert (and the reader) to decipher the target behind the name (for example, Arthur Rainbow is Quilty's version of the French poet Arthur Rimbaud), in other cases, he has to do a bit more work, and he is particularly agitated to come across the name "Ted Hunter, Cane, NH" which is an anagram of "The Enchanted Hunter," the place where Quilty first saw Dolly in Humbert's company (*L* 251). Although well-educated readers undoubtedly derive satisfaction when they are able to decode Quilty's puzzles, many of the allusions behind the names remain a challenge not only to Humbert but to these readers as well, and they can be grateful to Alfred Appel, Jr. and Carl Proffer for identifying the specific allusions contained in what Humbert calls a "cryptogrammic paper chase" (*L* 250).

Enmeshed in his tormentor's "demoniacal game," Humbert fails to learn the man's identity, but he acknowledges that "his type of humor [...] the tone of his brain, had affinities with my own" (L 249). Indeed, as we shall see later, the broad affinities that can be detected between Humber and Quilty have led many commentators to view Quilty as a kind of double or alter ego for Humbert, and it may be Humbert's own belief that by eliminating this figure who "mimed and mocked" him (L 249), he, Humbert may be purged of some of his own sins and deficiencies.

Be that as it may, Humbert does not find out the name of his identity for several years, and he describes the period following Dolly's disappearance as "three empty years" (L 253). He spent part of that time in a Canadian sanatorium, for he felt he was "losing contact with reality" (L 255). He suffers from grotesque nightmares and he writes desperate poems combining grief over Dolly's loss with a smoldering desire to wreak vengeance on her lover. Nor was he able to overcome his "pederosis." He continues to seek out glimpses of young girls, but he claims that he no longer had fantasies of dwelling in bliss "with a little maiden" in some remote locale. *That* was all over," he states, "for the time being at least" (L 257). The last phrase represents a characteristic Humbertian equivocation. The implication is that such fantasies had *not* vanished; they simply lay dormant, and possibly could awaken at a future point should the right circumstances arise. It was partly in an effort to prevent this from happening that Humbert felt the need to find another, older substitute for Dolly, and this time he discovers a woman named Rita, whom he describes as "the most soothing [...] companion" that he had ever had (L 259). She served as a willing traveling and drinking companion, and Humbert's description of his relationship with her resonates with a spirit of fondness noticeably absent in his earlier account of his marriages to Valeria and Charlotte.

At some point during his period of cohabitation with Rita, Humbert decides to revisit Briceland and the Enchanted Hunters Hotel. He writes to reserve a room, but receives a reply addressed to "Professor Hamburg" saying that there were no rooms available. The distorted form of his name, together with a statement on the hotel stationery stating that the hotel was located "near churches," leads one to conclude that the hotel management is determined to preserve their establishment for the exclusive use of Gentiles. Humbert settles for a visit to the town library where he hopes to find a newspaper photo that might show him in the lobby of the hotel. As he scans the relevant issue, he notes in passing a quotation from "the author of *Dark Age*" (*L* 262). This author is, as a reader with a good memory might recognize, Clare Quilty, whose name is still meaningless to Humbert. Quilty had refused to be photographed, and as a consequence, Humbert does not have the chance to identify his pursuer from such a photograph. And as if to complement the absence of Quilty's photograph, the photograph of the hotel clientele that night shows no trace of Humbert Humbert either.

So Humbert's life continues until one fateful day in September 1952.

Coalmont

Humbert describes for the reader how the play of light in the entrance hall of his building would sometimes mislead him into thinking that the handwriting on letters in his mailbox was Dolly's, when in fact it was someone else's. In a characteristic reversal of expectation, he now discovers that a letter he had thought was written by Rita's mother turns out to be from Dolly herself. But, before providing that letter to the reader, Humbert discusses another letter he received in that day's mail—from John Farlow. Farlow surprises Humbert by stating that he is now married to a very young Spanish girl and that he is "building a family" (*L* 266). He is writing to Humbert to settle the financial affairs of the Haze estate, and in order to wrap this up, he suggests that Humbert "better produce Dolly quick" (*L* 266).

It is at this very point, with the mention of Dolly's name, that another letter, as Humbert puts it, "began *talking* to me in a small matter-of-fact voice" (*L* 266, emphasis added). This letter is from Dolly. What's noteworthy about the way Humbert introduces the letter is his use of the image of Dolly's "voice." Once free of Humbert's control, Dolly is able to find and express a voice of her own. What is more, in writing this letter, she joins Humbert as a producer of written texts. Although she is no poet, her words ring with pathos nonetheless. She writes that she is now married, pregnant, and needs money so that her husband can pay their debts and move to Alaska. The letter concludes with a poignant plea: "Write, please. I have gone through much sadness and hardship" (*L* 266). It is signed "Dolly (Mrs. Richard F. Schiller)." The reader will note that Dolly does *not* use Humbert's pet name for her, Lolita. What is more, the attentive first-time reader may recall that John Ray, Jr. had stated in his foreword that a "Mrs. Richard F. Schiller" had died in childbirth. The stark impact of that news now strikes home.

The sudden appearance of this letter on the heels of John Farlow's letter demanding that Humbert produce Dolly quick has led at least one reader, Alexander Dolinin, to speculate that Dolly's letter is itself an invention of Humbert's, who makes up this version of Dolly's life in response to Farlow's demands.[19] Dolinin theorizes that Dolly may never have recovered from her illness in Elphinstone and that Humbert is now providing an alternate vision of a possible life for Dolly, drawing upon elements taken from Farlow's letter (marriage, pregnancy) and applying them to Dolly. We shall have more to say about this theory in the next chapter, but for the moment we should point out that the possibility that Dolly has already died would rob the novel of one of its richest and most moving scenes, Humbert's reunion with Dolly in Coalmont.

Significantly, Humbert's determination to visit Dolly in person rather than sending the funds by mail or wire seems to be motivated as much by his desire for vengeance as for any desire to see Dolly herself. He tells the reader that he took his gun with him and that he "rehearsed Mr. Richard F. Schiller's violent death" as soon as he reached a secluded spot outside the city on his way to Coalmont (*L* 267). Once in Coalmont, he makes his way to the Schiller home, which is nothing more than a "clapboard shack" with a "waste of withered weeds all around" (*L* 269). This is a far cry from the visions of Hollywood that Dolly had nurtured during her time with Humbert. Humbert is greeted by a "nondescript cur," which represents the final evolution of the canine theme in Dolly's life, from the car-crazed setter that triggered Charlotte's fatal accident, to the cocker spaniel that she had patted when they checked into the Enchanted Hunters Hotel, to the puppy she had frolicked with in front of Quilty's leering gaze, and the cocker spaniel puppy Quilty had brought her when he picked her up at the Elphinstone hospital. The transformation in these images, from the house to the dog, testify to the degradations that Dolly has experienced in life.

For many readers, Humbert's reunion with Dolly shines as the richest and most emotionally resonant scene in the novel. Several features in the scene stand out, from the new image of Dolly as a more mature woman who has experienced hardship in life and yet has achieved a kind of resigned acceptance, to Humbert's relinquishment of his fantasy of the nymphet and his appreciation of the woman that Dolly has become. The new image of Dolly appears before Humbert and the reader at the very beginning of the reunion scene when Dolly opens the door. Humbert notices that she has lost her tan, gained two inches in height as well as a pair of glasses, and is "hugely pregnant" (L 269). Gone is the girl whom Humbert described as the "ideal consumer" focused on clothes, pop music, and tourist trinkets. In her place is a woman coping with severely reduced circumstances yet confidently showing a warm solicitude for her new husband and her unborn child. This concern for others is unfamiliar to Humbert, both because he has not seen this before in Dolly, and because it is alien to his own narcissistic nature. Yet while Dolly may have shed some of her brashness, she has not been entirely crushed, and she retains a spirit of hope. Her dreams of stardom in Hollywood may have disappeared, but she now dreams of her husband's success in Alaska. She does not become a movie star, but she will end up in Gray Star. What is more, she is doggedly focused on the future and not on the past, which of course is what Humbert has come to see her about. When he presses her for the name of the man she left him for in Elphinstone, she initially balks, not wanting to rake up "all that muck" (L 271). He intimates that if she wants money from him, she will need to tell him the man's name, and she finally acquiesces.

In an interesting narrative maneuver, Humbert himself does not pass on to the reader the name that Dolly utters. Instead, he writes that she emitted "the name that the astute reader has guessed long ago," and he provides what seems to be an enigmatic substitute — "Waterproof" (L 272). Perhaps the astute reader *has* guessed the name long ago, but it is also likely that many first-time readers will still be in the dark. Humbert's inclusion of the word "Waterproof" and his subsequent question: "Why did a flash from Hourglass Lake cross my consciousness?" (L 272) are meant to send the reader back to Chapter Twenty in Part One, where Charlotte had uttered the word in reference to Humbert's watch just before John Farlow showed up and interrupted the "indecent story" about Ivor Quilty's nephew. With this bit of detective work, the reader may be able to get closer to guessing the man's name, which Humbert himself inserts into the narrative in a coded form at this point in his account of the scene: "*Quietly* the fusion took place, and everything fell into order" (L 272). What Humbert is striving for is to have his reader experience the same type of "golden peace" of recognition that he himself felt when Dolly uttered the long-awaited name, but it may be a sign of Humbert's continued self-absorption here that this golden peace may be felt by him alone. The reader may still be trying to put the puzzle together, and it is not until some eighteen pages later that Humbert finally names his nemesis (see page 290). Once readers learn Quilty's name, of course, they can go back and see the many points at which the figure is evoked: this is one of the great pleasures in rereading Nabokov's text.

After Dolly has uttered Quilty's name, Humbert is eager to hear all the details of their relationship. As she talks about Quilty, Dolly's lingering appreciation of the man is clear. She calls him "a genius" and "a great guy in many respects" (L 275, 276), but says that he was a "freak in sex matters" (L 276). Having promised to get her a small part in a Hollywood movie, he instead tried to get Dolly to participate in a homemade erotic or pornographic film. She refused to take part, and he threw her out. What is so striking about Dolly's account of the past is how little bitterness or anger she harbors, either toward Quilty or toward Humbert. Quilty, she states, was "the only man she had ever been crazy about" (L 272). When Humbert asks her about his own place in her emotional life, she does not immediately respond, and Humbert surmises that in her eyes: "our poor romance was for a moment reflected, pondered upon, and dismissed like a dull party [...] like a bit of dry mud caking her childhood" (L 272). It is, of course, characteristic of Humbert to view his relationship with Dolly as a "romance," when it was from her perspective anything *but* that. Indeed, when she finally does respond to his question, she does not refer to the emotional or even physical aspect of the relationship, but simply acknowledges that he "had been a good father, she guessed" (L 272), which is a rather generous assessment, all things considered. Dolly seems to regard all that has happened to her not with rancor or resentment, but with a kind of bemused wonder. When she tells Humbert that the ranch where she lived with Quilty for a time had later burned down, she remarks that this was "so *strange*, so *strange*" (L 277). Speaking more broadly about her experiences she states that "if somebody wrote up her life nobody would ever believe it" (L 273). Little does she realize that Humbert would, in his own fashion, write a compelling account of her life, one that readers have been discussing for decades.

Humbert pays close attention to the way Dolly talks and moves, and his description makes it clear that he no longer sees her as the little nymphet he had first fantasized about. In fact, watching her smoke a cigarette, he identifies physical gestures that he had seen in her mother, and he even comments that Charlotte "rose from her grave" (L 275). Paramount in all this is his acceptance of the new Dolly. Although he had fretted earlier about what he would do with Dolly after she outgrew her prepubescent form (see page 174), he now proclaims his devotion to just such an older person. Observing her "adult, rope-veined" hands, and commenting that she was "hopelessly worn at seventeen," Humbert nevertheless declares: "I looked and looked at her, and knew as clearly as I know I am to die, that I loved her more than anything I had seen or imagined on earth, or hoped for anywhere else" (L 277). The key word here might be "imagined," for Humbert's obsession with Dolly originally consisted in large part of an obsession with a fantasy figure of his own creation. The reader will recall what Humbert had written about this earlier: "What I had madly possessed was not she, but my own creation, another, fanciful Lolita" (L 62). Now, he expresses his love for the real person he sees before him. In one of the most famous passages in the book, Humbert declares: "I insist the world know how much I loved my Lolita, *this* Lolita, pale and polluted, and big with another's child, but still gray-eyed, still sooty-lashed, still auburn and almond, still Carmencita, still mine" (L 278).

We have already noted in an earlier chapter that some readers remain unconvinced that Humbert's declaration represents a genuine change in his attitude toward Dolly. The reference to "Carmencita" and the emphasis on the possessive phrase "still mine" give such readers grounds for skepticism. On the other hand, it is entirely possible that Humbert folds into his appreciation of the new Dolly Schiller his memories of the girl he had desired so intensely years earlier. The present has been superimposed over the past, but it has not eradicated it. Perhaps the years of separation from Dolly helped Humbert to realize that what he missed was not just a body, or a fantasy image, but a real person with a spirit and personality of her own. Indeed, his last affirmation in this passage conveys an evocation and appreciation of both the present Dolly and the remembered Dolly. No matter what how the ravages of time affect her body, Humbert says: "even then I would go mad with tenderness at the mere sight of your dear wan face, at the mere sound of your raucous young voice, my Lolita" (L 278). The epithet "wan" evokes the cares that life have now borne upon her, while the epithet "young" suggests something vital and unchanging in her spirit. We should also note Humbert's statement that he would go mad with "tenderness" — not desire, or lust — at the sound of her voice. Tenderness, we recall, is one of the key attributes of aesthetic bliss defined by Nabokov in his essay on *Lolita* (see L 315).

As genuine as Humbert's love for Dolly might be, however, he has not suddenly turned into an altruistic, compassionate saint. He implores Dolly to leave her husband, the father of her unborn child, and to go off with him, and his language becomes unpleasantly vulgar at this point: "I want you to leave your incidental Dick, and this awful hole, and come to live with me" (L 278). On the other hand, despite Dolly's dismay when she thinks he will only give her the money if she goes off to have sex with him, he assures her that the money is hers regardless, and he not only pays her $4000 in accumulated rent from the Haze house, but he pays her $500 for their old car as well. She can also look forward to the proceeds of the sale of the Haze property. Once again, he asks her to leave with him, and this time, in a softened voice, she says: "No, honey, no" (L 279). It is the first time she has ever called him "honey."

Although Humbert's love for Dolly may have evolved, another aspect of his personality remains unchanged: his murderous desire to punish the man who took Dolly away from him. This is evident throughout his meeting with Dolly, from the moment he walks through the door looking for Dolly's husband, although when he sees the man and realizes that this is not his old nemesis, the husband is "instantly reprieved" (L 270), and it continues in his persistent attempts to get Dolly to reveal Quilty's whereabouts. The strain of aggression that courses through Humbert's blood also shows up in incidental asides, as, for example, when he comments that Dick Schiller's hands were far finer than his own. He comments: "I have hurt too much too many bodies with my twisted poor hands to be proud of them" (L 274). And, as he leaves the Schiller home, Humbert's murderous intentions resurface. Yes, he tells Dolly, he has to go. Then, mentally, he adds: "I had to go, and find him, and destroy him" (L 280).

After this emotionally complex scene in the Schiller household, Nabokov provides his readers with a moment of relative calm. We follow Humbert out of Coalmont and through a dreary experience of becoming lost on the back roads of rural America. Humbert's car becomes stuck in the mud, and he has to spend the night in a nameless town somewhere in Appalachia. Noteworthy are the images of death and stagnation evoked up in Humbert's narration: the rain "had been cancelled"; "the town was dead" (L 281). These images suggest both the death of the possibility of a life with Dolly for Humbert, and the death he anticipates bringing to Quilty. In his description of the town at night, however, Humbert also provides marvelous images of the play of light and shadow that would go unnoticed by the sleeping inhabitants of the town. Nabokov was fond of such scenes, and one thinks of similar moments in *Mary* and *Pnin*. Here, though, one image stands out for its suggestive significance: Humbert observes a neon restaurant sign depicting a large coffee pot. Every second or so, it bursts into "emerald life." Then it would go out, but as Humbert notes: "the pot could still be made out as a latent shadow teasing the eye before its next emerald resurrection" (*L* 282). This image leads Humbert to recall a comment Dolly had made about her camp on the way to the Enchanted Hunters Hotel: "We made shadowgraphs" (*L* 114). Humbert writes: "I was weeping again, drunk on the impossible past" (*L* 282). Dolly's past — her last moments of unsuspecting innocence at camp — have long gone, never to be resurrected. The image of resurrection, however, may have relevance for Humbert himself. As we shall see, in striving to kill Quilty, whom he has viewed as his "shadow," he may be trying to resurrect himself. Whether Humbert can succeed in such an attempt, either morally or in his art, has yet to be determined.

In the very next chapter, Humbert launches into a review of his treatment of Dolly. For the first time he acknowledges the extent of crimes toward her. Bemoaning the fact that nothing could make Dolly "forget the foul lust" he had inflicted upon her, Humbert reflects on the meaning of this injustice in the cosmic scheme of things. In lines that recall Ivan Karamazov's inquiry about the nature of divine justice in a world in which innocent children are made to suffer,[20] Humbert declares that unless it can be proven to him "that in the infinite run it does not matter a jot that a North American girl-child named Dolores Haze had been deprived of her childhood by a maniac, unless this can be proven (and if it can, then life is a joke)," then Humbert sees nothing for the treatment of his misery than what he calls the "very local palliative of articulate art" (*L* 283). Humbert would seem to agree with Ivan Karamazov that no vision of heavenly reconciliation can make up for the injury perpetrated on a child, but he moves beyond Ivan in suggesting that art may provide some small compensatory relief — not art that imposes its designs on other people — but genuine art that reflects and transmutes the pains and the beauty of life. Humbert now quotes a couplet written by an "old poet" (of course, by Nabokov himself):

> The moral sense in mortals is the duty
> We have to pay on the mortal sense of beauty. (*L* 283)

Vladimir Alexandrov interprets this formula as follows: "an individual's perception of something or someone as beautiful automatically awakens an ethical faculty in that person; this emerges as a function of being alive, or 'mortal.'"[21] Leland de la Durantaye, however, finds that the link between the "mortal sense of beauty" and the "moral sense in mortals" is not so automatic. Examining the couplet in light of a similar remark in E. A. Poe's "The Poetic Principle," de la Durantaye point out that there is a tension or contrast between our sense of beauty and our moral sense: the latter is the duty we have to pay; it is not necessarily easy or automatic.[22] In fact, Humbert's earlier affirmation of his artistic aspirations coincided with a profound blindness to the ethical implications of the behavior he carried out under the banner of those aspirations. Now, however, after seeing Dolly and thinking about his appreciation of her, he may be beginning to understand that authentic art does not turn a blind idea to issues of morality. This understanding may find fulfillment at the end of his memoir when Humbert decides to enshrine Dolly — and his wretched treatment of her — in the transcendent realm of art.

In the next chapter Humbert follows up on the ethical review he has now undertaken. He recalls several discrete episodes in his life with Dolly where he became acutely aware of what was going on inside her, but chose not to react or change his behavior because of it. In one such episode, Humbert overhears Dolly telling a friend that what is so "dreadful" about dying is that "you are completely on your own" (L 284). This image of isolation poignantly captures Dolly's own situation as Humbert's defenseless captive, and Humbert acknowledges that he now realized for the first time that he did not know anything about Dolly's mind and that "quite possibly, behind the awful juvenile clichés, there was in her a garden and a twilight, and a palace gate — dim and adorable regions which happened to be lucidly and absolutely forbidden to me" (L 284). Here Humbert introduces a new variation on the image of Dolly as princess — not the fairy tale beauty whom he wished to keep locked up for himself — but a being with an emotional and intellectual world entirely her own. He is characteristically self-pitying when he says that this realm was "forbidden" to him, for he had steadfastly chosen *not* to be interested in her imaginative world, which he was always quick to put down for its fascination with popular culture, music, film, and so on.

The last episode Humbert recalls has to do with a book Dolly was reading in which the main character's mother is described as a heroic woman who dissimulated her love for her child because she was dying and she did not want her child to miss her. When Humbert realizes that Dolly has been thinking of her own mother, and missing her, he resists the impulse to go to

Dolly and comfort her. He now sums up his habitual conduct: "it was always my habit and method to ignore Lolita's states of mind while comforting my own base self" (L 287). Humbert's insight into what he has done, and what he failed to do, as Dolly's protector and guardian, is absolutely lucid here, and it will feed into his imminent encounter with Clare Quilty.

The fact that Humbert positions his review of his "case" between his reunion with Dolly and his return to Ramsdale to obtain Quilty's present whereabouts from his uncle Ivor suggests that his quest to find and destroy Quilty may be linked with a recognition of his own culpability. In other words, although his primary motive for finding and killing Quilty is to punish the man for taking Dolly away with him, he may also hope to achieve some expiation for his own conduct by killing someone whom he sees as harboring similar sins. We shall return to this premise shortly.

On to Pavor Manor

In order to obtain Quilty's present location, Humbert must return to Ramsdale and interview Quilty's cousin Ivor. What he learns from Ivor is that Quilty now lives on "Grimm Road" near Parkington. When Humbert drives to the home, he dubs it "Pavor Manor" (*pavor* is the Latin word for "nightmare"). The associations raised by these names are quite apt for the ensuing scene, for Humbert's encounter with Quilty reminds one both of a nightmare and of the kind of dark encounters with grotesque beings that populate the fairy tales of the Brothers Grimm. The description of Pavor Manor itself has reminded some readers of E. A. Poe's House of Usher and of the crumbling edifices of the Gothic novel. Both Humbert and Quilty are visibly impaired during their encounter: Humbert has gotten drunk in preparation for the murder, and Quilty is so addled by a combination of drugs and alcohol that he initially mistakes Humbert for "some familiar and innocuous hallucination" and a "raincoated phantasm" (L 294, 295). At one point in the encounter Humbert characterizes the two of them as "two large dummies, stuffed with dirty cotton and rags" (L 299).

Humbert's linkage of the two men in this way is noteworthy. Many commentators have evaluated the relationship between Humbert and Quilty and have concluded that Quilty is a kind of double or alter ego for Humbert.[23] They can point to many similarities between the two men. As Humbert himself has already declared: "his genre, his type of humor [...] the tone of his brain, had affinities with my own" (L 249). When Humbert first sees Quilty in his home, the latter is wearing a purple bathrobe, which Humbert acknowledges is "very like one I had" (*L* 294). Quilty also has a "hirsute chest" (*L* 295), which recalls Humbert's description of himself as "wooly-chested" (*L* 44). Both men are fond of fine wine. Quilty boasts of having a "magnificent cellar" (*L* 301), while Humbert has remarked upon the Farlows' "good cellar," which he thinks is rather uncommon in the United States (*L* 101). Both men are fond of working French phrases into their speech. To Humbert's "*Soyons logiques*" (*L* 238) we can compare Quilty's "*soyons raisonnables*" (*L* 301). Both men are defensive (and deluded) when they proclaim their former concern for Dolly's well-being. When Quilty says: "I gave her a splendid vacation" (*L* 298), one recalls Humbert's desire to prove to his judges that he did everything in his power to give Dolly "a really good time" (*L* 163).

A more important affinity, perhaps, is the fact that Quilty, like Humbert, has a preference for little girls, and, he, like Humbert, has an interest in recording images of his girls on film. While Humbert laments the fact that he could have filmed Dolly playing tennis and kept her with him in the "projection room" of his pain and despair (*L* 231), Quilty once promised to give Dolly a role in a film about a tennis player and then tried to make her perform in a pornographic film. At this point, though, we must note that Quilty's film project is much seamier than Humbert's, and several commentators have remarked that when comparing Humbert and Quilty, the latter, with his collection of erotica, his interest in physical freaks, and his connections with executions, should be considered a more debased version of the former.[24] The final area of kinship between the two is the realm of literature. Quilty writes plays, and Humbert, who has written about French and English literature, fancies himself to be a poet upon occasion. In fact, the "sentence" he has given Quilty to read before his death is written in a poetic form, which allows Humbert to call it "poetical justice" (*L* 299). Humbert himself highlights the deep interconnection between the two when he describes their tussle: "I felt suffocated as he rolled over me. I rolled over him. We rolled over me. They rolled over him. We rolled over us" (*L* 299).

These numerous links between Quilty and Humbert, as well as the specific content of the poem Humbert gives Quilty to read may encourage the reader to discern in Humbert's desire to kill Quilty not only a thirst for revenge, but something like a desire to expunge his own deficiencies and guilt through this act. In other words, by highlighting and attributing to Quilty some of his — Humbert's — own negative attributes and then exterminating their bearer, Humbert may hope to free himself of those very attributes. Richard Bullock views the Quilty-Humbert relationship in precisely these terms. Calling Quilty "the repository and personification of Humbert's evil," Bullock further identifies Quilty as "the objectification of the evil Humbert must kill in order to become a successful artist."[25] Whether Humbert can actually achieve this goal through the act of murder is, however, very much in doubt, as we shall see below.

Humbert's poem alternates between acknowledgments of his own guilt — "Because you took advantage of a *sinner*" (*L* 299; emphasis added) — and affirmations of innocence — "Because you took advantage of my inner / essential *innocence*" (*L* 300; emphasis added), but he stresses the possibilities that evaporated with the loss of Dolly. Thus, Humbert asserts that in taking Dolly away from him, Quilty "cheated" him of his "redemption" (*L* 300); in other words, Quilty deprived Humbert of the chance to redeem himself by mending his ways with Dolly. And in the final lines of the poem, he strikes an intriguing contrast between himself and Quilty: "because of all you did / because of all I did not / you have to die" (*L* 300). The initial phrase — "because of all you did" — clearly indicts Quilty for his crimes, but the next phrase is more ambiguous. "[B]ecause of all I did not" could be another profession of innocence, or even a lament over the loss of possible future joys with Dolly, or it could be a recognition that Humbert had not done what he *should have done* in regard to Dolly, such as treat her with respect and compassion, not desire and domination. In other words, Quilty must die not only because he stole Dolly away from Humbert, but because Humbert himself had mistreated Dolly as well.

Some commentators have argued that in killing Quilty, Humbert *does* succeed in expunging his negative attributes. Robert Levine writes: "By the end of the novel, H. H. has fully recognized his crime, has seen that he is clearly guilty, has executed the offending part of himself — Clare Quilty."[26] Herbert Grabes offers a similar opinion: "Quilty's murder [...] appears [...] as the destruction of the personification of the 'selfish vice' whose mastery the narrator had just overcome himself."[27] This interpretation, however, not only runs counter to Nabokov's own deeply held views on the immorality of murder, but the very treatment the murder receives in the novel seems to undermine its validity. As noted earlier, the entire scene has a nightmarish, hallucinatory quality to it, and Humbert's actual attempts to shoot Quilty are marked first by ridiculous ineptitude, and then by an exaggerated display of gore and pain. Humbert's first shot makes, in his words, "a ridiculously feeble and juvenile sound," and the bullet merely hits the rug. Humbert remarks that he had the "paralyzing impression that it had merely trickled in and might come out again" (*L* 297). These images recall those from Humbert's earlier dream about attempting to commit murder, when "one bullet after another feebly drops on the floor from the sheepish muzzle" (*L* 47). Later, at the end of the scene, Humbert's attempts to shoot Quilty seem only to inject "spurts of energy" into the figure, who roams from room to room "bleeding majestically" (*L* 303), until he crawls into bed and Humbert fires one last bullet. This is still not the end for Quilty, however. He manages to crawl out onto the landing before collapsing once and for all.

The very difficulty that Humbert encounters when trying to kill Quilty suggests that his desire to expunge himself of his own guilt by attributing it to another and then killing that other is not so easily accomplished. Charles Mitchell offers elucidation here: he states that Humbert tries to kill Quilty as an externalization of "his own swinish and monstrous lower nature," but because Humbert tries to "transcend his lower nature by using his lower nature," the attempt cannot succeed.[28] Indeed, Humbert may sense this, for he writes: "Far from feeling any relief, a burden even weightier than the one I had hoped to get rid of was with me, upon me, over me" (*L* 304).[29] And, just a short time later, after leaving Quilty's home, Humbert recalls: "I was all covered with Quilty" (*L* 306). It is not as easy to cast off one's guilt as Humbert might have imagined.

What is more, despite the affinities between Humbert and Quilty, it should be noted that they they are not authentic doubles of the type one finds in nineteenth-century literature (such as Poe's "William Wilson" or Robert Louis Stevenson's *The Strange Case of Doctor Jekyll and Mr. Hyde*). As some commentators have pointed out, Nabokov's treatment of the Quilty-Humbert relationship suggests that he is parodying the classic double theme.[30] And although Humbert would like to see Quilty as more reprehensible than Humbert himself, it must rankle him that Dolly preferred Quilty to him in the past (and would still choose Quilty over Humbert in the present, if she had to [see page 279]). Quilty did not force her to leave Humbert, nor did he force her to perform sex acts when she was unwilling to do so; when she refused, she was free to leave. Perhaps Humbert's fury at Quilty is further fueled by his recognition that Quilty, and not Humbert, was the subject of Dolly's original infatuation and that he, Humbert, was merely his successor. In any case, Humbert may have succeeded in eliminating his old nemesis, but he has not freed himself from the burden of guilt he has been carrying around for the last several years.

Finale

Leaving Quilty's house, Humbert decides to drive on the wrong side of the road, reasoning that since he had "disregarded all laws of humanity," he might as well "disregard the rules of traffic" (*L* 306). This impulse to rebel against the strictures of society deserves comment, because in the latter stages of Humbert's memoir, one gets the impression that Humbert may be aware that he is not as much in control of his destiny as he might have liked. Earlier, he had thought that fate (or "McFate") was on his side, removing the obstacle of Charlotte Haze from his path, for example. Once be became aware of Quilty's pursuit, however, he began to view fate as a baleful force. After the killing of Quilty, an action that proved far more bizarre and problematic than he had anticipated, Humbert remarks: "This [...] was the end of the ingenious play staged for me by Quilty" (*L* 305).

This observation is highly significant. Although Humbert likes to feel as though it is *he* who calls the shots, the entire scenario of the second cross-country trip with Dolly, which led to her eventual disappearance, had apparently been designed and carried out by Quilty. And it is Quilty who had led Humbert on the futile "cryptogrammic paper chase." Now, Quilty's failure to die the way Humbert had envisioned represents one final insult to Humbert's desired self-image as the artist in control. But there is more to Humbert's comment than that. For although it is unlikely that Quilty actually "staged" the "play" Humbert feels himself to be in, Quilty's collaborator, Vivian Darkbloom, does survive him, and goes on to write a biography called *My Cue*. Since Vivian Darkbloom is an anagram for Vladimir Nabokov, it would not be unprecedented in Nabokov's work to have one of his characters sensing the presence or agency of his creator onsite or behind the scenes. [31]

Adding to the notion that Humbert's status as character is being underlined here is the fact that despite Humbert's conviction that he is somehow being bold and rebellious by disregarding the rules of traffic, his feeble rebellion has antecedents in Russian literature too. In Dostoevsky's late story "The Dream of a Ridiculous Man" (1877) the narrator is initially taken with the thought that if were planning to kill himself, then nothing in the world should have any significance for him, including the suffering of a little girl. But because the suffering of a child *does* matter to the narrator, he realizes that there must be a flaw in his reasoning. Nabokov himself used a variant on this theme in his short novel *The Eye* (1930), where his first-person narrator also decides that if he is going to kill himself, then he can do anything he wants to beforehand, and his exercise in rebellion is just as trivial as Humbert's: he rips up a bank note and smashes his wristwatch. Humbert's gesture of defiance, then, serves to remind the reader that Humbert is, like Dostoevsky's Ridiculous Man or Nabokov's Smurov, a literary character, and a not entirely original one at that. Humbert's rebellion, such as it is, does not last for long. The police soon surround Humbert's car, and he drives off the road onto a hillside. This final action recalls in his mind the image of "two dead women" (that is, his mother and Charlotte Haze). Such evocations of death (and of his own role in at least one of these deaths) continue to haunt Humbert.

It is perhaps the hillside setting, (and perhaps together with the evocation of Charlotte's demise), that triggers within Humbert what he calls "a last mirage of wonder and hopelessness" (*L* 307). This is the famous scene that occurred, as Humbert recalls, not long after Dolly's disappearance when he parked along a mountain road above a mining town and heard "the melody of children at play" (*L* 308). In what many readers (including John Ray, Jr.) have seen as Humbert's "moral apotheosis" (*L* 5), Humbert comes to the sudden realization that "the hopelessly poignant thing was not Lolita's absence from my side, but the absence of her voice from that concord" (*L* 308). For the moment, at least, Humbert seems to move beyond his selfish obsession with possessing Dolly and acknowledge that she could have had — and should have had — a life of her own among other children her age.

As we have noted earlier, not everyone accepts the notion of an enlightened Humbert. David Rampton speculates: "Humbert's regret for Lolita's loss of her childhood is a threnody for time passing, including the loss of his own childhood, not a confrontation with his guilt. She was hardly a child when she met him, and he took from her, not playtime with friends [...] but the possibility of normal adult experience."[32] Kellie Dawson skeptically wonders "whether, had he been close enough to see (not just hear) the children, he might not have scanned them for the nymphet in their midst."[33] And Brian Boyd points out that Humbert's epiphany only comes to him now because he has *lost* Dolly; his innate selfishness and self-absorption continue to manifest themselves in his desire to avenge that loss by killing the man Dolly went off with.[34] Is Humbert's placement of this scene (which occurred long before the Quilty murder scene) merely a calculated attempt on his part to distract the reader from the gruesome reality of that murder?

Or is this entire quandary another example of the fundamental complexity which Nabokov has instilled into his portrait of Humbert? While Humbert is ready to acknowledge his guilt before Dolly (and would sentence himself to at least thirty-five years in prison for rape), he does not feel any guilt for the murder of Quilty. Clearly, Humbert's epiphany on the hillside overlooking the mining town did not transform the man entirely, and perhaps, Humbert remains a richer literary character for that very fact.[35] He himself seems to acknowledge this when he writes: "This, then, is my story [...] It has bits of marrow sticking to it, and blood, and beautiful bright-green flies" (*L* 308). This sentence contains a telling mix of violence and beauty. It may be that Humbert has recognized the extent of the devastation he had brought to Dolly's life, but he has not (and cannot?) eradicated the corrosive forces that led to the taking of Quilty's life.

Humbert's evocation of Dolly's absence from the concord of children at the end of his narrative serves to remind the reader of the crime that was most consistently before the reader earlier in the novel — Humbert's mistreatment of Dolly. Perhaps as the scene overlooking the valley suggests, he has recognized the nature of the injury he has done to her, and now, at the end of his narrative, he indicates some desire to make amends. He cannot repair the damage he has done to her life, but perhaps he can transform the pain and loss into something of transcendent value — a timeless work of art. To do so, of course, Humbert must extend the same kind of understanding he has arrived at in regard to his feelings for Dolly to his notion of the rights and responsibilities of the artist. For too long he had failed to see and appreciate Dolly Haze for what she was — a young girl trying to make her way in life much like the other children she knew at school. What is more, he had compounded that failure by choosing to regard his vision as essentially artistic, not realizing that authentic artists do not treat those around them as figures to be manipulated according to their egocentric artistic designs. What he may now have learned is that the real Dolly has a charm, a beauty, and an appeal all her own, and that from the point of view of the artist, such "reality" can be a marvelous springboard for artistic transformation. Artists must not impose their personal visions *onto* human experience, but they can draw upon that experience as the basis for the creation of new, original, and wholly autonomous works of art.

Humbert's last words seem to communicate both an appreciation of how the real Dolly Schiller has chosen to live her life and an appreciation of the transcendent potential of art. At the same time, his words also indicate that he has not been totally transformed (or reformed) by his experience, and that he retains some of the roughness and crudity that has percolated to the surface of his story throughout his memoir. Although he has stipulated that the memoir cannot be published during Dolly's lifetime because he does not want to subject her to public display, he mentally addresses her in Alaska: "Be true to your Dick. Do not let other fellows touch you. Do not talk to strangers. I hope you will love your baby. I hope it will be a boy" (*L* 309).

This sequence of simple sentences goes through a remarkable set of transitions. The first utterance — "Be true to your Dick" — comes across as a tasteless joke; Humbert cannot resist making one more vulgar pun. Buth then he expresses concern for Dolly's well-being, urging her not to let other men interfere with her. In the injunction, "Do not talk to strangers," one catches an echo of the reference work on the theater that Humbert had consulted in the prison library, where the entry under Dolores Quine noted that she had been in a play entitled *Never Talk to Strangers* (*L* 32). It is also an echo of the advice Humbert had given Dolly at the Enchanted Hunters Hotel just before she had gone to the lobby to be ogled at by Clare Quilty (see page 138). This complex set of echoes may allude to Dolly's sojourn with Quilty, which continues to rankle Humbert to this moment. Finally, however, Humbert settles on a more positive note. He tells Dolly not only that he hopes she will love her baby, but that he hopes it will be a boy. This is a crucial disclosure, because when Humbert had previously reflected upon the idea of Dolly having children, he had fantasized that she might have daughters, who would then become new prey for his own lecherous attention. Humbert may be signaling here that he is trying to overcome his wretched predilections.

In the last lines of the text one finds a palpable change of tone. Humbert momentarily switches to the third person when referring to himself, and he uses initials rather than full names: "And do not pity C. Q. One had to choose between him and H. H., and one wanted H. H. to exist at least a couple of months longer, so as to have him make you live in the minds of later generations" (*L* 309). This shift in the form of address has led some commentators to assert that the speaking voice has now shifted from Humbert to Nabokov himself, and that the final sentence, which begins "I am thinking of aurochs and angels," now belongs to Nabokov himself.[36] One could counter this proposition, however, by pointing out that on the previous page, the narrating Humbert had used the both the first-person and the third-person points of view *in the same sentence*: "Had I come before myself, I would have given Humbert at least thirty-five years for rape, and dismissed the rest of the charges" (*L* 308). Nabokov was given the opportunity to address this issue when Alfred Appel, Jr. asked him whether one is supposed to hear "a different voice" when the narrator begins "And do not pity C. Q." Nabokov replied: "No, I did not mean to introduce a different voice. I did want, however, to convey a constriction of the narrator's sick heart, a warning spasm causing him to abridge names and hasten to conclude his tale before it was too late" (*SO* 73).

With the final two sentences of his memoir, Humbert lays out his most radiant and hopeful vision for the fate of his work. Speaking of his desire to have Dolly live "in the minds of later generations, Humbert explains: 'I am thinking of aurochs and angels, the secret of durable pigments, prophetic sonnets, the refuge of art. And this is the only immortality you and I may share, my Lolita'" (*L* 309). Humbert's choice of imagery in his penultimate sentence provides an exquisite summary of the kind of art that aspires to transcend the moment. The phrase "aurochs and angels" is not only wonderfully euphonic, it links the creatures depicted in ancient cave drawings with those depicted in a myriad of religious paintings throughout the ages. Humbert is not only thinking of their longevity ("the secret of durable pigments"), but also of their status as emblems of their makers' belief in something larger or greater than themselves. Such art as Humbert envisions here is not created merely for an idle spectator's aesthetic enjoyment. Rather, it has deeply spiritual qualities that can uplift and inspire.

Humbert's very last sentence contains a distinctive combination of ardent hope of reunion with Dolly and a somber recognition of the impossibility of that hope. As he acknowledges, it is only in the "refuge of *art*" that he and Dolly may share immortality. If there is a heaven and a hell, then Humbert is sure that he will not be going to the same destination as Dolly. I think that these final lines convey the full range of Humbert's remorse, regret, and love in all their complexity and richness.

Notes

1. Alexander Pushkin, *The Captain's Daughter and Other Stories*, trans. T. Keane (New York: Vintage, 1936), 143, 144.
2. Martin Amis, "*Lolita* Reconsidered," *Atlantic* (September 1992): 109.
3. Dieter E. Zimmer, *A Guide to Nabokov's Butterflies and Moths 2001* (Hamburg: 2001), 211.
4. Fyodor Dostoevsky, *Crime and Punishment*, trans. Richard Pevear and Larissa Volokhonsky (New York: Vintage, 1993), 479–80.
5. We might further note that although Humbert faults Charlotte for her use of French, he himself resorts to French frequently. Indeed, right after mocking Charlotte for trying to get Dolly to be more modest when tying her shoes ("*ne montrez pas vos zhambes*"), Humbert refers to himself as a "poet *à mes heures*" (*L* 44). Perhaps his grammar is better than hers (he is a native speaker of French, after all), but the effect on the reader is not dissimilar: it comes across as rather pretentious at times. For a discussion of the use of French in the novel, see Brian T. Quinn, "The Occurrence of French Idiomatic Phrases in Nabokov's *Lolita*," *Eigo to Eibungaku. Studies in English Language and Literature* 39 (1989): 85–100.
6. See, for example, Alfred Appel, Jr.'s comments in *The Annotated Lolita* (*AnL* 345–47).
7. In his detailed commentary on all the names in the class list, Gavriel Shapiro points out that Nabokov further emphasized the boy's Jewishness by changing his name to "Fleishman, Moisei." See Shapiro, "*Lolita* Class List," *Cahiers du Monde russe*, 37.3 (1996): 323.
8. Sarah Herbold, "'(I have camouflaged everything, my love)': *Lolita* and the Woman Reader," *Nabokov Studies* 5 (1998/1999): 83.
9. Fyodor Dostoevsky, "White Nights," trans. David Magarshack, in *Great Short Works of Fyodor Dostoevsky* (New York: Harper and Row, 1968), 148.
10. See Vladimir Alexandrov, *Nabokov's Otherworld* (Princeton: Princeton University Press, 1991), 179–81.
11. For a brief discussion of the *rusalka* theme in *Lolita*, see Julian Connolly, "Why are Nymphets 'Demonic'?: Remarks on the Cultural Roots of Nabokov's *Lolita*," in *The Real Life of Pierre Delalande: Studies in Russian and Comparative Literature to Honor Alexander Dolinin*, ed. David M. Bethea, Lazar Fleishman, and Alexander Ospovat (Stanford: Department of Slavic Languages and Literatures, 2007), 2:674–86.
12. A similar ignorance on Humbert's part occurs during his description of his cross-country trip with Dolly: he mistakes moths for "creeping white flies" (*L* 156) at one point, and for "hummingbirds" at another (*L* 157). As Alfred Appel, Jr. notes, it would be up to his creator, Nabokov, to point out Humbert's errors (*AnL* 390).

13. Perhaps the most famous association of swine and the demonic, however, is in the Gospel of Luke, where demons cast out by Jesus went into a herd of swine which then leapt off a cliff into the water (see Luke 8.27–32). This passage plays a prominent role in Dostoevsky's *The Devils*.

14. The 1947 film *Gentleman's Agreement* focuses on this very atmosphere.

15. Dostoevsky, *The Double*, trans. George Bird, *Great Short Works of Fyodor Dostoevsky*, 40.

16. For an excellent discussion of the cultural prejudices and preconceptions Humbert brings to America, see John Haegert, "Artist in Exile: The Americanization of Humbert Humbert," *English Literary History* 52.3 (1985): 777–94.

17. And yet, such things do happen. The *Washington Post* ran a story in 1995 about a man who fathered two children with his *granddaughter*, who was eleven years old when the man began having sex with her. See "Man Who Fathered Great-Grandkids Gets 5-Year Term," *Washington Post*, 30 November 1995, sec. A, p. 17.

18. Humbert does not seem to notice, but in his formulation of what attracted Dolly to the film musical — a "grief-proof sphere of existence wherefrom death and truth were banned" — sounds remarkably similar to his fantasy of an "intangible island of entranced time" where his nymphets dwell, impervious to the outside world (see *L* 16–17).

19. See Alexander Dolinin, "Nabokov's Time Doubling: From *The Gift* to *Lolita*," *Nabokov Studies* 2 (1995): 33–35.

20. See Book Five, Chapter Four of Dostoevsky's *The Brothers Karamazov*.

21. Alexandrov, *Nabokov's Otherworld*, 183.

22. Leland de la Durantaye, *Style is Matter: The Moral Art of Vladimir Nabokov* (Ithaca: Cornell University Press, 2007), 62–63.

23. Andrew Field, for example, labels Quilty "Humbert's perverse *alter ego*." Field, *Nabokov: His Life in Art* (Boston: Little, Brown and Co., 1967), 342. Thomas R. Frosch calls Quilty "the double." Frosch, "Parody and Authenticity in *Lolita*," in *Nabokov's Fifth Arc: Nabokov and Others on His Life's Work*, ed. J. E. Rivers and Charles Nicol (Austin: University of Texas Press, 1982), 178.

24. Dana Brand declares that "Quilty is the monster, the debased image of Humbert himself." Brand, "The Interaction of Aestheticism and American Consumer Culture in Nabokov's *Lolita*," *Modern Language Studies* 17.2 (1987): 20.

25. Richard H. Bullock, "Humbert the Character, Humbert the Writer: Artifice, Reality, and Art in *Lolita*," *Philological Quarterly* 63.2 (1984), 197, 199.

26. Robert T. Levine, "'My Ultraviolet Darling': The Loss of Lolita's Childhood," *Modern Fiction Studies* 25.2 (1979): 473.

27. H. Grabes, *Fictitious Biographies: Vladimir Nabokov's English Novels* (The Hague: Mouton, 1977), 43.

28. Charles Mitchell, "Mythic Seriousness in *Lolita*," *Texas Studies in Literature and Language* 5.4 (1964): 341. David Rampton offers a similar analysis: "Trying to find and kill Quilty means trying to make a sinister 'second self' responsible for

what has happened, to isolate evil in a fundamentally narcissistic and unreal way." Rampton, *Vladimir Nabokov: A Critical Study of the Novels* (Cambridge: Cambridge University Press, 1984), 119.

29. Lucy Maddox comments about Humbert's attempts at expiation or release through murder: "The expiatory release that Humbert had anticipated may be achieved through the artistic restaging of the murder in the metaphors of the commentary [...] but for Humbert the actual killing of the real person is ugly, muddled, and untransfigurable"; see Maddox, *Nabokov's Novels in English* (Athens: The University of Georgia Press, 1983), 71.

30. See Alfred Appel, Jr.'s essay "*Lolita*: The Springboard of Parody," *Wisconsin Studies in Contemporary Literature* 8.2 (1967). There he writes that Quilty "is at once a projection of Humbert's guilt and a parody of the psychological double" and "By making Quilty too clearly guilty, Nabokov is assaulting the convention of good and evil 'dual selves' found in the traditional Double tale" (229).

31. See, for example Franz's discomfort at meeting a Nabokov surrogate in the form of an exotic foreigner with a butterfly net in *King, Queen, Knave*. The most distinctive example of this is the contact of the mind of the authorial surrogate and his creation Adam Krug at the end of *Bend Sinister*.

32. David Rampton, *Vladimir Nabokov* (New York: St. Martin's Press, 1993), 99.

33. Kellie Dawson, "Rare and Unfamiliar Things: Vladimir Nabokov's 'Monsters'," *Nabokov Studies* 9 (2005): 129.

34. See Brian Boyd, *Vladimir Nabokov: The American Years* (Princeton: Princeton University Press, 1991), 254.

35. It is eminently worth noting that Nabokov based his description of this scene on an important moment in his own life. It was on just such a hillside above Telluride, Colorado in July 1951 that Nabokov found the first female specimen of the butterfly *Lycaeides argyrognomon* (now *idas*) *sublivens* that he had been desperate to find for some time. He wrote about this event to several people, and in a letter to Edmund Wilson he describes the sounds from the town below: "all you hear are the voices of children playing in the streets — delightful!" (*NWL* 294). One wonders whether he would have conferred such a meaningful experience onto Humbert if he did not want the reader to view it as something unique and important, and not just another exercise in cynicism or deceit. For Nabokov's account of his lepidopteral explorations, see *Nabokov's Butterflies*, ed. Brian Boyd and Robert Michael Pyle (Boston: Beacon Press, 2000), 476–82.

36. See, for example, Sarah Herbold, "'(I have camouflaged everything, my love)': *Lolita* and the Woman Reader," 76; and Maurice Couturier, "Narcissism and Demand in *Lolita*," *Nabokov Studies* 9 (2005): 43.

Chapter Six

LOLITA'S AFTERLIFE:
CRITICAL AND CULTURAL RESPONSES

CRITICAL RECEPTION

With the early debates over whether *Lolita* should even be published now a distant memory, the novel has attained near canonical status in the literary world. In 1998, the board of Random House's Modern Library division ranked *Lolita* fourth on the list of the top 100 novels of the twentieth century (James Joyce's *Ulysses*, which Nabokov himself had pronounced the greatest masterpiece of the twentieth century [*SO* 57], was ranked number one). *Lolita*'s importance has found reflection in scholarly criticism as well. In 2008 Zoran Kuzmanovich reported that of the more than 2500 scholarly pieces written about Nabokov, approximately one-fifth were devoted to *Lolita*.[1] In the following sections, we will briefly examine both the immediate critical reaction to the novel and the evolution of criticism among literary scholars over the past five decades since *Lolita*'s initial publication.

Contemporary Reviews

From *Lolita*'s first appearance in the light green covers of the Olympia Press edition in 1955, readers have been wrestling with the question of how to react to the text: Shock? Delight? Outrage? Joy? The early exchange of opinions began with much heat and little light. To Graham Greene's unadorned nomination of the novel as one the best books of 1955, John Gordon responded with outrage: "Sheer unrestrained pornography," he declared, and the debate was on. The controversy slowly spread to the United States, where, in the first American review, John Hollander wrote: "There is no clinical, sociological, or mythic seriousness about *Lolita*, but it flames with a tremendous perversity of an unexpected kind."[2] Noting that the word "nympholepsy" was "a common word for a commonly cultivated state," Hollander surmises that Nabokov wanted to "literalize the word's metaphor," and to write of a class of "real" nymphets who could inspire their admirers to produce "romantic writing." Thus, Hollander concludes, "*Lolita*, if it is anything *'really,'* is the record of Mr. Nabokov's love affair with the romantic novel." It is also, Hollander asserts, "just about the funniest book I remember having read."[3] Hollander's 1956 review established one prominent early approach to dealing with *Lolita*, underscoring its status as a work of words, a verbal performance.

The first extended excerpts from *Lolita* to appear in the United States came out in *The Anchor Review* in 1957. F. W. Dupee's preface to the excerpts seemed designed to help pave the way for the publication of the full novel the following year. He summarized the plot and then sought to convey the essence of Nabokov's vision. The essay begins with an endorsement of Hollander's image of the novel as flaming with "a tremendous perversity of an unexpected kind," but Dupee goes beyond Hollander to assert the novel's "seriousness" and he dwells on the "human" dimensions of the novel.[4] In the elements of mistrust, hostility, and lack of communication between Humbert and Dolly, Dupee sees a "monstrous picture" of a "desperately common experience."[5] Although he confesses that he is not entirely persuaded by Humbert's "belated love cries" for Dolly, he concludes that the novel is "partly a masterpiece of grotesque comedy" and partly "a wilderness where the wolf howls — a real wolf and a real Red Riding Hood."[6] Dupee's essay registers both the comedy and the pain evoked in the novel. In another review published in 1957, Howard Nemerov discussed both the humor in the novel and its moral message. Following Hollander's declaration that *Lolita* was "just about the funniest book I remember having read," Howard Nemerov wrote that *Lolita* "may well be the funniest tragedy since *Hekuba*."[7] Tackling the ever-important issue of the novel's morality, Nemerov asserts that *Lolita* is indeed a moral work, for "if Humbert Humbert is a wicked man, and he is, he gets punished for it in the end. Also in the middle. And at the beginning."[8]

As the novel approached its release date in the United States of August 18, 1958, newspapers and journals began to publish commentary on the novel. Brian Boyd notes that a dozen reviews came out just before the novel appeared, and roughly two-thirds of these were enthusiastic, while one-third were "puzzled, taxed, peeved, irked, or outraged."[9] The early reviews continued to highlight the comic aspects of the novel. Charles

Rolo exulted that the *Lolita* seemed to be "an assertion of the power of the comic spirit to wrest delight and truth from the most outlandish materials. It is one of the funniest serious novels I have read."[10] Granville Hicks voiced a similar opinion, writing that *Lolita* "is in large part an extremely funny book."[11] But there were a few dissenting voices. Orville Prescott, in a review in the *New York Times* that came out on the day *Lolita* was released, called the book "dull, dull, dull in a pretentious, florid and archly fatuous fashion" and declared that "Mr. Nabokov fails to be funny."[12] Predictably, perhaps, the *Catholic World* took a similar view: "The aura of evil, the implications of a decadence universally accepted and shared — this is a romp which does not amuse."[13] Elizabeth Janeway, writing in the *New York Times Book Review* the day before Prescott, adopted an intermediate position. Speaking of the excerpts published in the *Anchor Review*, Janeway states: "The first time I read Lolita I thought it was one of the funniest books I'd ever come on [...] The second time I read it, uncut, I thought it was one of the saddest."[14]

These reviewers also addressed the issue of the novel's morality. While Prescott declared that the novel is "disgusting" and "highbrow pornography,"[15] Janeway found the opposite to be true: "As for its pornographic content, I can think of few volumes more likely to quench the flames of lust than this exact and immediate description of its consequences."[16] Dorothy Parker agreed: "I do not think that *Lolita* is a filthy book. I cannot regard it as pornography, either sheer, unrestrained, or any other kind. It is the engrossing, anguished story of a man, a man of taste and culture, who can love only little girls."[17] To a certain degree, the evaluation of *Lolita* in the early reviews rested in part on how the reviewer evaluated the subject of child abuse in the novel. Those who saw this as the most prominent element in the novel tended to offer a negative opinion of the work. Those who foregrounded the style, the humor, and the satirical elements (while downplaying the sexual elements) tended to be more positive. Todd Bayma and Gary Alan Fine have argued that the prevalence of a stereotype of the "bad girl" in American society in the 1950s "provided reviewers with a tool for making sense of their mixed attitudes toward Humbert, with Lolita's assumed immoral character explaining and (in part) excusing the narrator's offenses."[18] The broad issue of the readers' identification with Humbert and their attitudes toward Dolly would play a significant role as the debate about *Lolita* shifted from the popular press to the scholarly journal.

Lolita *in Criticism*

Over time, *Lolita* has been subject to a shifting array of critical approaches. Broadly speaking, an early focus on the romantic element in the novel gave way to an exploration of Nabokov's predilection for creating games, puzzles, and patterns in his work. That in turn was followed by a re-centering of attention on the novel's ethical implications, and this, in turn, has been succeeded by a wide-ranging discussion of the politics of literary representation. The following discussion is a brief attempt to take note of some of the more distinctive mileposts on a long and winding critical journey.

Lolita *as Love Story and Quest*

Lionel Trilling published an essay in *Encounter* in October 1958 that had a significant impact on subsequent discussions of *Lolita*. He begins by acknowledging that *Lolita* is a shocking book but that it is not porno-graphic, and one of his aims in the essay is to explain the precise nature of the shock that the novel triggers in the reader. His essay is one of the earliest to address the issue of reader identification and the way that Humbert's discourse affects the reader. He confesses that in recounting the plot of the novel he was "not able to muster up the note of moral outrage" that might be expected in such a situation. Although Humbert is "perfectly willing to say that he is a monster," and "no doubt he is," but "we find ourselves less and less eager to say so." As Trilling continues, it becomes clear that he has largely accepted Humbert's viewpoint on events: Humbert, he says, is dealing with "a Lolita who is not innocent" and we "naturally incline to be lenient towards a rapist [...] who eventually feels a deathless devotion to his victim!" Trilling acknowledges, however, that when we pull away from the text and think about this situation happening to twelve-year-olds in real life, we again feel outrage, and that we feel this all the more "because we have been seduced into conniving in the violation, because we have permitted our fantasies to accept what we know to be revolting."[19] Trilling's outline presents a clear model of what happens when one identifies too closely with Humbert's perspective, even to the point of underestimating the extent of the damage done to Dolly Haze.

Trilling goes on to argue that Nabokov's ultimate aim in *Lolita* is to revive the love story in western literature. In his view, Humbert's obsession represents a modern incarnation of the "passion-love" that appeared in European literature that once flourished in European literature but has disappeared in modern times. Those who experienced this kind of love were sick, and their passions put them beyond the pale of societal convention. Their love was scandalous. How, Trilling wonders, can one depict this type of love in modern society, when adultery no longer has the power to shock or be scandalous? His conclusion is itself startling: "a man in the grip of an obsessional lust and a girl of twelve make the ideal couple for a story about love written in our time."[20] Trilling has come up with an intriguing premise, but his argument displays one glaring flaw. He seems to assume that Humbert and Dolly are in fact real "lovers," like the famous couples of the past. The fact is, however, that Dolly did not "love" Humbert as Anna Karenina did Vronsky, and that Humbert's sexual abuse of Dolly remains just that, no matter how poetically he himself wishes to dress it up.

Denis de Rougemont also explored the scandalous aspect of the Humbert–Dolly relationship, and he, like Trilling, saw in it shades of the myth of Tristan and Isolde. But he moves beyond Trilling and acknowledges that a "touch of irony" accompanies the allusion to the Tristan legend.[21] The reason for this, he points out, is that Humbert and Dolly have never known what he calls "unhappy reciprocal love": "Lolita has never responded to the fierce and tender passion of her elder lover." The result of this imbalance, de Rougement claims, is the reduction of the novel "to the dimension of a genre-study of mores in the matter of Hogarth." Unlike Trilling, he states that as readers, we "laugh often," but "are never moved."[22]

Nevertheless, the image of Humbert as a man on a quest for an unattainable ideal held sway in much of the criticism of the 1960s. Thus, Charles Mitchell writes about Humbert's experience in terms of "the quest myth,"[23] and G. D. Josipovici states that "Humbert's desire for nymphets [...] was never that of a sex maniac. It was the manifestation of a desire for unpossessable beauty, for that which is beautiful precisely because it is unpossessable."[24] Josipovici's formulation, however, seems to overlook the fact that Humbert's desire for "beauty" was first and foremost a *sexual* longing, grounded in the body of a prepubescent girl, and not for something more remote or abstract.

A slightly different take on the quest theme, but one that was striking enough to draw Nabokov's attention, was Diana Butler's article, "Lolita Lepidoptera," in which she draws an analogy between Humbert's pursuit of Dolly and the lepidopterist's quest to capture butterflies. Although the article contains some useful observations, it also exhibits a significant degree of overreaching, as for example, in Butler's comment that "Lolita's eyes are wide-spaced and poor-sighted, like a butterfly's."[25] More unsettling, however, is Butler's interpretation of the emotional shift that occurs in Humbert's memoir as he moves from the "moment of ecstasy on the tennis court" to the specter of death raised by Dolly's illness in Elphinstone. Butler speculates that this emotional shift "recreates, perhaps, Nabokov's guilt at attaining ecstasy by the capture of a rare butterfly, and then being forced to kill his specimen."[26] It is therefore no surprise that Nabokov took a dim view of the article, writing to Page Stegner that it is "pretentious nonsense from beginning to end" (*SL* 393).[27]

The Art of the Novel

After the publication of *Pale Fire* in 1962, Nabokov's readers began to pay increasing attention to the writer's penchant for constructing worlds of artifice in which puzzles, patterns, and enigmatic allusions played a prominent role. The title of Page Stegner's book — *Escape into Aesthetics: The Art of Vladimir Nabokov* (1966) — is very telling in this respect. Stegner gave his chapter on *Lolita* a revealing subtitle as well: "A Palliative of Articulate Art." Commenting on the novel's word play, its allusiveness, and its parodic content, Stegner dwells on the ways in which Humbert's narrative evokes the reader's sympathy and pity for the narrator. He is somewhat less interested in Dolly ("Lolita is in reality a rather common, unwashed little girl whose interests are entirely plebeian, though, in certain respects, precocious"[28]). Perhaps privileging technique over content, Stegner asserts: "The immortality of *Lolita*, Humbert the artist's immortality, exists in the telling, in the farce and the anguish of his narrative, and not in the bizarre facts of the story told. It is the telling that matters."[29] One might modify this assertion, however, by pointing out that the sensitive reader will note how much space Humbert devotes to his feelings and sensations, and how little he tells us about Dolly. Humbert's treatment of these "facts" is itself a crucial feature of "the telling."

Alfred Appel, Jr. made several important contributions to this line of Nabokov criticism in the mid-1960s. Most important for *Lolita* was his "*Lolita*: The Springboard of Parody," which appeared in *Wisconsin Studies in Contemporary Literature* in 1967 and was subsequently incorporated into his extensive preface to *The Annotated Lolita*. His article makes the bold assertion that *"parody* is the 'keyword' in *Lolita*, and it provide a key to all of Nabokov."[30] Appel's central point about parody is that "by definition, parody and self-parody suspend the possibility of a fully 'realistic' fiction, since their referents are either other literary works or themselves, and not the world of objective reality which the 'realist' or 'impressionist' tries to reproduce."[31] On the other hand, although he concentrates on parody, Appel is not oblivious to the presence of pathos, and he finds that in *Lolita* and *Pale Fire* alike, "the parody and the pathos are always congruent."[32] What is more, Appel asserts, Nabokov uses the grotesque to "express the anguish behind Humbert's rhetoric, the pain at the center of his playfulness."[33] Like Stegner, Appel tends to focus on Humbert ("Humbert is both victimizer and victim"), and as a result, he tends to overlook Dolly or view her as a stereotypical figure: she "affords Nabokov an ideal opportunity to comment on the Teen and Sub-Teen Tyranny."[34] Nonetheless, the article contains a wealth of useful observations about the novel and its relationship to other texts, and Appel would supplement these observations with the highly informative notes he prepared for *The Annotated Lolita*, which came out in 1970.

Complementing Appel's annotated version of the novel is Carl Proffer's book, *Keys to Lolita* (1968), which contains chapters on literary allusion, the subtle markers of Quilty's presence in Humbert's narrative, and the novel's stylistic features (including sound play, rhythm, metaphors, etc.). As Proffer himself acknowledged in his foreword, he did not concern himself "with the character of the hero or the heroine, the meaning or morality of the novel," but instead set out to offer "keys to some of the technical puzzles [...] an introduction to the realms hidden in Nabokov's secretly sliding panels and double-bottomed drawers."[35]

Picking up the theme of parody but approaching it from a different angle was Thomas Frosch, whose article "Parody and Authenticity in *Lolita*" (1982) revised John Hollander's declaration in 1956 that *Lolita* is the record of Nabokov's love affair with the romantic novel. Frosch argues that Nabokov deployed parody to undermine or lay to rest the traditional romantic novel in order to give it new life in contemporary fiction. As he puts it, "parody is Nabokov's way of getting as close to the romantic novel as possible and, more, that he actually does succeed in creating it in a new form, one that is contemporary and original, not anachronistic and imitative."[36] *Lolita*, Frosch argues, can only be a love story "through being a parody of love stories."[37]

In his 1966 article, "The Morality of *Lolita*," Martin Green took an original approach to the issue of the novel's "gamesmanship" by contrasting the principles of Nabokov's art to those that Leo Tolstoy articulated in his tract *What is Art?* (1897–98). Whereas Tolstoy prized sincerity in art and privileged works promoting a feeling for the brotherhood of man, Nabokov was "a man of tricks" whose work "flies in face of all ordinary usable morality."[38] In Green's view, Nabokov was striving to move away from the romantic and the idyllic associated with Europe and toward a realism that incorporates ugliness and pain as well as beauty and pleasure. Thus, if we read *Lolita* according to Tolstoy's principles, we would have to condemn it. But, if we give it a "perfect reading" and understand it "from the inside," we find the novel to be "a brilliant and beautiful experience, satisfying our most purely moral sense as well as all the others."[39]

Julia Bader's 1972 monograph, *Crystal Land: Artifice in Nabokov's English Novels*, pursued the premise that Nabokov's novels are primarily concerned with "the artistic imagination and consciousness."[40] In her chapter on *Lolita*, Bader treats the characters depicted in Humbert's narrative as his creations. Thus, the disembodied voice of Clare Quilty at the Enchanted Hunters Hotel represents a "still uncreated Quilty." It is not until Humbert decides to kill Quilty "that the playwright actually begins to 'exist.'"[41] Bader points out that unlike the other characters in the narrative, Dolly is described in minute detail, but Humbert does not realize until it is too late "that he has given her no soul."[42] One could dispute this formulation, however, and argue that the problem is not that Humbert has "given" Dolly no soul (it is not his to give, after all), but that he has failed to notice or appreciate that soul. Bader's focus on the aesthetic dimension of the novel leads her to pronounce that the "questions tackled by *Lolita* are artistic, or aesthetic, and the 'moral' dilemma is treated in aesthetic terms." Using this criterion, Bader finds that the "grossest violation" is Quilty's for he is a commercial artist, and his crime "is so monstrous that it merits the greatest punishment in a novel about artistic creation: he is left deliberately half-created."[43] That would certainly seem to be Humbert's judgment, but is it the reader's?

The problems inherent in identifying too closely with Humbert's artistic strivings is perhaps best illustrated by Douglas Fowler's chapter on *Lolita* in his book *Reading Lolita* (1974). Regarding Humbert as Nabokov's "favorite," Fowler declares that Nabokov "shifts moral responsibility" away from Humbert first by killing Charlotte for him and then by having Dolly, whose "sexual corruption" predated Humbert, seduce him.[44] What is more, according to Fowler, Humbert "goes to enormous lengths" to try to make Dolly happy.[45] Dolly herself is characterized as "meretricious and far less vulnerable than Humbert," and when Humbert has his epiphany about the absence of Dolly's voice from the concord of children's voices, Fowler declares that he is demonstrating "a moral sensitivity completely beyond" Dolly's capabilities; she is left busy "incubating a philistine fetus in her stretched belly."[46] Humbert's ultimate crime, then, is "a crime against his own ethical sense rather than against Lolita, for she is quite as indifferent to the injury he supposes he has done her as she is indifferent to his love of her. In this instance, 'crime' is a wholly subjective affair, existing only in the mind of the criminal."[47] Due to his persistent focus on Humbert's internal world, Fowler seems to make the same error that Humbert made: he fails to perceive the value of Dolly Haze's simple humanity.

Perhaps the strongest statement of the primacy of the game element in Nabokov's art is Mark Lilly's essay, "Nabokov: Homo Ludens," first published in 1979. Lilly opens his essay with the declaration: "Nabokov's work is a joke,"[48] and although he does not linger on *Lolita*, he makes an intriguing claim about the spirit of ambiguity readers have detected while reading the work. In this novel, he states, we find "an incongruity between the immorality of deed, and the amoral way in which it is narrated." As he sees it, the purpose of this incongruity "is not to replace one form of morality with a new one, but to direct us away from morality altogether, and toward the specially enchanted world where the logic and delight of games replaces everyday reality."[49] A few years later, David Packman further highlighted the prominence of the game element in *Lolita*. In his 1982 monograph, *Vladimir Nabokov: The Structure of Literary Desire*, Packman argued that *Lolita* is a "polyvalent text" that operates in terms of literature itself, "so that the realistic elements in the novel are actually false leads or snares," much like the "cryptogrammic paper chase" that confronted Humbert after Dolly's disappearance.[50] Packman finds that all the texts in the novel, and Nabokov's own text, refer to other texts, and these in turn refer to still other texts, so that the hope to discover "some final signified" can never be realized. Such an approach, of course, tends to undervalue the possible connections the novel might have to the real world, and Dolly Haze once more becomes something of an abstraction, not a representation of a recognizably human being. Packman also investigates the way in which Nabokov's text illustrates the dynamics of literary desire. In his view, the desire displayed by Humbert for Dolly mirrors the operations of the reader's desire for the narrative itself. Thus, the "desire represented in the text and the reader's desire for the text double each other."[51]

The culmination of this line of criticism may be Trevor McNeely's 1989 article, "'Lo' and Behold: Solving the *Lolita* Riddle." McNeely's basic premise is that Nabokov's ultimate aim in *Lolita* is to get revenge on the whole industry of literary criticism, "the Freudians, the New Critics, the Existentialists, the Structuralists, and all their bastard progeny."[52] While all these critics have been busy looking for the novel's "real theme," the only meaning the novel has to Nabokov, according to McNeely, "is as an exhibition of his own verbal skill, his linguistic and literary sophistication, nothing more."[53] McNeely argues that Nabokov's novel is carefully designed to trap both those critics who celebrate the aesthetic virtues of the novel and those who dwell on the humanity of the characters. The incidents of child abuse depicted in the novel work to undermine the arguments of the former group, while the latter group fail to recognize that both Dolly and Humbert are "deliberately created absurd in their exaggeration."[54] McNeely's radical critique lays waste not only to those critics and readers who have been enthralled by Nabokov's novel for decades but also to Nabokov himself, as it seems to dismiss the writer's very description of art as something containing the qualities of "curiosity, tenderness, kindness, ecstasy" (*L* 315). As we shall see below, other readers of *Lolita* have found more compelling meaning in the work.

The Ethical Turn

Indeed, one of the best treatments of the complexities of *Lolita* that takes into account both its aesthetic and its human dimensions was Ellen Pifer's 1980 monograph *Nabokov and the Novel*. Responding to the line of criticism that tended to privilege Humbert's artistic aspirations over his actual impact on those around him, Pifer took a broader view of the novel's landscape and sought to bring Dolly Haze back into the discussion by reminding readers of the genuine damage Humbert inflicted upon her. Acknowledging Humbert's artistic aspirations, Pifer drew a bright line between the freedom granted artists in their private worlds and the ethical obligations that come into play when artists deal with people around them. Pifer provides a cogent formulation of this relationship: "The power and passion of the imagination do not grant the ardent dreamer any ultimate authority over his fellow man, who has an unquestionable claim to his own dreams and desires."[55] Pifer's persuasive reorientation of critical focus onto the ethical implications of Nabokov's novel had the effect of bringing to life a prediction Nabokov had made about his own reputation in 1971: "In fact I believe that one day a reappraiser will come and declare that, far from having been a frivolous firebird, I was a rigid moralist kicking sin, cuffing stupidity, ridiculing the vulgar and cruel—and assigning sovereign power to tenderness, talent, and pride" (*SO* 193).

The ethical issues raised by Pifer now became the subject of con-centrated study in Nabokov criticism. In her article, "Humbert Humbert and the Limits of Artistic License," Gladys M. Clifton also pointed out the problems involved in accepting too readily Humbert's artistic posturings, perhaps at the expense of recognizing the pain he caused Dolly. She criticizes Douglas Fowler's denigration of Dolly's capacities for moral sensitivity, and she tries to bring forward Dolly's own perspective on her relationship with Humbert and with Quilty. She notes, for example, that in reading through the scene at the Enchanted Hunters, although "we may be invited to smile at Humbert's situation and find it comical, this is not true for Lolita, even though she is part of the same situation."[56] Clifton finds that Nabokov has achieved a finely balanced artistic creation in this novel: "Humbert's self-portrait is a fascinating combination of artistic triumph (as he intended) and moral failure (as Nabokov intended)." It is these balanced oppositions, Clifton declares, that makes *Lolita* a literary masterpiece.[57]

David Rampton's monograph *Vladimir Nabokov*, published in 1984, provides a very fine reading of *Lolita* that delves into the way the novel "subverts the judgment-making capacity" of the reader.[58] Skillfully ex-ploring the contradictions raised by the text, Rampton shows how spe-cific episodes (such as Humbert's belated recognition and sorrow for the way he treated Dolly) can be interpreted in different ways: some readers will accept Humbert's expressions of remorse as sincere, while others might remain suspicious that this is just another attempt at duping the reader. Rampton offers an especially sensitive discussion of Dolly Schiller's situation at the end of the novel. He concludes: "Nabokov, in this one scene, shows us all the poignancy of Lolita's attempt to build a future for herself in a world that was not of her making. Such a scene does not 'solve' the problem of *Lolita* [...] But it does remind us why *Lolita* matters and why we go on talking about it."[59]

Richard Rorty devoted an illuminating chapter to Nabokov in his book *Contingency, Irony, and Solidarity* in 1989. For Rorty, Nabokov holds special interest as a writer because of his concern with a distinctive form of cruelty — "incuriosity" — the failure to notice the pain and suffering of others, even if we ourselves are the cause of that suffering. While Humbert Humbert is the prime representative of incuriosity in the *Lolita*, Rorty argues that the reader too might be implicated in this failing, and he cites the episode of the Kasbeam barber who talks about a son who, Humbert is startled to realize, had died long ago. The fact that Nabokov listed this episode as one of "the nerves of the novel" (*L* 316), Rorty suggests, indicates that Nabokov may have felt that the reader too, like Humbert, would have failed to notice this untimely death and its consequences. For Rorty, then, the "moral" of the novel is "not to keep one's hands off little girls, but to notice what one is doing, and in particular to notice what people are saying. For it might turn out, it very often does turn out, that people are trying to tell you that they are *suffering*."[60]

Feminist Approaches

The fresh attention paid to the plight of Dolly Haze in *Lolita* in the 1980s received additional energy from readers who addressed the novel from a feminist perspective. In her 1989 article "Framing *Lolita*: Is There a Woman in the Text?" Linda Kauffman excoriates masculinist readings such as Lionel Trilling's and Thomas Molnar's that seemed to replicate Humbert Humbert's pattern of overlooking Dolly Haze and her suffering. As Kauffman sees it, "sophisticated readers of *Lolita*, avid to align themselves with 'aesthetic bliss,' fall into the [...] trap by ignoring the pathos of Lolita's predicament."[61] The text of the novel "elides the female by framing the narrative through Humbert's angle of vision," and it is up to the feminist critic to resist "the father's seductions" and to "expose the lack, the trap [...] by reading symptomatically" and dismantling "the misogyny of traditional critical assessments of Lolita's wantonness."[62] When one inscribes the female body in the text, one discovers that "Lolita is not a photographic image, or a still life, or a freeze frame preserved on film, but a damaged child."[63] Kauffman thus joins Pifer and Clifton in calling upon readers to bring Dolly Haze out of the shadows of Humbert's dazzlingly distracting rhetoric.

Picking up on Kauffman's criticism of readings that seem to minimize or look past the pain and trauma depicted in *Lolita*, Elizabeth Patnoe suggested in a 1995 article that Dolly was not alone in suffering such trauma, and she sought to extend the reader's awareness of abuse beyond the boundaries of the text. Writing in the journal *College Literature*, Patnoe calls on her readers — students and teachers, women and men — not to retreat from the trauma of the book, but to "confront its messages and challenges" and "address its personal and cultural implications."[64] Other feminist critics in the mid-1990s drew attention to the specific challenges Nabokov's text posed for the female reader. Colleen Kennedy, for example, warned about the dangers that feminist critics, eager to share in the power inherent in the position of being a "producer and proper reader," would accept Nabokov's emphasis on aesthetic bliss and join with him in disdaining "the culture Lolita represents."[65] In her reading, Nabokov's novel indicates that the "seduction of a twelve-year-old girl becomes the 'reality' the reader must 'overcome,' in the same way that Humbert must overcome the vulgarity of Dolly; and this training of the reader becomes the means by which Nabokov may overcome the vulgarity of the culture."[66] Virginia Blum put forth a slightly different view of the author-reader relationship, although she too draws an analogy between Humbert's dominating attitude toward Dolly and Nabokov's dominating attitude toward the reader. Blum holds that both postures reflect a consummate narcissism. Of Dolly's death while giving birth to a stillborn child, Blum writes: "There is no place for the other of reproduction in the narcissistic economy [...] There is no place for the reader when the text is its own superior reader."[67]

Responding to Blum and Kennedy in an article published at the end of the 1990s, Sarah Herbold agreed that Nabokov's text attempts to manipulate its readers, but she went on to say that *Lolita* also "covertly acknowledges its need for and indebtedness to female readers, characters, and writers."[68] The novel's "manipulativeness, sexiness, and difficulty," she writes, "are as complimentary to women as they are insulting"; through his text, Nabokov "challenges women not to remain victims and acknowledges his dependence on their considerable power."[69] After explaining the contradictions and ambiguities Humbert's narrative seems to put before female readers, Herbold argues that Nabokov encourages the female reader to read "aggressively — and playfully."[70] Such a reading yields the discovery that behind the image of Dolly as an "ill-educated and naive girl" there lurks "a sophisticated partner/antagonist," and that behind the image of Charlotte as a "dopey small-town bridge-player and pretentious book club member stands a highly sophisticated female rival/co-author of

Lolita."[71] Herbold argues that Charlotte may have worked to foil Humbert's designs on Dolly from the outset, and that in giving Charlotte her name, Nabokov established a complex allusion to Charlotte Bronte, whose novel *Jane Eyre* should be taken into account when interpreting Humbert's fate in *Lolita*. In making her arguments, however, Herbold implicitly conflates Humbert and Nabokov in ways that many critics would strongly resist.

Proliferating Perspectives

The 1990s not only saw a surge of articles addressing *Lolita* from a feminist perspective; the decade also witnessed the proliferation of a broad array of critical approaches. One significant event was the publication of Vladimir Alexandrov's monograph *Nabokov's Otherworld* in 1991. Alexandrov delved into the metaphysical dimensions of Nabokov's work, finding that the oft-discussed metaliterary element in Nabokov's fiction "is camouflage for, and a model of, the metaphysical."[72] In his chapter on *Lolita,* Alexandrov examines Humbert's episodes of clairvoyance and intermittent perspicacity, and he matches them up with his understanding of Nabokov's own metaphysical doctrines. Tracking the appearance of signs of "fate" and other elements of patterning that Humbert is not aware of, Alexandrov suggests that the character's destiny is affected by contact with the otherworld. Of particular interest is Alexandrov's assertion that Charlotte may become an "occult presence" after her death. Indeed, Alexandrov argues that Charlotte's spirit may have prompted Humbert to go to the Enchanted Hunters Hotel to set in motion Dolly's eventual escape from Humbert. Thus, "Charlotte's spirit is a constituent element of Humbert's fate."[73] While other critics have found evidence of an otherworldly theme in Nabokov's work (most notable, perhaps, is Brian Boyd's monograph on *Pale Fire*), Alexandrov's chapter offers the most extensive exploration of this theme in *Lolita*.

The mid-1990s also saw the blossoming of a debate over the very "reality" of some of the most crucial scenes in *Lolita*. Several readers, beginning with Elizabeth Bruss in 1976, and followed by Christina Tekiner in 1979 and Leona Toker in 1989, took note of a peculiar problem involving some of the calendric dates that appear in *Lolita*.[74] According to Humbert, Dolly Schiller's letter reached him on September 22 (1952), and he later states that he worked on the manuscript of his memoir for fifty-six days (see *L* 267 and *L* 308). According to the information provided by John Ray,

Jr. in his foreword, Humbert died on November 16, 1952. If John Ray is correct, and if Humbert is accurate when he says that he had been working on the manuscript for fifty-six days, then he would have had to have begun the manuscript on the very day that he received Dolly's letter and finished it on the day he died. It would therefore not have been possible for him to have traveled to Coalmont, visit with Dolly, and then move on to Pavor Manor and kill Quilty as his narrative indicates. These crucial scenes — the reunion with Dolly and the murder of Quilty — would of necessity be Humbert's creative fabrications.

Although Bruss first discovered this calendric quandary, and it was then developed by Tekiner and Toker, the most detailed examination and defense of the thesis was conducted by Alexander Dolinin in the second issue of *Nabokov Studies*.[75] In the same issue of the journal, I contributed an article exploring the question of what it means for our understanding of Humbert and of the novel if these two major scenes are merely his invention.[76] Of course, if Humbert had never seen Dolly again (and indeed, if she had died in Elphinstone as Dolinin suggests), then our view of the characters and the novel would radically change. Brian Boyd, for one, strenuously objected to this "revisionist" theory, and he provided an extended rebuttal to the theory in the same issue of *Nabokov Studies* as the Dolinin and Connolly articles.[77] In his article Boyd marshals an impressive array of arguments to refute the notion that Humbert's visit with Dolly and the murder of Quilty never occurred, including the fact that Nabokov himself was very prone to making (and not finding) errors in his work. If one changes the date of Humbert's death by one digit (November 16 to November 19), the time discrepancy disappears and Dolly Schiller and Quilty are restored to full being in the novel. Boyd's arguments are indeed persuasive, but scholars being what they are, it is likely that some will continue to pursue the revisionist design.

Rachel Bowlby took an entirely different approach to the novel in her 1993 book, *Shopping with Freud*. In a chapter entitled *"Lolita* and the Poetry of Advertising," Bowlby examines the themes of consumerism and advertising in the novel. She demonstrates that the seeming distinction that Humbert sees between the high culture of his educated European background and the low (American) culture embraced by Charlotte and Dolly is not really sustained by the narrative itself. Both Humbert and the Hazes are oriented on pre-existing stereotypes and they are all drawn to the magic of words. Ultimately, Bowlby argues, there is no separation of form between Humbert's "literary world" and Dolly's "consumerly world"; "the gap is in the incompatibility of particular wishes and dreams that make them up."[78] In fact, Bowlby asserts, the "language of consumption" seems to "take over the poetic force of the novel" even as Humbert tries to resist it; "the infiltration of high and low language goes in both directions."[79]

Bowlby's defense of Dolly's enchantment with language represents another step in the reevaluation of Dolly's personality in the 1990s. Michael Wood's magnificent study *The Magician's Doubt: Nabokov and the Risks of Fiction* (1994) also helps the reader to locate Dolly within the daunting thicket of Humbert's discourse. But Wood's chapter on *Lolita* does much more. He offers a stimulating discussion of language in the novel, and he provides pithy and thought-provoking characterizations of the main figures. Most importantly, he helps the reader negotiate a path through the ambiguities and contradictions embedded in Humbert's narrative. He provides a thoughful perspective on the question of whether Humbert has truly learned to love Dolly in a new way at the end of his narrative. Wood himself is skeptical, stating that "there is noting in his self-portrait to suggest he can rise to it," but he goes on to point out that what is "unmistakable is [Humbert's] desire to see himself, and to project himself, as supremely conscious of his grisly errors."[80] Wood continues: "We need to work through our skepticism, I think, but then we can let it go, because we can all, without question, believe in Humbert's loss, his sense of dereliction [...] We don't have to admire Humbert in order to feel his pain."[81]

In recent years critics have been bringing ever new perspectives to the study of Nabokov's *Lolita*. One productive line of inquiry examines the novel as a response to the cultural and social conditions of post-war America. Articles illustrating this line include Douglas Anderson's "Nabokov's Genocidal and Nuclear Holocaust in *Lolita* (1996), Susan Mizruchi's "*Lolita* in History" (2003), and Steven Belletto's "Of Pickaninnies and Nymphets: Race in *Lolita*" (2005).[82] Taking a very different tack, however, is Eric Naiman. His 2006 article "A Filthy Look at Shakespeare's *Lolita*" uses the tradition of Shakespearean bawdy language as a lens to analyze the language of Nabokov's novel, and he discovers numerous references to sexual organs and acts encoded in the text through puns, anagrams, and word play. Naiman asserts that for Humbert, bawdy language may be a way of "obtaining mastery over the body's essential drives, but we can also see bawdy talk as a self-perpetuating verbal prison that traps the speaker in lexical solipsism that never reaches the flesh."[83] If this be the case, then Humbert's penchant for expressing himself in eroticized language makes up just one more bar in the cage he draws as he sits in his cell and contemplates his past. In sharp contrast to the solipsism of Humbert's text, however, is the text of Nabokov's novel. As we have seen, it remains an open-ended work of art, and continues to invite new and original interpretations.

CULTURAL RESPONSES

Translation into Russian

Early in 1963, Nabokov began toying with the idea of translating his novel into Russian. He explained to an interviewer that year that when he imagined someone else tackling the project in the future, he saw that "every paragraph, pockmarked as it is with pitfalls, could lend itself to hideous mistranslation" (*SO* 38).[84] So, to rescue his creation from "vulgar paraphrases or blunders," he undertook the task himself (*SO* 38). He found the effort quite challenging. In his postscript to the Russian edition he devised a charming image for the difficulty he encountered: "Alas, that 'wondrous Russian tongue' that, it seemed to me, was waiting for me somewhere, was flowering like a faithful springtime behind a tightly locked gate, whose key I had held in safekeeping for so many years, proved to be nonexistent, and there is nothing behind the gate but charred stumps and a hopeless autumnal distance, and the key in my hand is more like a skeleton key."[85]

When the book appeared in 1967, some readers felt that the Russian language of Nabokov's translation was stilted or ungainly,[86] but others, including several of Nabokov's most sensitive readers, have argued to the contrary. Gennady Barabtarlo, for example, states that the Russian *Lolita* is "not merely an unrivaled triumph of an exceedingly sophisticated translation technique but also an ultimate masterpiece of Russian prose [...] a piece of art of the highest order and quality."[87] Alexander Dolinin concurs: "For twentieth-century Russian prose *Lolita* was a miracle of resurrection, a rebirth of its modernist panaesthetic tradition."[88] One reason why some Russian readers found the language "unnatural" is that during the Soviet era, the language itself had, as Brian Boyd put it, "undergone a steady vulgarization."[89] Thus, as Barabtarlo notes, that there are "very few Russians extant who can appreciate the opulent beauty of the thing because of the tragically rapid deterioration of the language."[90] It is the opinion of these critics that Nabokov's translation may ultimately enrich the Russian literary language with its contribution of new vocabulary, pliant syntax, and even those echoes of English idiom and constructions faulted by its critics.

As far as the relationship between the Russian version and the English version is concerned, there are many places where the original is faithfully mirrored, but there are also many places where significant emendations, clarifications, and additions appear. Often, Nabokov would add or word or two to explain a literary allusion. Thus, when Humbert referred to Dolly's piano teacher as a "Miss Emperor" (L 202) and added the remark "as we French scholars may conveniently call her," Nabokov intends his readers to make a connection between this piano teacher and the piano teacher Emma Bovary was supposed to be taking lessons from in Flaubert's *Madame Bovary*. For his Russian readers, Nabokov made the allusion more transparent, and changed "French scholars" to "connoisseurs of Flaubert" ("znatoki Flobera"). He also added a glossary of names and terms at the end of the text. In some cases, he changed the target of an allusion from an Anglo-American cultural context to a Russian one. Thus, in the series of false names left by Quilty to torment Humbert, "A. Person, Porlock, England" (L 250), which refers to the English poet Samuel Taylor Coleridge, becomes in Russian "P. O. Temkin, Odessa, Texas," a reference to the mutiny on the battleship Potemkin that took place in Odessa on the Black Sea in 1905. One of the effects of these changes is to strengthen the connection between Humbert's aesthetic world and that of the Russian Silver Age. As Dolinin points out, in dealing with the name "Carmen," the Russian version loses the simple word play of "car men," but it gains rich associations with Alexander Blok's cycle of poems on the Carmen theme.[91] Finally, Nabokov took advantage of the opportunity opened up by translating his novel into Russian both to heighten the dreamlike quality of the last portion of Humbert's memoir and to add chronological markers that help the reader locate events in time.[92] All in all, one can fairly agree with Dolinin's formulation that Nabokov's Russian *Lolita* can be considered "a *new redaction* of the novel, its second avatar in a parallel linguistic and cultural reality, rather than a bleak copy of the dazzling original."[93]

Nabokov's Screenplay, Kubrick's Film

In the summer of 1959, Nabokov was contacted by James Harris and Stanley Kubrick with an offer to write the screenplay for *Lolita* (they had acquired the film rights in 1958). Nabokov was not inclined to tamper with his novel, but he met with the two in California in July. According to Nabokov, the producers' concern about how the relationship between Humbert and Dolly would be received led them to ask Nabokov whether he might insert a scene hinting that "Humbert had been secretly married to Lolita all along" (*Lo Screen* vii). Nabokov decided that he could not undertake the job and he departed. With time, however, Nabokov began to regret his decision, and fortunately, he was offered the chance to change it; in January 1960 he received a telegram from his agent, Irving ("Swifty") Lazar, stating that Kubrick and Harris would pay him $40,000 to write the screenplay, plus an additional $35,000 if he received sole credit, plus travel and living expenses for six months.[94] Nabokov now agreed to reconsider the project.

On March 1, 1960, Nabokov met with Kubrick to discuss the screenplay. As Nabokov recalls it, they had an "amiable battle of suggestion and countersuggestion" in which Kubrick "accepted all my vital points," and Nabokov "accepted some of his less significant ones" (*Lo Screen* ix). That spring, Nabokov and his wife lived in a rented house in Mandeville Canyon and he submitted portions of his screenplay to Kubrick at regular intervals. By mid summer, he had finished the screenplay, which now totaled about 400 pages. Kubrick declared to him that the screenplay "was much too unwieldy, contained too many unnecessary episodes, and would take about seven hours to run" (*Lo Screen* x–xi). Nabokov went back to work, deleted some scenes, trimmed others, and "devis[ed] new sequences" as well. After receiving the new screenplay in September, Kubrick pronounced himself satisfied with the result, and went off to England to make the film. Nabokov never visited the set during the shooting of the film, and when he finally saw it at a private screening a few days before its New York premiere on June 13, 1962, he was surprised to see how much Kubrick has altered his work. Years later, in an effort to convey his own vision of how the work should be filmed without interference by another, he revised his script and published it as an autonomous work in 1974. In his foreword to this publication he tried to be charitable as he recalled his initial impression of the film. At that time, he recalled, he discovered that "Kubrick was a great director, that his *Lolita* was a first-rate film with magnificent actors, and that only ragged odds and ends of my script had been used [...] When adapting *Lolita* to the speaking screen he saw my novel in one way, I saw it in another — that's all." (*Lo Screen* xii–xiii). In his private diary, however, he was somewhat less gracious, and compared the experience of watching the film to "a scenic drive as perceived by the horizontal passenger of an ambulance."[95]

Nabokov faced several challenges in trying to transform his novel into a film. Most importantly, the loss of the intimate first-person narrative perspective meant that he would have to devise other means to convey the full range of emotions, the humor, and the contradictions that lie at the core of Humbert's memoir. Secondly, Nabokov was faced with the disappearance of his exquisitely crafted language, with its palpable lyricism and abundant word play. Nabokov never quite makes up for these losses, although one senses that he was perhaps loath to surrender his carefully wrought phrases, for many of the stage directions in his screenplay are direct quotations from the novel. On the other hand, the speeches of the characters are often simplified, and the most ornate turns of phrase found in the novel are stripped away. Although Nabokov retained the main plot and characters from his novel, he essentially re-imagined the work anew, and made numerous substantive changes right from the outset.

Indeed, his original screenplay opens not with John Ray Jr.'s foreword, or with Humbert's account of his childhood, but rather with the scene of Humbert's murder of Quilty. This is a dramatic change. Although the reader of the novel knows at the outset that Humbert died in jail awaiting trial, and that Humbert calls himself a "murderer" (*L* 9), the reader doesn't know who's been murdered. Quilty himself is only a shadowy presence for much of the first part of the novel. In the screenplay, however, the image of Humbert as murderer and Quilty as victim is front and center, and so the dramatic interest of the work shifts somewhat from the question of who it is that Humbert murders to curiosity about what his specific motivation for the murder is. The foregrounding of Humbert's act of murder may have the effect, as Alfred Appel, Jr. speculates, of deflecting attention from Humbert's identity as pedophile to his identity as murderer, "on the assumption [...] that a killer is more acceptable than a pervert" to the censors.[96] Certainly Nabokov's screenplay tones down the sexual content of the novel. It does not include the infamous masturbation scene on the Haze's living room couch, nor does it include any reference to the French prostitute Monique or Humbert's wretched attempt to procure a liaison with an underage girl who turns out to be "at least fifteen" (*L* 24). To compensate for this, Nabokov included a scene in which Humbert suffers a mental breakdown while addressing a women's club and begins to rant about the attraction of nymphets, and this represents a highly condensed version of Humbert's description of the nymphet in Part One, Chapter Five. It is as a result of this breakdown that Humbert is introduced to the care of John Ray, Jr. Curiously enough, the published version of the screenplay also softens Humbert's image as murderer. Although Nabokov's original screenplay (and Kubrick's film) retained much of the dialogue between Humbert and Quilty, the published screenplay does not, and the murder becomes simply a wordless sequence of actions.

Equally striking is the way Nabokov handled the problem of the novel's reliance on written texts, particularly John Ray, Jr.'s foreword, and Humbert's memoir itself. In his screenplay (though not in Kubrick's film), Nabokov has both men address the camera at certain points in the story. John Ray, Jr. is given a particularly prominent role at the beginning of the screenplay. He is first shown sitting at a desk and then he turns to face the camera and delivers a long speech that encapsulates many of the pronouncement's he makes about Humbert's story and personality in the novel. But this does not end his appearance in the projected film. He temporarily cedes the narrative role to Humbert who gives a brief summary of his childhood and makes comments to the audience much like a film director: "I would now like a shot of two hands" (*Lo Screen* 5). It is Humbert who tells the audience about his abortive affair with Annabel, but when his story reaches the point where he weds Valeria, Dr. Ray's voice suddenly becomes extraordinarily intrusive. When Humbert and Valeria enter the taxi driven by Valeria's lover, Ray begins making comments like "I think the cab driver ought to have turned left here. Oh, well, he can take the next cross street" and "Look out! Close shave. When you analyze those jaywalkers you find they hesitate between the womb and the tomb" (*Lo Screen* 12, 13). Clearly, Nabokov uses the figure of John Ray, Jr. to insert humorous notes into the film, perhaps to compensate for the humor that disappeared along with Humbert's narrative monologue.

When working on his screenplay, Nabokov made other additions to his basic story. In one of his revisions, Nabokov added a quirky scene involving Humbert's arrival at the remains of the McCoo house, which has just been destroyed in a fire: the distraught McCoo takes Humbert on a tour of the charred ruins, pointing out the charms of the room that he *would* have had if it were not for the fire. The most striking additions, though, involve the characters of Clare Quilty and Dolly. Nabokov introduces Quilty into the action of the screenplay at a much earlier point than he appears in the book. In the first version of the screenplay that Nabokov wrote, Quilty encounters Dolly in the dentist's chair at his Uncle Ivor's office. In the revised version, Quilty sees Dolly at a school dance. Neither scene is in the novel. Later in the story, Dolly and Quilty are shown talking with each other more than once in Beardsley, and Dolly expresses real determination and resourcefulness in her desire to escape from Humbert with Quilty. The effect of these changes is to make their entire story somewhat more conventional or accessible. In the novel, Humbert's memoir is intensely solipsistic, and the other characters (particularly Quilty) are shadowy emanations given life by Humbert's imagination. In the screenplay, the characters breathe with a life of their own. What is more, the haunting ambiguity and sense of mystery found in Humbert's narrative is diminished. Mindful of the fact that the film viewer does not have the luxury of a rereader to stop the narrative, go back, and retrieve whatever information might be necessary to clarify an event, Nabokov simplifies certain crucial points. Thus, the death of Dolly Schiller is announced by Dr. Ray's voice at the end of the screenplay, rather than in the foreword to the novel, when the first-time reader does not even know who "Mrs. Richard F. Schiller" is. Nabokov's screenplay is a fascinating work, but it is no substitute for his original novel.

When Stanley Kubrick set out to make a movie out of Nabokov's *Lolita*, his major concern was not to run afoul of the so-called Production or Hays Code, a set of guidelines adopted by the motion picture industry in the 1930s to prohibit the depiction of activity that might be deemed immoral or offensive to society, especially in a way that seemed to condone the activity in question. Several years later, Kubrick lamented to an interviewer that because of his concern over the Production Code and the Catholic Legion of Decency, "I wasn't able to give any weight at all to the erotic aspect of Humbert's relationship with Lolita; and because his sexual obsession was only barely hinted at, it was assumed too quickly that Humbert was in love. Whereas in the novel this comes as a discovery at the end."[97] In his effort to avoid a confrontation with the Code, Kubrick made several strategic decisions that significantly altered Nabokov's *Lolita*. He cast Sue Lyon as Lolita, and the actress, who was fifteen when the film was completed, looked even a few years older than that. Kubrick also eliminated any references to Humbert's pedophiliac desires in the years before his entrance into the Haze household (in fact, Humbert is given almost no pre-history at all, and thus there is no Annabel, only a fleeting reference to Valeria, and no mad rant about nymphets). James Mason's Humbert Humbert is a refined, slightly sad and inept gentleman who seems sincerely devoted to his love. Therefore, as Bosley Crowther noted in a *New York Times* film review on the day after the opening, "the factor of perverted desire that is in the book" is removed, and the hero's passion becomes "more normal and understandable [...] Older men have often pined for younger females. This is nothing new on the screen."[98]

Instead of dark eros and obsession, Kubrick emphasized the comic aspects of the novel. Shelley Winters, as Charlotte Haze, plays a blowsy suburban housewife desperate for love. She stalks Humbert more frantically than Humbert pursues Dolly and comes across as more of a panting sex fiend than he does. Their interaction creates an opening for much double-entendre. At one point in the bedroom she says: "Hum, you just touch me and I go limp as a noodle." Mason makes the deadpan response: "Yes, I know the feeling." But the greatest source of comedy in the film is provided by Peters Sellers as Clare Quilty. Although Nabokov made Quilty a more visible figure throughout the screenplay than in the novel, Kubrick made Quilty's role even larger. Thus, the conversation between Humbert and Miss Pratt about Dolly's conduct at the Beardsley School is replaced by a conversation between Humbert and a psychologist named Dr. Zempf, played to the hilt by Peter Sellers with a thick German accent that anticipates his appearance in *Dr. Strangelove*. In that scene, Zempf threatens Humbert with the prospect of having a team of psychologists come to inspect "the home situation," and suggests that he can avoid this by letting Dolly participate in the school play: "Let's stop Dr. Cutler [pronounced Cuddler] from fiddling around with the home situation," Zempf says with a leer. In several scenes, Kubrick let Sellers improvise, and this added a manic energy to the proceedings. Although Nabokov may not have been entirely pleased with what he saw on screen, he did remark favorably on certain episodes, such as the mad ping-pong game that Quilty tries to initiate with Humbert in the opening scene (see *Lo Screen* xiii); Sellers himself came up with the idea.

Not only did Kubrick change the tone of Nabokov's novel and screenplay, he made substantial cuts and revisions. Appel states that Kubrick used only about twenty percent of the Nabokov's screenplay.[99] As noted above, there are no scenes involving Annabel or Valeria. The intrusive appearance of John Ray, Jr. is entirely eradicated. What is more, the time setting of the action is advanced by about ten years. Instead of the late 1940s, the action in the film occurs in the late 1950s. Because he shot the film in England, Kubrick unfortunately did not reproduce the rich streak of Americana that runs through Nabokov's novel and screenplay alike. Many of the shots are characterless interiors, and some of the external shots (such as that of the Schiller house) do not match up at all with Nabokov's vision. Kubrick even stamped the film with a marker of his own directorial presence when he has Sellers emerge from a chair in Pavor Manor wrapped in a sheet and intone "I'm Spartacus." *Spartacus* was Kubrick's previous film, released in 1960. A final, yet crucial change that Kubrick made to Nabokov's novel and script is his failure to tell the audience what happened to Dolly Schiller. Although Humbert's demise is announced in rolling titles at the end of the film, no mention is made of Dolly's fate. Kubrick would go on to make several distinguished films, including *2001: A Space Odyssey* (1968), *A Clockwork Orange* (1971), and *The Shining* (1980), but Nabokov's novel would have to wait for more than a quarter of a century for a film maker who would come closer to reproducing its essential setting and tone.

In 1990 the director Adrien Lyne approached the production company Carolco with the idea of making a new film version of *Lolita*. Carolco procured the rights and Lyne set about finding a script that he was comfortable with. Lyne was known for glossy films steeped in eroticism or suspense, such as *Flashdance* (1983), *Nine 1/2 Weeks* (1986), and *Fatal Attraction* (1987). When word got out that Lyne was going to film *Lolita*, some critics feared the worst. Yet Lyne did not seem interested in making a superficial, sensationalist film, and he went through three separate screenwriters (James Dearden, who had worked with Lyne on *Fatal Attraction*, Harold Pinter, and David Mamet) before settling on the relatively unknown Stephen Schiff.[100] Schiff, who admitted that he had not much experience in writing film scripts, wanted to write something that captured the spirit of Nabokov's novel. He rejected the idea of setting the action in the present day, and insisted that the film should reproduce the atmosphere of the late 1940s.[101] The resulting film does indeed capture the look and feel of America in the late 1940s, particularly during the travel scenes, and the moody score by Ennio Morricone provides a lush accompaniment to the film's action.

In terms of plot, the Lyne film is much closer to Nabokov's original than the Kubrick version. Humbert's relationship with Annabel is restored to the story (and it is even made into a clear rationale for Humbert's later obsession with Dolly), and the role of Quilty in the first part of the film is reduced. On the other hand, the film begins with a shot of Humbert's car driving along a rural road; there is a bloody gun on the front seat, and Humbert is spattered with blood himself. At this point, however, the audience does not know whose blood this is, or what has transpired before this moment. The film then moves on to Humbert recalling his relationship with Annabel. As even this transition indicates, Humbert's voice (uttering words largely derived from the novel) is heard much more frequently in the Lyne film than in the Kubrick version. Schiff's screenplay uses many voiceovers, and several of the most important passages in the novel are transmitted this way. Prime examples include Humbert's affirmation of love for Dolly Schiller, "pale and polluted and big with another's child," and a condensed version of the final lines of the book, including "this is the only immortality you and I may share, my Lolita."[102] In fact, unlike Kubrick's film, where Peter Sellers as Quilty seems to dominate the film, this is very much *Humbert's* film. Lyne believed, and Schiff supported him in this, that the audience has to "sympathize with and, yes, love him even though his deeds revolt us."[103] Jeremy Irons portrayed Humbert as a tormented lover, one who suffers mightily from Dolly's increasing lack of regard for him. He seems in thrall to Dolly's caprices, and not her captor. Viewing the film, one thinks that this is very much how Humbert would like his readers to view him. The monstrosity of his abuse of a twelve-year-old child recedes into the background.

This effect is heightened by the character of Dolly as portrayed by the fifteen-year-old Dominique Swain. She emphasized both the childish capriciousness of the character and a kind of sexual precocity that surpasses what the novel allows us to see. In fact, the film makes one crucial distortion in its treatment of Dolly's sexual relationship with Humbert. Humbert declares to the reader quite explicitly: "Never did she vibrate under my touch, and a strident 'what d'you think you are doing?' was all I got for my pains" (*L* 166). Just one page earlier, he had described Dolly sitting on his lap reading the newspaper, "as indifferent to my ecstasy as if it were something she had sat upon [...] and was too indolent to remove." In the Schiff-Lyne version of this scene, however, Dolly is shown reacting with clear sexual pleasure to the experience. Schiff's screenplay reads: "She is breathing hard, and her eyes are very bright. She moans again. Thre seems no dividing line between her sexual pleasure and the pleasure she takes in the comics."[104] The effect of this is to further undermine the notion that Humbert is a callous pedophile. What emerges instead is the image of an unusual romance that eventually becomes a bore to one of the lovers.

The supporting actors fulfill their roles competently. Melanie Griffith as Charlotte Haze tones down the extreme shrewishness of Shelly Winters, but portrays a certain steeliness that contrasts nicely with Irons's reserve. Frank Langella as Quilty eschews the antic comedy expressed by Peter Sellers and revives the atmosphere of sinister menace that Humbert tried to evoke in his depiction of Quilty in the novel. One can find a marvelous contrast in acting styles and intentions when one compares the two film versions of the scene involving Quilty and Humbert at the Enchanted Hunters Hotel. Whereas Peter Sellers rambles on in a mad monologue about how "normal" Humbert looks and what a "normal guy" he is, Langella solemnly intones the lines written for Quilty by Nabokov, and this is accompanied by shots of an electronic bug zapper that emanates sharp sizzling sounds and bursts of artificial light, an apt accouterment for a demonic being. Whereas Kubrick's film highlighted the comic dimension of Nabokov's *Lolita*, Lyne's film foregrounds the melancholy. And, unlike in Kubrick's film, the concluding titles in Lyne's film announce that "Lolita" died in childbirth on Christmas Day, 1950.

Although one might think that a director making a film of *Lolita* in the mid-1990s would have less to worry about in terms of censorship than one making a similar film some thirty years earlier, Lyne and his associates became aware of a new censorship threat during the filming itself. In 1996, the U. S. Congress passed the Child Pornography Prevention Act, which was designed to criminalize pornographic materials involving not only real children, but actors or altered photographic images that make it appear as if children were involved. Lyne began editing his film in the presence of a lawyer who specialized in pornography law, and the resulting film contains fewer erotic moments than the original screenplay had envisioned. Nonetheless, fears about a public reaction to such a film were heightened by the media frenzy that developed around the sensational murder of six-year-old beauty pageant contestant Jon Benet Ramsey in December 1996. American film distributors now wanted no part of Lyne's film. Eventually, the film had its premiere in September 1997 at a film festival in Spain. After circulating in Europe, it was finally shown in the United States on the Showtime cable channel in August 1998 and had a limited theatrical release the following month.

While *Lolita* found moderate success in its cinematic incarnations, attempts to mold the story into other media have been less fortunate. *Lolita, My Love*, a musical version of the novel written by Alan Jay Lerner (lyrics) and John Barry (music) struggled during tryouts in Philadelphia and Boston in 1971, and never made it to its intended destination on Broadway. Edward Albee, who had achieved distinction with plays such as *The Zoo Story* (1959) and *Who's Afraid of Virginia Woolf* (1962), wrote a stage adaptation of *Lolita* that opened in March 1981 in New York. Albee's script lacked the lyricism and subtlety of Nabokov's original, and he foregrounded the concept of artifice by including a character called "A Certain Gentleman" who was supposed to represent the author Nabokov and who interacted with Humbert throughout the play. Albee changed certain plot elements (Charlotte Haze dies from falling down the stairs after threatening Humbert with a gun), and he makes Dolly Haze a more knowing and hardened child than Nabokov's Dolly.[105] None of this found favor with the audience. The reviews were uniformly critical, and the play closed two weeks later.[106] A Russian composer, Rodion Shchedrin, wrote an opera based on *Lolita* that was performed in Swedish and produced in Stockholm in December 1994 and January 1995; it did not fair particularly well with the critics either.

Despite these misadventures, *Lolita* continues to inspire artists, writers, and composers to introduce elements from the novel into their work. One can point to several contemporary novels that have been directly inspired by *Lolita*, from Pia Pera's *Lo's Diary* (1995), a rather grim attempt to depict Dolly's experience with Humbert from the child's point of view, to Emily Prager's *Roger Fishbite* (1999), which provides an updated account of abuse from the perspective of a knowing and articulate child living in Manhattan and dreaming of having her own talk show. Other novels resonating with echoes of Nabokov's creation include Donald Harrington's *Ekaterina* (1993), A. M. Homes's *The End of Alice* (1996), and Victor Pelevin's *The Sacred Book of the Werewolf* (2005). Moreover, the novel has proved inspirational in contexts other than fiction. Azar Nafisi's 2003 memoir, *Reading Lolita in Tehran*, describes how a group of women gathered informally to discuss literature in Tehran away from the prying eyes of the conservative regime. One of the central texts they discussed was *Lolita*. The women in the group had a somewhat different take on the novel than what is generally found in Western literary criticism. As Nafisi put it: "The desperate truth of *Lolita*'s story is *not* the rape of a twelve-year-old by a dirty old man but *the confiscation of one individual's life by another*. We don't know what Lolita would have become if Humbert had not engulfed her. Yet the novel, the finished work, is hopeful, beautiful even, a defense not just of beauty but of life, ordinary everyday life, all the normal pleasures that Lolita [...] was deprived of."[107]

Nabokov's *Lolita* has clearly left a significant impression in highbrow culture, but its impact on popular culture is far greater. The notion of an older man's obsession for a school-age girl has captured the imagination of a wide swath of readers, writers, film makers, musicians, and journalists. The 1980 song by the British rock group The Police entitled "Don't Stand So Close to Me" features a schoolgirl's crush on her teacher and the teacher's anxiety over the feelings he has for her. The final words before the refrain are: "It's no use, he sees her / He starts to shake and cough / Just like the old man in / That book by Nabakov." Other emanations of *Lolita* in popular music include band names, such as Clare Quilty and Vivian Darkbloom, and album names such as *Lolita Nation* by Game Theory.

The most striking and most widespread legacy of Nabokov's novel in mass culture, however, stems from the spread of the concept of the "nymphet" and even of "Lolita" as terms to denote a sexually precocious and desirable girl. Thus, the *New Oxford American Dictionary* (2001) defines "Lolita" as "a sexually precocious young girl" and explains that the term comes from the name of a character in Vladimir Nabokov's novel *Lolita*; a "nymphet," the same dictionary informs us, is "an attractive and sexually mature young girl." The *Merriam-Webster's Collegiate Dictionary* (1998) offers similar definitions: "Lolita" is "a precociously seductive girl" and a "nymphet" is "a sexually precocious girl barely in her teens." These terms soon became common in popular usage. Thus, a 1962 pulp fiction book featuring two young people in a steamy embrace on the cover was entitled *The Lolita Lovers*, and the tag line above the title read: "They Lived For Violence, Sin and Sensation."

Journalists in particular have had a field day with the term, labeling any young, attractive female with the soubriquet "Lolita," particularly if there is a hint of involvement with an older man. The most notorious example of this, perhaps, was the treatment of a seventeen-year-old girl's shooting of her lover's wife in Massapequa, New York in 1992. The girl, Amy Fisher, had begun a relationship when she was sixteen with a thirty-five-year-old man name Joey Buttafuoco. When her identity as assailant was released, Amy was immediately dubbed "The Long Island Lolita." She ended up serving seven years in prison. Her lover, Joey Buttafuoco, served six months in jail for statutory rape. The wife, Mary Jo, survived. Three television films based on the story were made, and two of them ended up with "Lolita" in the title (*Amy Fisher: My Story* was given the new title of *Lethal Lolita*, while the second film was called *Casualties of Love: The Long Island Lolita Story*). The media has a special fondness for naming young Russian females "Lolita": the tennis star Anna Kournikova was called the "Lobbing Lolita" when playing tennis in the United States.

The broad concept of "Lolita" as combining the innocence of a child with the knowledge or desires of an adult has had a major impact on fashion as well. An enduring style of fashion that started in Japan and spread to the West is called "Lolita." Although there are several distinct subsets of the style, in general, girls and young women dress in frilly outfits reminiscent of the Victorian era; often the women carry parasols. One popular variation of this is called "Gothic Lolita," in which the dominant tone is black. There is even a glossy publication entitled the *Gothic and Lolita Bible*. All kinds of consumer products, from purses to shoes, have been given the name "Lolita."

While these fashion trends are relatively innocuous, the underlying notion that children can be sexually appealing to adult men has led to the association of the name "Lolita" with a broad panoply of soft and hard core erotica. In Japan, the term "lolicon" (or "rorikon") denotes an attraction to young girls, and both comics and animated films featuring such subjects have been produced with names such as "Lolita Anime." What is more, the name "Lolita" has become broadly associated in the soft and hard core pornography industry with the theme of sexually charged teenagers. A search of the Internet Movie Database (IMDb) turns up titles such as *Emanuelle e Lolita* (1978), *Lolita vib-zeme* (also known as *Lolita Vibrator Torture* [1987]), and *Lolita 2000* (1998), a soft-core science fiction film. In the porn world, "Lolita" has come to mean a sexually adventuresome young female, ready and willing to take on all interested parties. This is a far cry from the vulnerable twelve-year-old girl that Nabokov brought to life in his novel, and he himself was pained at how easily people misinterpreted the child's status. Contrasting Dolly's age with that of young women who are mentioned in the tabloids in the company of older men, he pointed out in an interview: "Humbert was fond of 'little girls' — not simply 'young girls.' Nymphets are girl-children, not starlets and 'sex kittens.' Lolita was twelve, not eighteen, when Humbert met her" (*SO* 93). Yet although his novel deplores the abuse of little girls, the name he popularized has become indelibly associated with licentiousness and young women. While Nabokov could consider himself "the perfect dictator" in the "private world" of his art (*SO* 69), and he regarded his characters as "galley slaves" (*SO* 95), he could only be surprised at the way his characters could take on life of their own once they were out of his hands. "Lolita" has certainly done that. He once said that of all his novels, he had the "most affection" for *Lolita* (*SO* 92). He was also wise enough to know that he would be remembered for *Lolita* (*SO* 106). As he so aptly put it: "*Lolita* is famous, not I" (*SO* 107). This may largely be true, but both *Lolita* and her maker have found a secure place in the halls of world culture.

Notes

1. Zoran Kuzmanovich, "Commentary on *Lolita*," in *Approaches to Teaching Nabokov's* Lolita, ed. Zoran Kuzmanovich and Galya Diment (New York: The Modern Language Association, 2008), 20.
2. John Hollander, "The Perilous Magic of Nymphets," *Partisan Review* 23.4 (1956): 557.
3. Ibid., 560.
4. F. W. Dupee, "A Preface to *Lolita*," *The Anchor Review* 2 (New York: Doubleday, 1957), 1, 2.
5. Ibid., 11.
6. Ibid., 12, 13.
7. Howard Nemerov, "The Morality of Art," *The Kenyon Review*, 19.2 (1957): 314.
8. Ibid., 320–21.
9. Brian Boyd, *Vladimir Nabokov: The American Years* (Princeton: Princeton University Press, 1991), 364.
10. Charles Rolo, "Reader's Choice," *Atlantic*, September 1958, 78. Rolo further echoes John Hollander when he declares that "*Lolita* blazes [...] with a perversity of a most original kind."
11. Granville Hicks, "*Lolita* and her Problems," *Saturday Review*, 16 August 1958, 12.
12. Orville Prescott, "Books of The Times," *New York Times*, 18 August 1958, 17.
13. Riley Hughes, review of *Lolita, Catholic World*, October 1958, 72.
14. Elizabeth Janeway, "The Tragedy of Man Driven by Desire," *New York Times Book Review*, 17 August 1958, 5.
15. Prescott, "Books of the Times," 17.
16. Janeway, "The Tragedy of a Man Driven by Desire," 25.
17. Dorothy Parker, "Sex — without the asterisks," *Esquire*, October 1958, 103.

18. Todd Bayma and Gary Alan Fine, "Fictional Figures and Imaginary Vixens: The Transformation of Lolita from Victim to Vixen," *Studies in Symbolic Interaction* 20 (1996): 174.
19. Lionel Trilling, "The Last Lover: Vladimir Nabokov's *Lolita*," *Encounter* 11.4 (1958): 14.
20. Ibid., 17.
21. Denis de Rougemont, *Love Declared: Essays on the Myths of Love*, trans. Richard Howard (Boston: Beacon Press, 1963), 52.
22. Ibid., 53.
23. Charles Mitchell, "Mythic Seriousness in *Lolita*," *Texas Studies in Literature and Language* 5.4 (1964): 330.
24. G. D. Josipovici, "*Lolita*: Parody and the Pursuit of Beauty," *Critical Quarterly* 6.1 (1964): 43.
25. Diana Butler, "Lolita Lepidoptera," *New World Writing* 16 (Philadelphia: Lippincott, 1960), 64.
26. Ibid., 79.
27. Nabokov also criticized the Butler article (without naming its author) in an interview with Herbert Gold: "The essay might have been amusing had she known something about Lepidoptera. Alas, she revealed complete ignorance and the muddle of terms she employed proved to be only jarring and absurd" (*SO* 96).
28. Page Stegner, *Escape into Aesthetics: The Art of Vladimir Nabokov* (New York, Dial Press, 1966), 114.
29. Ibid., 114.
30. Alfred Appel, Jr., "*Lolita*: The Springboard of Parody," *Wisconsin Studies in Contemporary Literature* 8.2 (1967): 212.
31. Ibid., 216.
32. Ibid., 214.
33. Ibid., 228.
34. Ibid., 225, 219.
35. Carl Proffer, *Keys to* Lolita (Bloomington: Indiana University Press, 1968), vii.
36. Thomas R. Frosch, "Parody and Authenticity in *Lolita*," in *Nabokov's Fifth Arc: Nabokov and Others on His Life's Work*, ed. J. E. Rivers and Charles Nicol (Austin: University of Texas Press, 1982), 182.
37. Ibid., 182.
38. Martin Green, "The Morality of *Lolita*," *The Kenyon Review*, 28.3 (1966), 359, 364.
39. Ibid., 376, 377.
40. Julia Bader, *Crystal Land: Artifice in Nabokov's English Novels* (Berkeley: University of California Press, 1972), 4.
41. Ibid., 76, 77.
42. Ibid., 77.

43. Ibid., 79–80.
44. Douglas Fowler, *Reading Nabokov* (Ithaca: Cornell University Press, 1974), 149.
45. Ibid., 151.
46. Ibid., 165. It appears that Fowler is mistaken about the time when this epiphany occurred. He indicates that Humbert experienced the epiphany itself right after the murder of Clare Quilty, when it actually occurred years earlier and is only recalled by Humbert at this moment.
47. Ibid., 166. And what of the other crime in the novel — the murder of Quilty? Well, it is Fowler's view that Quilty is a "*real* monster" whose murder is an act "we of course fully approve of" (ibid., 164–65).
48. Mark Lilly, "Nabokov: Homo Ludens," in *Vladimir Nabokov: A Tribute*, ed. Peter Quennell (New York: William Morrow, 1980), 88.
49. Ibid., 96.
50. David Packman, *Vladimir Nabokov: The Structure of Literary Desire* (Columbia: University of Missouri Press, 1982), 42.
51. Ibid., 47.
52. Trevor McNeely, "'Lo' and Behold: Solving the *Lolita* Riddle," *Studies in the Novel* 21.2 (1989): 183.
53. Ibid., 184.
54. Ibid., 194–95.
55. Ellen Pifer, *Nabokov and the Novel* (Cambridge, MA: Harvard University Press, 1980), 166.
56. Gladys R. Clifton, "Humbert Humbert and the Limits of Artistic License," in *Nabokov's Fifth Arc*, 155.
57. Ibid., 169.
58. David Rampton, *Vladimir Nabokov: A Critical Study of the Novels* (Cambridge: Cambridge University Press, 1984), 107.
59. Ibid., 115.
60. Richard Rorty, *Contingency, Irony, and Solidarity* (Cambridge: Cambridge University Press, 1989), 164.
61. Linda Kauffman, "Framing *Lolita*: Is There a Woman in the Text?," in *Refiguring the Father: New Feminist Readings of Patriarchy*, ed. Patricia Yaeger and Beth Kowalski-Wallace (Carbondale: Southern Illinois University Press, 1989), 138–39.
62. Ibid., 138, 133, 149.
63. Ibid., 148.
64. Elizabeth Patnoe, "Lolita Misrepresented, Lolita Reclaimed: Disclosing the Doubles," *College Literature* 22.2 (1995): 98.
65. Colleen Kennedy, "The White Man's Guest, or Why Aren't More Feminists Rereading *Lolita?*," in *Narrative and Culture*, ed. Janice Carlisle and Daniel R. Schwartz (Athens: University of Georgia Press, 1994), 53, 51.
66. Ibid., 51.

67. Virginia Blum, *Hide and Seek: The Child between Psychoanalysis and Fiction* (Urbana: University of Illinois, 1995), 232.

68. Sarah Herbold, "'(I have camouflaged everything, my love)': *Lolita* and the Woman Reader," *Nabokov Studies* 5 (1998/1999): 75.

69. Ibid., 75.

70. Ibid., 96.

71. Ibid., 93.

72. Vladimir E. Alexandrov, *Nabokov's Otherworld* (Princeton: Princeton University Press, 1991), 18.

73. Ibid., 179, 181.

74. See Elizabeth Bruss, *Autobiographical Acts: The Changing Situation of a Literary Genre* (Baltimore: Johns Hopkins University Press, 1976), 145–46; Christina Tekiner, "Time in *Lolita*," *Modern Fiction Studies* 25.3 (1979): 463–69; and Leona Toker, *Nabokov: The Mystery of Literary Structures* (Ithaca: Cornell University Press, 1989), 209–11.

75. Alexander Dolinin, "Nabokov's Time Doubling: From *The Gift* to *Lolita*," *Nabokov Studies* 2 (1995): 3–40.

76. Julian W. Connolly, "'Nature's Reality' or Humbert's 'Fancy': Scenes of Reunion and Murder in *Lolita*," *Nabokov Studies* 2 (1995): 41–61.

77. Brian Boyd, "'Even Homais Nods': Nabokov's Fallibility or How to Revise *Lolita*," *Nabokov Studies* 2 (1995): 62–86.

78. Rachel Bowlby, *Shopping with Freud* (London and New York: Routledge, 1993), 70–71.

79. Ibid., 65, 67–68.

80. Michael Wood, *The Magician's Doubts: Nabokov and the Risks of Fiction* (London: Pimlico, 1995), 139, 141.

81. Ibid., 141.

82. See Douglas Anderson, "Nabokov's Genocidal and Nuclear Holocaust in *Lolita*, *Mosaic* 29.2 (1996): 73–90; Susan Mizruchi, "*Lolita* in History," *American Literature* 75.3 (2003): 629–52; and Steven Belletto, "Of Pickaninnies and Nymphets: Race in *Lolita*," *Nabokov Studies* 9 (2005): 1–17.

83. Eric Naiman, "A Filthy Look at Shakespeare's *Lolita*," *Comparative Literature* 58.1 (2006): 19.

84. For an account of Nabokov's work on the translation, see Brian Boyd, *Vladimir Nabokov: The American Years* (Princeton: Princeton University Press, 1991), 472–73, 488–91, 503.

85. Vladimir Nabokov, "Postscript to the Russian Edition of *Lolita*," trans. Earl D. Sampson, in *Nabokov's Fifth Arc*, ed. J. E. Rivers and Charles Nicol, 190.

86. See, for example, Jane Grayson's comment that the Russian *Lolita* "is an ingenious and talented translation, but much of the language is indeed awkward, unnatural, and strongly influenced by English idiom and English constructions." Grayson, *Nabokov Translated: A Comparison of Nabokov's Russian and English Prose* (Oxford: Oxford University Press, 1977), 183.

87. Gennady Barabtarlo, "*Onus probandi*: On the Russian *Lolita*," *Russian Review*, 47 (1988): 242–43.

88. Alexander Dolinin, "*Lolita* in Russian," in *The Garland Companion to Vladimir Nabokov* (New York: Garland, 1995), 324.

89. Boyd, *Vladimir Nabokov: The American Years*, 490.

90. Barabtarlo, "*Onus probandi*," 243.

91. Dolinin, "*Lolita* in Russian," 322. Dolinin also notes that the Vladimir Nabokov anagram of "Vivian Darkbloom" becomes "Vivian Damor-Blok" (328n2). Blok was one of Nabokov's favorite poets when he was a young poet himself.

92. See Dolinin, "*Lolita* in Russian," 326–27, and Barabtarlo, "*Onus probandi*," 249–50.

93. Dolinin, "*Lolita* in Russian," 323.

94. Boyd, *Vladimir Nabokov: The American Years*, 404.

95. Quoted in Boyd, *Vladimir Nabokov: The American Years*, 466.

96. Alfred Appel, Jr., *Nabokov's Dark Cinema* (New York: Oxford University Press), 230.

97. Interview with Stanley Kubrick by Gene Phillips, *Film Comment* 7.4 (1971–72): 32.

98. Bosley Crowther, review of *Lolita*, *New York Times*, 14 June 1962, 23.

99. Appel, *Nabokov's Dark Cinema*, 231.

100. For a discussion of some of the properties of the four scripts prepared for the film, see Christopher C. Hudgins, "Lolita 1995: The Four Filmscripts," *Literature/Film Quarterly* 25.1 (1997): 23–29.

101. Stephen Schiff, "Introduction," *Lolita: The Book of the Film* (New York: Applause, 1998): xii–xiii.

102. Schiff, *Lolita*, 201, 225

103. Ibid., xvi.

104. Ibid., 120.

105. In Albee's published screenplay, Dolly had several lovers before Humbert, and she tells him that she preferred their sexual practices to his: "Wham, bam, thank you, ma'am; simple, pure and simple. Not these *hours* and *hours* of pawing, and licking, and..." *Edward Albee's Lolita: Adapted from the Novel by Vladimir Nabokov* (New York: Dramatists Play Service, Inc., 1984), 50.

106. For further discussion of the play, see Graham Vickers, *Chasing Lolita: How Popular Cutlure Corrupted Nabokov's Little Girl All Over Again* (Chicago: Chicago Review Press, 2008).

107. Azar Nafisi, *Reading Lolita in Tehran: A Memoir in Books* (New York: Random House, 2004), 33.

A GUIDE TO FURTHER READING IN ENGLISH

Books about *LOLITA*

Bloom, Harold, ed. *Lolita*. Major Literary Characters. New York: Chelsea House, 1993. Contains excerpts from early reviews as well as a selection of critical essays.

___, ed. *Vladimir Nabokov's* Lolita. Modern Critical Views. New York: Chelsea House, 1987. A collection of seminal essays on the novel, from Lionel Trilling to Thomas Frosch.

Clegg, Christine, ed. *Vladimir Nabokov:* Lolita. *A Reader's Guide to Essential Criticism*. Duxford, Icon Books, 2000. Provides summary and excerpts from major critical essays on *Lolita* from the time of publication through the end of the twentieth century.

Corliss, Richard. *Lolita*. BFI Film Classics. London: British Film Institute, 1994. An extended commentary on Stanley Kubrick's film version of *Lolita*.

De la Durantaye, Leland. *Style is Matter: The Moral Art of Vladimir Nabokov*. Ithaca: Cornell University Press, 2007. A detailed examination of the interplay of aesthetics and ethics in Nabokov's work, with a focus on *Lolita*.

Kuzmanovich, Zoran and Galya Diment, eds. *Approaches to Teaching* Lolita. New York: Modern Language Association, 2008. Aimed at teachers and students, contains numerous brief essays on a broad variety of topics along with references to further study.

Nakhimovsky, A. and S. Paperno, compilers. *An English-Russian Dictionary of Nabokov's* Lolita. Ann Arbor: Ardis, 1982. A list of words and phrases from Nabokov's Russian translation of *Lolita* with their English equivalents.

Olson, Lance. Lolita: *A Janus Text*. Twayne's Masterwork Studies 153. New York: Twayne, 1995. Contains chapters on the literary and historical context of the novel as well as essays on the work's moral and aesthetic dimensions.

Pifer, Ellen. *Vladimir Nabokov's* Lolita: *A Casebook*. Oxford: Oxford University Press, 2003. An excellent anthology of essays covering a broad range of topics.

Proffer, Carl. *Keys to* Lolita. Bloomington: Indiana University Press, 1968. An important early study of the style and literary allusions in *Lolita*.

Vickers, Graham. *Chasing Lolita: How Popular Culture Corrupted Nabokov's Little Girl All Over Again*. Chicago: Chicago Review Press, 2008. A detailed commentary on the relationship of Nabokov's novel to developments in popular culture.

Books about Nabokov Containing Chapters on LOLITA

Alexandrov, Vladimir E. *Nabokov's Otherworld*. Princeton: Princeton University Press, 1991. Shows how the metaliterary elements of Nabokov's fiction point to its metafictional dimensions.

Alexandrov, Vladimir E., ed. *The Garland Companion to Vladimir Nabokov*. Garland Reference Library of the Humanities 1474. New York: Garland, 1995. Essays on a broad range of topics, including *Lolita*.

Andrews, David. *Aestheticism, Nabokov, and* Lolita. Studies in American Literature 31. Lewiston, NY: Edwin Mellon, 1999. Contrasts the aesthetic positions of Humbert and Nabokov; discusses film adaptations of the novel.

Appel, Alfred, Jr. *Nabokov's Dark Cinema*. New York: Oxford University Press, 1974. Reveals the deep connections between Nabokov's work and the cinema.

Bader, Julia. *Crystal Land: Artifice in Nabokov's English Novels*. Berkeley: University of California Press, 1972. *Lolita* chapter focuses on themes of aesthetics and creativity.

Clancy, Laurie. *The Novels of Vladimir Nabokov*. New York: St. Martin's Press, 1984. Explores the intersection of the artistic and the human.

Connolly, Julian W., ed. *The Cambridge Companion to Nabokov*. Cambridge: Cambridge University Press, 2005. Provides essays on various topics, including a discussion of *Lolita* by Ellen Pifer.

Cornwell, Neil. *Vladimir Nabokov*. Plymouth: Northcote House, 1999. Contains brief introduction to *Lolita* and its subsequent effect on culture.

Fowler, Douglas. *Reading Nabokov*. Ithaca: Cornell University Press, 1974. Offers a sympathetic interpretation of Humbert Humbert.

Grabes, Herbert. *Fictitious Biographies: Vladimir Nabokov's English Novels*. The Hague: Mouton, 1977. Examines Humbert's moral growth.

Hyde, G. M. *Vladimir Nabokov: America's Russian Novelist*. Critical Appraisals Series. London: Marion Boyars, 1977. Explores literary antecedents in Nabokov's art.

Lee, L. L. *Vladimir Nabokov*. Boston: Twayne, 1976. Discusses parodic elements in *Lolita* and Humbert's development of self-knowledge.

Maddox, Lucy. *Nabokov's Novels in English*. Athens, GA: University of Georgia Press, 1983. Outlines Humbert's struggle with moral issues and Quilty's role in this struggle.

Morton, Donald E. *Vladimir Nabokov*. New York: Frederick Ungar, 1974. Investigates the way Nabokov uses the structure of *Lolita* to balance aestheticism and moralism.

Moynahan, Julian. *Vladimir Nabokov*. Minneapolis: University of Minnesota Press, 1971. Explores Nabokov's manipulation of genre and the role of artistic consciousness.

Packman, David. *Vladimir Nabokov: The Structure of Literary Desire*. Columbia, MO: University of Missouri Press, 1982. Shows how desire depicted in *Lolita* mirrors the reader's desire for the story.

Page, Norman, ed. *Nabokov: The Critical Heritage*. The Critical Heritage Series. London: Routledge and Kegan Paul, Ltd, 1982. Excerpts from reviews of *Lolita* and other novels.

Parker, Stephen Jan. *Understanding Vladimir Nabokov*. Columbia, SC.: University of South Carolina Press, 1987. Provides concise introduction to *Lolita*.

Pifer, Ellen. *Nabokov and the Novel*. Cambridge, MA: Harvard University Press, 1980. Pioneering study brings to fore the ethical dimensions of Nabokov's art.

Rampton, David. *Vladimir Nabokov*. New York: St. Martin's Press, 1993. Delves beneath Humbert's rhetoric to expose his deceptions and desires.

____. *Vladimir Nabokov: A Critical Study of the Novels*. Cambridge: Cambridge University Press, 1984. A sensitive discussion of the emotional contradictions raised in Nabokov's novel.

Sharpe, Tony. *Vladimir Nabokov*. London: Edward Arnold, 1991. Explores both the sadness and the comedy of the novel and views Humbert's memoir as an act of expiation.

Stegner, Page. *Escape into Aesthetics: The Art of Vladimir Nabokov*. New York: Dial Press, 1966. Explores role of allusions; finds touching element in Humbert's story.

Strathern, Paul. *Nabokov in 90 Minutes*. Chicago: Ivan Dee, 2005. Brief discussion highlights the enjoyment of reading *Lolita*.

Tammi, Pekka. *Problems of Nabokov's Poetics: A Narratological Analysis*. Suomalaisen Tiedeakatemian Toimituksia Annales Academiae Scientiarum Fennicae B 231. Helsinki: Suomalainen Tiedeakatemia, 1985. Investigates narrative intricacies in *Lolita*.

Toker, Leona. *Nabokov: The Mystery of Literary Structures*. Ithaca: Cornell University Press, 1989. Discusses ambiguities in *Lolita* and underscores ethical import of the novel.

Wood, Michael. *The Magician's Doubts: Nabokov and the Risks of Fiction*. Princeton: Princeton University Press, 1995. Masterful discussion of problems raised through Humbert's carefully-wrought monologue.

Wyllie, Barbara. *Nabokov at the Movies: Film Perspectives in Fiction*. Jefferson, NC: McFarland, 2003. A detailed study of the centrality of cinematic elements and techniques in Humbert Humbert's narrative.

Selected Articles

Amis, Martin. "*Lolita* Reconsidered." *The Atlantic Monthly* 270.3 (September 1992): 109–20. Notes prominence of images of death and injury in *Lolita* as well as distinctive humor.

Appel, Alfred, Jr. "Introduction." In Vladimir Nabokov, *The Annotated Lolita*. Ed. Alfred Appel, Jr. New York: Vintage International, 1991. xvii–lxvii. A multifaceted introduction to the novel.

———. "*Lolita*: The Springboard of Parody." *Wisconsin Studies in Contemporary Literature* 8.2 (1967): 204–41. A detailed examination of the uses of parody in *Lolita*.

Bayma, Todd and Gary Alan Fine. "Fictional Figures and Imaginary Vixens: The Transformation of Lolita from Victim to Vixen." *Studies in Symbolic Interaction* 20 (1996): 165–78. A study of the cultural climate affecting *Lolita*'s reception.

Blum, Virginia L. "Nabokov's *Lolita* / Lacan's Mirror." In *Hide and Seek: The Child between Psychoanalysis and Fiction*. Urbana: University of Illinois Press, 1995. An analysis of Humbert's profound narcissism.

Bowlby, Rachel. "*Lolita* and the Poetry of Advertising." In *Shopping with Freud*. New York: Routledge, 1993. 46–71. Explores the allure of language, both literary and commercial.

Boyd, Brian. "'Even Homais Nods': Nabokov's Fallibility or How to Revise *Lolita*." *Nabokov Studies* 2 (1995): 62–86. Rebuttal of theory that last episodes of *Lolita* are merely Humbert's fantasy.

Bruss, Elizabeth. "Vladimir Nabokov: Illusions of Reality and The Reality of Illusions." In *Autobiographical Acts: The Changing Situation of a Literary Genre*. Baltimore: Johns Hopkins University Press, 1976. 127–62. Points out Humbert's flaws as autobiographer.

Bruss, Paul. "*Lolita*: The Pursuit of Text." In *Victims: Textual Strategies in Recent American Fiction*. Lewisburg: Bucknell University Press, 1981. 52–66. Compares Humbert and Quilty as artists.

Butler, Diana. "Lolita Lepidoptera." *New World Writing* 16. Philadelphia: Lippincott, 1960. 58–84. Examines Humbert's pursuit of Dolly in terms of a pursuit for butterflies.

Clifton, Gladys. "Humbert Humbert and the Limits of Artistic License." In *Nabokov's Fifth Arc: Nabokov and Others on His Life's Work*. Ed. J. E. Rivers and Charles Nicol. Austin: University of Texas Press, 1982. 153–70. Explores Humbert's desires and Dolly's humanity.

Couturier, Maurice. "Narcissism and Demand in *Lolita*." *Nabokov Studies* 9 (2000): 19–46. A psychological approach to Humbert Humbert.

Dolinin, Alexander. "Nabokov's Time Doubling: From *The Gift* to *Lolita*." *Nabokov Studies* 2 (1995): 3–40. Detailed examination of theory that final episodes in *Lolita* are Humbert's fantasy.

Frosch, Thomas R. "Parody and Authenticity in *Lolita*." In *Nabokov's Fifth Arc: Nabokov and Others on His Life's Work*. Ed. J. E. Rivers and Charles Nicol. Austin: University of Texas Press, 1982. 171–87. Outlines the uses of parody in *Lolita*.

Green, Martin. "The Morality of *Lolita*." *The Kenyon Review* 28.3 (1966): 352–77. Analyzes the morality of *Lolita* in terms of Leo Tolstoy's views on the morality of art.

Haegert, John. "Artist in Exile: The Americanization of Humbert Humbert." *English Literary History* 52.3 (1985): 777–94. View Humbert's experience as émigré writer's encounter with America.

Herbold, Sarah. "'(I have camouflaged everything, my love)': *Lolita* and the Woman Reader." *Nabokov Studies* 5 (1989/1999): 71–98. Argues that Nabokov respects his (female) readers more highly than some feminist critics recognize.

Josipovici, G. D. "*Lolita*: Parody and the Pursuit of Beauty." *Critical Quarterly* 6.1 (1964): 35–48. Explores Humbert's desire to capture and express upossessable beauty.

Kauffman, Linda. "Framing *Lolita*: Is There a Woman in the Text." In *Refiguring the Father: New Feminist Readings of Patriarchy*. Ed. Patricia Yaeger and Beth Kowalski-Wallace. Carbondale: Southern Illinois University Press, 1989. 131–52. Argues that *Lolita* is not about love but abuse and betrayal, with Dolly as a damaged child.

Kennedy, Colleen. "The White Man's Guest, or Why Aren't More Feminists Rereading *Lolita*?" In *Narrative and Culture*. Ed. Janice Carlisle and Daniel R. Schwartz. Athens: University of Georgia Press, 1994. 46–57. Decries readings of *Lolita* that ignore abuse of child in the novel.

McNeely, Trevor. "'Lo' and Behold: Solving the *Lolita* Riddle." *Studies in the Novel* 21.2 (1989): 182–99. Claims that *Lolita* must be seen above all as a game.

Mizruchi, Susan. "Lolita in History." *American Literature* 75.3 (2003): 629–52. A reading of *Lolita* against larger events in the twentieth century.

Naiman, Eric. "A Filthy Look at Shakespeare's *Lolita*." *Comparative Literature* 58.1 (2006): 1–23. Examines use of bawdy language in *Lolita*.

O'Connor, Katherine Tiernan. "Rereading *Lolita*, Reconsidering Nabokov's Relationship with Dostoevskij." *Slavic and East European Journal* 33 (1989): 64–77. Investigates relationship of *Lolita* to Dostoevsky's novels.

Patnoe, Elizabeth. "Lolita Misrepresented, Lolita Reclaimed: Disclosing the Doubles." *College Literature*, 22.2 (1995): 81–104. Focuses on the reality of abuse depicted in the novel and its implications for readers.

Phelan, James. "Estranging Unreliability, Bonding Unreliability, and the Ethics of *Lolita*." *Narrative* 15.2 (2007): 222–38. Dissects the effects of narrative unreliability in *Lolita*.

Raguet-Bouvart, Christine. "That Intangible Island of Entranced Time: Vladimir Nabokov's *Lolita*." In *Sounding the Depths: Water as Metaphor in North American Literatures*. Ed. Gayle Wurst and Christine Raguet-Bouvart. Liège: Liège Language and Literature, 1998. 205–18. A detailed study of water imagery in the novel.

Rorty, Richard. "The Barber of Kasbeam: Nabokov on Cruelty." In *Contingency, Irony, and Solidarity*. Cambridge: Cambridge University Press, 1989. 141–68. Highlights the significance of Humbert's insensitivity and lack of curiosity toward others in the novel.

Tamir-Ghez, Nomi. "The Art of Persuasion in Nabokov's *Lolita*." *Poetics Today* 1.1–2 (1979): 65–83. An excellent description of the rhetorical devices used by Humbert and Nabokov.

Tekiner, Christina. "Time in *Lolita*." *Modern Fiction Studies* 25.3 (1979): 463–69. Discusses time discrepancy in *Lolita* suggesting that Humbert imagined later episodes in the novel.

Trilling, "The Last Lover: Vladimir Nabokov's *Lolita*," *Encounter* 11.4 (October 1958): 9–19. Early discussion of novel as modern depiction of "passion-love."

Twitchell, James. "*Lolita* as Bildungsroman." *Genre* 7.3 (1974): 272–78. Examines story of Dolly's maturation against nineteenth-century genre of female maturation.

Walter, Brian. "Romantic Parody and the Ironic Muse in *Lolita*." *Essays in Literature* 22.1 (1995): 123–43. Argues that Nabokov renews romanticism in *Lolita*.

Whiting, Frederick. "'The Strange Particularity of the Lover's Preference': Pedophilia, Pornography, and the Anatomy of Monstrosity in *Lolita*." *American Literature* 70.4 (1998): 833–62. Treats *Lolita* as exemplification of society's anxiety about pedophilia and pornography in mid to late twentieth century.

Biographical Studies

Boyd, Brian. *Vladimir Nabokov: The American Years*. Princeton: Princeton University Press, 1991. With its companion volume below, this is the definitive biography of Nabokov, and it contains an insightful analysis of *Lolita* by Boyd.

____. *Vladimir Nabokov: The Russian Years*. Princeton: Princeton University Press, 1990.

Field, Andrew. *Nabokov: His Life in Art*. Boston: Little, Brown and Co., 1967. Focuses on Nabokov's literary works.

____. *Nabokov: His Life in Part*. New York: Viking Press, 1977. Begun with Nabokov's cooperation, the finished biography contains errors.

____. *VN: The Life and Art of Vladimir Nabokov*. New York: Crown, 1986. Marred by speculation.

Grayson, Jane. *Vladimir Nabokov*. Illustrated Lives. London: Penguin, 2001. A brief, nicely illustrated overview.

Schiff, Stacy. *Véra (Mrs. Vladimir Nabokov)*. New York: Random House, 1999. Biography of Véra Nabokov complements studies of Nabokov's life.

Bibliographies and Online Resources

Bryer, Jackson R., and Thomas J. Bergin, Jr. "Vladimir Nabokov's Critical Reputation in English: A Note and a Checklist." *Wisconsin Studies in Contemporary Literature* 8.2 (1967): 312–64.

Field, Andrew. *Nabokov: A Bibliography*. New York: McGraw-Hill, 1973. Lists works and translations and some reviews.

Jones, Nancy J. "Vladimir Nabokov's *Lolita*: A Survey of Scholarship and Criticism in English, 1977–1995. *Bulletin of Bibliography* 54.2 (1999): 129–47. An annotated list of articles on *Lolita*.

Juliar, Michael. *Vladimir Nabokov: A Descriptive Bibliography*. Garland Reference Library of the Humanities 656. New York: Garland, 1986. Contains detailed information on the publication of Nabokov's work.

Lolita USA: A Geographical Scrutiny of Vladimir Nabokov's Novel Lolita (1955/1958). By Dieter E. Zimmer. <http://www.d-e-zimmer.de/LolitaUSA/LoUSpre.htm> A reconstruction of the itinerary Humbert and Dolly may have followed in their cross-country travels.

Nabokov Online Journal. <http://etc.dal.ca/noj/main_menu_en.shtml> Resource dedicated to publishing new research on Nabokov.

Parker, Stephen Jan, et al. "Annual Bibliography" in *The Vladimir Nabokov Research Newsletter* (1978–84) and *The Nabokovian* (1984–), published semi-annually at the University of Kansas by the Vladimir Nabokov Society. Annual listing of published works by and about Nabokov.

Schuman, Samuel. *Vladimir Nabokov: A Reference Guide*. Boston: G. K. Hall, 1979. Annotated listing of works on Nabokov, mainly in English, from the 1930s to 1977.

Zembla. <http://www.libraries.psu.edu/nabokov/zembla.htm> Online website devoted to Nabokov and his work.

INDEX